I_____

Dear Abbie,
Why think straight
when you could
THINK KINK?!

♡ Catherine

Thinking Kink

*The Collision of BDSM,
Feminism and Popular Culture*

C ATHERINE S COTT

McFarland & Company, Inc., Publishers
Jefferson, North Carolina

LIBRARY OF CONGRESS CATALOGUING-IN-PUBLICATION DATA

Scott, Catherine, 1983–
    Thinking kink : the collision of BDSM, feminism and popular
culture / Catherine Scott.
        p.   cm.
    Includes bibliographical references and index.

    ISBN 978-0-7864-9863-5 (softcover : acid free paper) ∞
    ISBN 978-1-4766-2039-8 (ebook)

    1. Bondage (Sexual behavior) in mass media.   2. Sexual
dominance and submission in mass media.   3. Sadomasochism
in mass media.   4. Feminism in mass media.   5. Popular
culture—United States—21st century.   I. Title.

P96.B75S36 2015
306.77'5—dc23   2015009180

BRITISH LIBRARY CATALOGUING DATA ARE AVAILABLE

On the cover: Lady Byron in a BDSM collar, 2004 (photograph by
Grendelkhan)

Printed in the United States of America

McFarland & Company, Inc., Publishers
  Box 611, Jefferson, North Carolina 28640
    www.mcfarlandpub.com

For Brian

Acknowledgments

The author would like to thank the following for their contributions to the creation of this book: Meg John Barker, Robin Bauer, Thomas Bliss, Emily Brady, Heather Carper, Brian Dillingham, Breanne Fahs, Stacey May Fowles, Lidija Haas, Charlie Hale, Andy Harris, Kathryn Klement, Mira Mattar, Katherine Martinez, Michelle Martinez, Shiloh McCabe, Michael McIntyre, Kathy Navin, Cliff Pervocracy, Marisol Smalls, Clarisse Thorn, Sara Vibes, Antony Whitehead and Mollena Williams. I would also like to thank my family for their continued love and support for all that I do, especially Rosslyn Scott, Richard Scott, Jonathan Scott and Cathryn Bishop.

Table of Contents

Preface

BDSM first appeared in popular culture in 2012.

That's what you could be forgiven for thinking if you scanned 20th and 21st century media for evidence of when kink became an acceptable topic in the mainstream press. Those in and outside of the kink scene with more of a taste for nuance know that the story isn't quite that simple, but one thing is for sure; there were never more discussions of what BDSM *really meant*—for society, for individuals, for gender relations, for feminism—than after *Fifty Shades of Grey*, a trilogy of mildly BDSM-themed novels became hugely popular in spring 2012. In order to placate those (including myself) who were already sick of hearing the books discussed at the time, and are even sicker of them two years later, but also acknowledge that they occupy a valid place within the discussion, I'll hereafter only be referring to them as *that trilogy* or *that book*.

This book follows on from a blog series I wrote for *Bitch* magazine in summer 2012 named "Thinking Kink: A Blog on BDSM, Feminism and Pop Culture." It aims to develop upon and more deeply explore the themes I considered back then, as well as introducing new examples of and angles on the intersections of BDSM, feminism and pop culture. My chosen method has been to individually examine particular kink tropes—the female dominant, the male submissive, the male dominant, the female submissive, the switch—how they turn up in pop culture, and how they respond to a feminist analysis: I've also looked at how pop culture represents the intersection of BDSM and the LGBT community, and BDSM and non-white people. I've examined how kink and consumerism dovetail, the implications of certain language that has emerged from the BDSM community, and the ever-important issues of safety and consent. I've also looked at, and I hope debunked, many of the uninformed assumptions made around kink and those who practice it.

1

Before I get started, however, I think it's worth explaining what started the whole thing off.

In February 2012, I was lucky enough to leave the grey and cloudy shores of Britain to undertake a three-month internship for *Ms.* magazine in Los Angeles in 2012. As an aspiring feminist writer who had been blogging furiously for four years already, it was fantastic to be working at the original feminist magazine and have a job where objecting to the often shitty portrayals of women in popular culture did not instantly render you the office pariah. I would come into work, scan the news for stories relevant to feminism, and spend my days blogging, fact-checking and researching, stopping only to drink the PG Tips tea I had brought five thousand miles with me.

After a couple of months at *Ms.*, one of my fellow interns mentioned *that book* to me. I hadn't heard of it, but we had a copy in our review section, so I had a quick flick. It was trashy, it was badly written, it was in need of a huge edit, but the kinky bits were mild at best. As someone who had indulged in kink in my private life and was well familiar with much more hardcore BDSM–themed literature such as *The Story of O*, I saw little to be shocked by; however, my friend's assertion that it was massively popular with women started alarm bells ringing in my head. I could already predict that, for that reason alone, this phenomenon wasn't going to go unreported, and I wasn't wrong.

Soon every blog or magazine was carrying an opinion piece on the apparently stunning revelation that women were enjoying erotic literature. The media labeled this type of fiction "mommy porn," a highly patronizing label I find more offensive than any amount of gags, floggers or restraints. And sure enough, here came the shit-stirring.

In April 2012, the *Newsweek* cover story "The Fantasy Life of Working Women: Why Surrender Is a Feminist Dream" appeared in print and online, written by Katie Roiphe, who is renowned for claiming that campus rape statistics are overstated/fabricated, and who is certainly not viewed as any friend to feminism. Roiphe suggested that the popularity of *that book* plus some sex scenes from the TV show *Girls* were evidence that "free will" has become "a burden" for modern women, so that they now want to "play at surrendering."[1] She went on to say that perhaps women are submitting in the bedroom (assuming that somehow she was suddenly party to the sexual activities of a nation, rather than merely aware of a new trend in reading habits) because they are finding that equality is a chore, "that power and all of its imperatives can be boring."

Roiphe also suggested, "The relentless responsibility of a contemporary woman's life … the pressure of economic participation … all that strength and independence and desire and going out into the world" is making scenes of sexual submission appealing to modern women. It was hardly a new argument—any time women make choices that are seen as deviating from the perfect feminist template, such as deciding to be stay-at-home parents, some commenter usually claims it is because the pressure of participating fully in society is just too damn much. If women are getting cancer, suffering from mental health problems, or struggling to conceive, let's blame feminism for pushing women to do too much in the first place.

This piece bothered me more than other feminist-baiting articles because of its total ignorance about how BDSM actually functions, especially that which involves scenes of male domination and female submission. I expected that the feminist community would have my back and start shooting Roiphe's lazy, poorly evidenced piece of provocation out of the water immediately; however, it didn't quite work out like that. On the excellent U.S. feminist blog Feministing, editor Maya Dusenbery wrote an article that purported to be defending submissives against Roiphe's sneering supposition. However, Dusenbery undid any good work she aimed to do by including the phrase, "I am in no way surprised that many women, who have been socialized in a culture in which male sexuality is linked to domination and in which women are taught their sexual power comes from being wanted, have fantasies of submission."[2]

This was hardly the robust defense of female agency and women's right to sexual freedom that I expected from a 21st century feminist. Instead it was simply advancing Roiphe's argument by another name. Whether we agreed with Roiphe that women were submitting because the pressure to participate in society was too great, or we agreed with Dusenbery that they were doing so because they were told by society that their role should always be passive, we were still being pushed to end up at the same conclusion—women always participated in BDSM due to one terrible societal pressure or another, and never *simply because it got them horny.*

I exorcised some of my irritation posts on my personal blog, All

That Chas, where I wondered why, even though the average feminist wouldn't dream of telling someone to "pray away the gay," if your kink preference happens to bear any vague resemblance to oppressive social structures, you're automatically accused of having been socialized into it.[3] I enjoyed reading Pat(rick) Califia and Gayle Rubin's articulate and impassioned defenses of lesbian BDSM in their respective works *Speaking Sex to Power, Public Sex* and *Deviations*. I plundered the well-stocked feminist library of the *Ms.* offices for further feminist analyses of kink that went beyond simple condemnation of BDSM as unsalvageably misogynistic. However, it was noticeable that there was still very little writing that addressed the particular problem of heterosexual women's submission being labeled anti-feminist. The only essay which I could find defending the right of the heterosexual female to practice BDSM, and as a sub at that, was Canadian writer Stacey May Fowles' excellent essay "The Fantasy of Acceptable Non-Consent: Why the Female Sexual Submissive Scares Us, and Why She Shouldn't."[4] I felt that, in the rush to explain why women were so keen to read *that book*, too many people, including feminists, were happy to erase the agency of heterosexual female submissives. No one was really speaking back to this trend in a way that I found satisfactory, so I decided I would do it myself.

Although there are plenty of books that separately deal with feminism, pop culture, or BDSM, I could never find any literature that attempted to deal with all three. Since the very debate that inspired my writing was precisely caused by the collision of the three, and the subsequent failure of any critics to truly address the complex facets of each of those worlds, it made sense that I would take on that task. This was helped by the fact that my chosen platform, *Bitch* magazine, operates under the tagline "A feminist response to pop culture."

On August 10, 2012, I published the final article of a 24-post blog series for *Bitch*. It had taken me eight weeks, 19,500 words, a great deal of research on and offline, and had sparked some fantastic discussions. It had taken me to play parties, munches, sex shops and online kink forums, places I'd never dared dip a toe into before. I had sampled the kink scene in both the U.S. and UK, and made good friends in both, as well as encountering people I looked upon a lot less favorably. There was more PVC in my wardrobe, but perhaps more significantly, there were also a hell of a lot more books on my shelf; works by Jay Wiseman,

Margot Weiss, Clarisse Thorn, Morpheous, Mollena Williams, Dossie Easton and Janet Hardy had all helped to educate me about the BDSM scene, while feminist anthologies such as *Yes Means Yes!, Pleasure and Danger, Sex Exposed,* and *Jane Sexes It Up* had shown me there were feminists writing about BDSM in tones other than prurient disapproval. I had spent hours on YouTube watching videos from Madonna, Grace Jones, Rihanna and Lady Gaga to name but a few, and more hours yet on the couch with a notepad scribbling furiously about depictions of BDSM in movies and TV shows. My initial aim with the blog series had been to find a pop culture portrayal of a female heterosexual submissive who acted out of her own agency, not due to love, financial reasons, coercion or past trauma. I'm not sure I ever really found her, but by the end I wasn't so bothered—because I realized that demanding that any female, whether real or a pop culture construct, should fit a perfect feminist template is just rehashing patriarchy's tactic of finding women constantly wanting. Once I had dived into the heap of pop culture references to kink, I had also quickly come to realize there were many other issues and questions raised and that the female submissive wasn't by any means the only construct which merited analysis.

I have friends who don't own televisions, friends who don't go near celebrity or women's magazines, friends who don't read full stop. I sometimes envy them their existence unmolested by the questionable portrayals of women, men and sexuality that can be found in pop culture. However, that envy isn't enough to make me want to plug my ears and cover my eyes against the modern media. Born in 1983, I'm very much a child of my time: my teens were spent watching *Friends* and *Buffy the Vampire Slayer,* my university years watching *Sex and the City, Family Guy* and nervously glimpsing some of the porn that my fellow students downloaded off the campus file-sharing network. Since I learned to read, my whole life has been spent immersed in literature, ranging from *Sweet Valley High* to *100 Years of Solitude,* and since I was given Michael Jackson's *Bad* on cassette tape at age five, pop music has never been far from my ears or my stereo. I love music videos, and remember the excitement of watching *Top of the Pops* on a Thursday evening in the '90s, one of only two shows which played music videos on terrestrial UK television. I remember being terrified by the video to The Cure's "Lullaby" and later, aroused by Madonna's "Human Nature," and I still compulsively flick through the music channels, although it saddens me that in a medium with such potential for originality, shaking female buttocks still seems to constitute the majority of what music video producers think viewers want to see.

Regardless, my research showed that feminist readings were possible when it came to all kinds of kinky pop culture artifacts—music videos, songs, books, TV shows and movies. Furthermore, it showed me that there were gender politics to be analyzed in every power dynamic in kink, not just the ones that appeared instantly patriarchal and troubling; there was also much to say about female domme/male sub, gay and lesbian BDSM and play between individuals who don't identify with traditionally dictated gender roles. There were issues of clothing, consumerism, consent and safety. There was controversy about racial stereotypes in the kink scene and in pop culture. There was the unpicking of the assumption that BDSM is abuse, or that only those with abuse in their past could enjoy it. There were references to *Family Guy, Zoolander, Married with Children*, Beyoncé videos and to my surprise, Joan Armatrading lyrics, plus many more pop culture arenas. There was the moment I laughed out loud as one of my interviewees pointed out that Mr. Burns and Smithers from *The Simpsons* must be the longest running master/slave relationship on television. And of course, there was much consideration given to why pop culture producers feel the need to include kink in their media in the first place, and whether this is advantageous or ultimately derogatory to public understanding of BDSM.

In terms of the public response, the "Thinking Kink" blog series was a huge success, triggering fascinating and impassioned debates in the comments section, as well as confessions and gratitude for addressing certain topics. There were clearly a lot of feminists frustrated that no one was dealing with the intersection of kink and feminism in any intelligent way. Posts from the series were reprinted by AlterNet, Salon, and even as far afield as a Polish political magazine, *Forum*. The link to the series from my personal blog is never out of the "Top 5 Most Read" posts list and still gets thousands of hits, two years on.

After I finished the series, I pondered the idea of expanding it and turning it into a book and pitched the idea to a couple of independent, feminist-leaning U.S. publishers. The response was a polite no, and since I was now a freelance writer and had to get on with the business of earning money, I dropped the idea. In late 2013, I was invited to speak at the American Culture Association/Popular Culture Association national conference the following spring. The chair of the BDSM/Fetish Studies panel had found me via the *Bitch* blog and felt I had an interesting contribution to make. I was nervous but excited to be returning to the "Thinking Kink" series. I wasn't an academic, rather a freelance writer/ranter and hoped my presentation would be up to standard. In April 2014, I presented on "Navigating Kink While Feminist: What I Learned from Thinking Kink" to a room of attentive listeners, and breathed a sigh of relief as the applause began afterwards. I fielded questions, participated in the panel discussion, and then handed over copies of my paper to be sold on the front desk. I was later told that it was the first paper of the conference to sell out—again, reflecting the power of kink to draw attention.

The questions I received after my presentation showed me that the conversation that the blog series started had only grown. I was touched that several attendees already knew my name from having read it, and I wished I had more than an allotted time slot in which to deal with the topics they raised. There was so much more still to say, so much thought-provoking discourse that had resulted from my writing which deserved more of an airing. I had enjoyed revisiting the intersecting worlds of feminism, BDSM and pop culture.

While browsing the bursting book tables, effectively heaven for a bibliophile such as myself, I noticed McFarland's wide and colorful range of pop culture titles and started flicking through anything I could find that covered my interests of sexuality, feminism and TV, music and film. I then saw their sign, "Tell us about your nonfiction book proposal." I considered it, then thought, "Naaaw ... you've tried this already," and started to walk away. Then I reflected that I had come 4,000 miles, paid hundreds of pounds and worked for months to make this trip happen; why not just take a chance? So I approached the woman who was manning the stall, and said, "I don't really have a book proposal as such, but I've just presented on this ... and I wrote a blog series on this ... and I've always thought it would make a good book, I'm just not quite sure how. Would you be interested?"

"We would be very interested," the woman replied warmly. She handed me a card. "Email us when you get back to the UK."

And I did.

*   *   *

What you have in front of you, then, is the result of two years spent highly attuned to all pop culture discourse surrounding BDSM, a career spent heavily invested in feminism, and a life spent loving, hating and questioning pop culture. Once I knew I was going to revisit "Thinking Kink," I went back to every topic, every film, book, TV show and music video that I had examined during the blog series, and decided whether they merited further discussion. I also picked up multiple new examples of kink in pop culture, both modern stories that had emerged since my blog ended and older examples that I'd simply missed, and started addressing them. I looked at the comments prompted by the series, and found that several of them necessitated whole new discussions of their own. I re-immersed myself in the words of the interviewees who had agreed to give me their time and thoughts for the original series, and sought new interviewees too. I pulled out the multiple handouts, papers and email addresses I'd collected at the PCA/ACA conference and began contacting speakers to hear more of their thoughts on aspects of BDSM.

I hope you will enjoy joining me as I interrogate pop culture and all its tropes, presumptions and potential foundations for both bigotry and liberation. I will also explore how BDSM functions, both as a concept and a reality, an abstract space which bodies and minds occupy in private, as well as a community publicly inhabited by a cross-section of imperfect people. And finally, I will aim to critically examine how feminism fits into this. Only by looking at how our conceptions of power and gender roles intersect with a sexual culture that makes power explicit but also openly stages it as malleable, and then looking at whether pop culture can ever really depict such subtleties, can I hope to address the multiple misunderstandings about what it means to be kinky—for individuals, for communities, and for society at large.

1

Subversive or Complicit?

The Female Dominant

"To fall at the feet of an imperious mistress, obey her mandates, or implore pardon, were for me the most exquisite enjoyments...."—Jean-Jacques Rousseau, *The Confessions*[1]

The first time I was asked to dominate a man, it came as something of a surprise to me. I was attending my first play party, ostensibly as part of research for my writing. I had found some knee-high boots with pointed toes at a flea market the previous weekend, and with the help of sale racks and thrift stores, had put together an approximation of what I thought constituted a kinky enough outfit to allow me to blend in. An older man began chatting with me and complimented me on the boots, and then said, "Can I ask you a question?" I tentatively responded, "OK," and he said, "Would you kick me in the balls?"

Being asked to deliberately hurt another human being, especially in a way that women are taught to strenuously avoid unless the man in question is attacking us, disrupted my thought process to the extent that I was actually speechless for a good 30 seconds. The devil on my shoulder said, "Well, you *could*..." while the sensible voice in my head said, "Don't be ridiculous!" I finally opted for a terribly British and polite "No, thank you" and the man drifted off. I was later told that he found a woman to fulfill his desires, and I was glad for him, but also glad that I had said no. I figured that there was a right way to inflict that kind of pain, and since I didn't know what it was, it was best that I refuse. Later, while watching *The Notorious Bettie Page* as part of my research for this book, my experience as a reluctant domme came back to me as I watched the scene where one of Bettie's fans approaches her at a party. "Doesn't it just make you sick to see guys like me groveling?" he hisses lasciviously.

"Doesn't it just make you want to crush us, humiliate us, punish us?" he asks, hopefully. Bettie gently lets him down by saying, "No, I'm sure you're a very nice guy."

This brief and rather sweet scene highlights the difference between the female dominant as she is constructed on camera, and how she is in real life. Bettie Page may have been the first and most famous bondage model, but off the clock she had no interest in fulfilling her male fans' desires to be humiliated by her. Yet it can be hard to get past the mainstream media depiction of the female dominant (domme, dominatrix, domina, mistress, etc.) when we're given so few nuanced representations of her: movies, TV shows and music videos tend not to deviate from a fairly repetitive, and some might say unimaginative, stereotype. The domme must be a ball-buster (pun sort of intended, given my aforementioned experience), a man-hater, an aggressive, sadistic shrew. She must exhibit no traditionally "feminine" qualities, as these are equated with weakness. Her clothes must signal her role in an exaggerated fashion, be this through a uniform implying a position of authority, or the restrictive costume of corset and spike heels.

To the average feminist, the idea that strength can only be signified through aggression and the ability to inflict pain is little more than a belief that traditionally masculine qualities are superior ones—"might is right," if you will. Yet despite these troubling nods to a restrictive gender binary, in my research I repeatedly came across misguided attempts to defend BDSM as feminist via the very existence of the female domme. People's (sometimes understandable) discomfort with the idea of women submitting to men in kink, and inability to reconcile this with feminist thought, was often allayed with the argument "There are dominant women and submissive men too!" While I could understand where these people were coming from, I thought that their dividing of kinksters into "Acceptable/Feminist" and "Unacceptable/Anti-feminist" involved the kind of judgmental imposition of artificial categories that those fighting for free sexual expression should reject. I also thought it rested on a misperception of feminism that harks back to the ugly stereotypes put about by right-wing conservatives—that feminists wish to oppress, harm and possibly even kill men in their "FemiNazi" quest to create a matriarchy. To me, women dominating men is no more or less feminist than any other configuration of kink—male dom/fem sub, fem dom/fem sub, male dom/male sub—unless we believe that to take a spanking represents some kind of crushing defeat for one's gender, and furthermore, that what feminism wants *is* the crushing defeat of men.

The very fact that the female dominant is treated as such an artificial construct perhaps says the most about how we view power and femininity. Until Christian Grey came along, there were few, if any, images of a male dominant in a BDSM sense in popular culture. One might suggest that this is because dominance is assumed to be the default position for men, therefore there is no need to create a character to represent such a figure. Aside from the odd stereotype of the "leather daddy" turning up in shows such as *Arrested Development* (and usually in the context of gay male culture anyway), there is not much of a flipside to the female dominant—she stands alone, defined by her difference from her gender, whereas the figure of the male dominant often blends in as simply another man. The assumption that dominance is naturally a male state, and therefore unnatural for females, is another reason we should treat the pop culture depiction of the female domme with caution. There is much to suggest that she is held up as special, interesting, comical, a character with which to make a statement by pop culture producers, precisely because she doesn't "act like a typical woman."

The Damaged Domme

In the 2006 movie *Shortbus*, noted for the fact it featured real sex between the actors and that its storyline grew out of workshops run by the actors themselves, dominatrix Severin is described in the blurb on the DVD cover as "unable to connect." There we have stereotype number one about a woman who wishes to dominate men for a living—she is emotionless, cold and must fly in the face of the assumption that women are nurturing creatures far better able to communicate than the opposite gender. Interestingly, Severin's dominance is as much emotional as it is physical. The first client the viewer sees her with is a young man, who she castigates for being spoilt, rich and obnoxious. When he tries to get into her mind by asking, "Are you a top or bottom? I mean, in real life?" she screams, "Get on the fucking bed!" Her interactions with women and gay men are notably much gentler; she lies in an isolation tank with frustrated sex therapist Sofia and talks her through her lack of orgasms, even offering an exchange of skills, "I can help you have an orgasm, and maybe you can help me, like, have a real human interaction with someone." Although the physical contact and offers of sexual help may still only be another form of sex work for Severin, the way she offers this to Sofia comes across very differently to the way she harangues and attacks her heterosexual male clients. When Severin ends up in a closet with Jamie, a severely depressed gay man, she abandons her dominatrix persona and instead listens to him talk about his experience as a sex worker. However, her inability to connect with others emotionally is still made apparent by her discomfort when Jamie begins to cry.

Severin has some moments of intimacy with Sofia at sex club Shortbus, but ends up in tears, admitting, "I can't do it any more. I just want to have a house and a cat I can pet." It seems that underlying any hard, cold, female character, there must be an emotional and vulnerable girl, otherwise this poses too great a threat to the socially constructed narrative of femininity as frail and unstable. In her famous book on women and the law, *Eve Was Framed*, Helena Kennedy notes how women who match men in savage behavior are seen as dangerous aberrations: "When Martina Anderson and Ella O'Dwyer were sentenced after the Brighton bombing trial in 1986, the judge made a special comment about their cold-heartedness. On the evidence, they were no less feeling than their male co-accused, but of course 'caring' is not the province of men."[2]

A common quality of pop culture characters who participate in BDSM, and a frustratingly common assumption about real-life BDSM participants, is that they must be mentally damaged in some way. BDSM is still, whether explicitly stated or quietly believed, regularly assumed to be sick, freaky, deviant, wrong (much like the dominant view of homosexuality until recently, and before then, interracial relationships). The deliberate seeking of pain, humiliation and extreme sensations is pathologized and presumed to be the result of past trauma or mental illness, despite the fact no one has ever been included in the *DSM-IV* for playing rugby or appearing on *The X Factor*. Unfortunately, *Shortbus* does little to dispel this myth. Severin is portrayed as a deeply unhappy character who cannot reach out to other human beings—even in group scenes, she sits silently on the outskirts, her only participation being when she snaps Polaroids of certain moments and hands them wordlessly to those

Unable to connect? Severin the dominatrix and her "fucking trust fund hipster muppet" in *Shortbus* (Movie Stills Database).

who appear in the photograph. When Sofia's husband visits Severin, her contempt for him seems real, and the viewer sympathizes to an extent because they are aware that Rob is seeing a sex worker behind his wife's back. When Severin asks, "You never asked your wife to do this for you?" and Rob responds, "No. She wouldn't understand," the audience rolls its collective eyes along with Severin at the clichéd excuse given by a man for betraying his partner's trust: his wife doesn't understand him. However, Severin's anger boils over and the more she hurls abuse at Rob the more hysterical she becomes, screaming, "Don't fucking look at me!" as she collapses on the bed in tears.

Severin's descent into extreme emotion could, again, be seen as reflective of a misogynistic culture's need to see strong women "break." Female characters are only allowed to transgress traditional gender limits if the audience can be reassured by seeing the mask crack once in a while. Whether it's fearless and fiercely intellectual Lisbeth Salander being brutally raped in *The Girl with the Dragon Tattoo*, Katniss Everdeen sobbing to her male mentor, "Just help me get through this" in the movie *Catching Fire*, or Sarah Connor weeping as she holds a gun towards Dyson in *Terminator II: Judgment Day*, it can seem as if female characters on the silver screen are obliged to abandon their strength at some point to remind the audience they are still women, because they are still emotionally or physically weak, and therefore the threat they pose to men (assumed to always be physically strong and in control of all emotions) is limited. By contrast, if a male character does shed tears, panics or has a meltdown, it's explained away as momentary weakness, a brief show of femininity that allows us to see him as human before he reverts to default maleness. If a female character cries, she's just being a typical woman, and any show of femininity, however brief, is assumed to define her whole character, rendering her a loose cannon.

However, in the case of *Shortbus* there is also a sense of relief and release in Severin's meltdown. Kink is often described as cathartic by those who practice it and those who appreciate its power—what is often forgotten is that tops can experience this just as intensely as the bottoms upon whom they are inflicting pain, sensation or restriction. Much is written about "subspace" and "sub drop," experienced after intense kink play sessions, and therefore the importance of aftercare following these. However, much less is written about "top drop," and the possibility of dominants feeling drained, spaced out, overwhelmed with emotion or numb after play sessions, even though this happens too.

The fact that Severin experiences the intense release of emotion that she has implicitly been seeking throughout the whole of the movie can also be viewed as intensely positive for her character—her breakthrough, to use therapy terms. In the final scenes at the sex club, Severin is still sitting alone as other couples kiss and touch around her, but as the group begins to sing she yells and drums her feet as if experiencing a climax of her own. The fact that she is more thoughtful, humane and gentle when not doing her job says perhaps much less about gender and much more about the theatrical and artificial nature of BDSM. No one can be in 24-hour top mode, and few people would care to be. Her emotional outbursts with Sofia and Rob may have less to do with the apparent strain of having to be dominant when apparently this is an unnatural state for women, and much more to do with the therapeutic power of BDSM—it brings out feelings and sensations that are unexpected, and can be intense and troubling. However, it would be nice to see a pop culture depiction of a dominatrix who is unambiguously well adjusted, rather than the implication that any woman who does it must be emotionally troubled in some way.

The Man Hater

"The seductiveness of powerful women is mesmerizing but also frightening because of the unspoken notions that such power is won at the expense of men, and that powerful women consume and destroy."— Helena Kennedy[3]

Feminist concern about whether women wanting to play the submissive to a male partner signifies the victory of male aggression in shaping female sexuality comes somewhat undone when we consider the reverse scenario. If we truly believe that men who enjoy dominating their female partner in sex and play are misogynists, then do we believe that women who dominate men must be misandrists? That all female dominants are secretly using BDSM as an outlet for their anger and hatred at men and all their apparent crimes against women?

There are certainly pop culture tropes that support this notion. When the real-life memoir of sex worker Belle de Jour was turned into the mostly fictionalized TV series *Secret Diary of a Call Girl* in 2007 (appearing on ITV2 in the UK and Showtime in the U.S.), there was an inevitable kink-themed episode in the first season. To be fair, the episode did actually provide some useful information on BDSM—mentioning ground rules, safe words and negotiation, and noting that "hurting people is a very special talent"—albeit still within the context of white, heterosexual, cisgendered interactions.

In the episode, Belle asks Stephanie, her agent, for advice on how to add BDSM to her repertoire. Stephanie muses, "I was a domme for a while…. You do this job long enough, you want to kick the shit out of a man eventually." The line is played for comedy, but BDSM practitioners may bridle at the notion that (a) the desire to dominate must be necessarily borne from hatred and aggression, and (b) that domming someone is as simple as, or equivalent to, "kicking the shit out of" a person. The conflation of BDSM with real violence is a misperception that many kinksters spend a lot of time patiently refuting to those outside of the community, and it can feel like efforts to educate the public about the difference between a nonconsensual attack, and a pleasurable, consensual beating, are set back every time TV show producers decide to mix the two up. However, there are those who would say that due to physical and social differences in power, a woman saying she wants to "kick the shit out of men" simply does not carry with it the same threat that a man saying the same about women would. Anne McClintock writes, "Some dominas confess to potent expressions of feminist anger, outrage and power when they work," therefore for us to assume that "S/M *never* involves real anger or hate runs the risk of disavowing the intense emotional voltages that can be S/M's appeal."[4]

This brings us back to the question of what is seen as default behavior for each gender. Women's aggression is treated as an aberration, whereas men's is treated as natural, and still far too often unquestioned. However, this imbalance may actually mean that women are more likely to get a "pass" when it comes to exhibiting aggression against men. Much like the vicious punishments which Lisbeth Salander doles out to misogynists throughout the novels in Stieg Larsson's *Millennium* trilogy, female aggression against men is sanctioned by popular culture if it is a justified response to the crimes of the male sex. One example of this is the Gulabi Gang, an organization of Indian women who patrol a district of Utter Pradesh wielding sticks, taking on men who abuse or desert their female relatives (with force if necessary). The group has won bravery awards and their work has been reported on with fascination by the Western media, including the BBC and *Ms.* magazine. There is a sense that violent vigilantism is an understandable response from women in a country where social and legal protection for them is incredibly poor. So, in *Secret Diary of a Call Girl,* the appalling behavior from men that Stephanie has apparently witnessed during her time in sex work is justification enough to want to flog them bloody.

When Belle meets Sirona, a professional dominatrix who comes over to give Belle some pointers, the exchange between Sirona and her sub is again played for laughs—the spectacle of a man forbidden to speak, made to strip and kneel, and drink out of a dog bowl is handled very differently than if the submissive was a woman—if so, one wonders if the scene would even have made it in to the show. Again, is this because of the differing power dynamics that mean men being humiliated is funny, whereas women being dominated is simply too close to the reality of pervasive violence against women for an audience to perceive it as comedic or even watchable?

The episode also bursts an important myth about BDSM; namely, that sex is always involved. Belle is surprised to learn that being a dominatrix does not (necessarily) involve any sexual contact with a sub at all, and that a scene ends not with an orgasm, but with the dominatrix's watch beeping. Some dominatrices do offer sexual services, and obviously many private, non-financial relationships between female dommes and male subs do involve sex, but it is perhaps telling that the line is drawn so strictly here. Here, it appears that part of the domme's power over a man is to withhold sex from him. To allow sexual contact would muddy the power boundaries, either because it would mean allowing him too much pleasure or indulging him in physical intimacy. Sirona makes her view of power dynamics clear when she says, "I'm a goddess to my slaves; I wouldn't stoop to sex with them." It is certainly an interesting comment on gender relations that men are seen as exercising power over a woman by having sex with her, "fucking her," whereas women's power over men is exercised by denying them this very pleasure.

This assumption is troubling from a sex positive feminist viewpoint—it seems to feed into the belief held both by conservative antifeminists, and radical anti-pornography feminists, that sex is something which degrades women while empowering men. It also implies that women themselves don't enjoy sex, but only "stoop" to it for men's sake. In "A Scandal in Belgravia," the BDSM–themed episode of BBC series *Sherlock*, dominatrix Irene Adler tells Watson she is gay, which neatly sidesteps the issue of her having any sexual contact with men outside of her job. However, her frission with Sherlock implies otherwise, and it is this attraction that ultimately undoes her. Adler's attraction to Sherlock is what leads her to inadvertently give away an important piece of information that she has been concealing from him, and as a result she ends up begging him for help. It seems that any genuine attraction towards a man immediately renders a dominatrix weak; that women's only real power over men comes from retaining a steely indifference to them.

The Female Dominant Through the Male Gaze

> "We live in a world which worships the unreal female body and despises real female power."—Laurie Penny[5]

Another area in which the female dominant in popular culture and feminism clash most severely is the narrow category of physical appearances into which dommes must fit. The assumption that dommes are somehow feminist warriors comes unstuck when we consider how rarely the figure of the female dominant is actually freed from the restrictive confines of typically feminine clothing. If the submissive or masochist is meant to be the party on the receiving end of physical discomfort, why is it that the female dominant is so often depicted as squeezed into a bone-crushing corset or skin-smothering latex, and tottering on six-inch heels? Why is she usually heavily made up (with black eyeliner, pale face powder and red lipstick being the absolute minimal standard), with her hair fully styled? If female dominants were truly empowered, one might wonder why we do not see them more often wearing jeans, t-shirts, running shoes and no make-up, with their hair tied back? Dominating someone is sweaty work, after all!

Part of the answer lies in the fact that dom/sub relationships are more of an exchange than is often recognized, and that both parties aim to derive pleasure from the other—it is not a one way street whereby the dominant merely gets their own way and the submissive suffers. Many of the men who seek out dominatrices are aroused not just by the treatment meted out to them, but the clothing and appearance of the woman dominating them (I'm sure more than one man has fantasized about being lassoed by Wonder Woman...). Going to a dominatrix allows men with latex or shoe fetishes to indulge their fantasies in a way that simply is not available in everyday life, so when we wonder why female dommes always seem to be wearing those ridiculously high-heeled shoes, the answer may simply be "So her submissive can lick them." As I found out when I donned the flea-market high-heeled boots that I mentioned at the beginning of this chapter, the response from a submissive/masochist man was immediate. Another fetish that non-kinksters may be unaware of is the practice of trampling, whereby a woman walks on a man's back while she is wearing high heeled shoes. While this is a delicate skill that must be practiced safely, it is one that brings satisfaction via a certain amount of pain and pressure—ergo, the higher and more spiky the heel, the more fun for the man lying under the domme's feet.

However, we have to ask ourselves if this isn't a rather chicken-and-egg scenario—if women weren't traditionally expected to shoehorn their feet and bodies into horrendously uncomfortable shoes and clothes,

Is the female dominant in pop culture truly powerful, or is she merely objectified through the male gaze? "Worship" (courtesy www.naughtyart.co.uk).

would the fetish for such wear have developed in the first place? As Germaine Greer wrote in her book *The Whole Woman,* "The high-heeled shoe is a marvelously contradictory item. It brings a woman up to a man's height but makes sure she cannot keep up with him."[6] Anyone who has watched Beyoncé's 2007 music video "Green Light" and winced at the sight of her dancers standing on tiptoe in restrictive ballet-style high heels inevitably wonders what exactly is supposed to be empowering about wearing shoes so uncomfortable one can barely stand in them, and instead of walking, can only totter like an unsteady infant.

An online commenter on some of my writing wrote that they found expectations for female dress in the BDSM community restrictive, despite the assumption that because BDSM is a counterculture, it must automatically be liberating. Talking about the expectation that dominatrix footwear must automatically mean high heels, they wrote, "It's tough to get lost in the scene when you've got fresh blisters on your feet. Tough to wield a flogger when you can barely stand. On one particularly memorable occasion, I pitched forward as soon as I got in the door of the dungeon, grabbing on to the front desk to keep from falling on my face. Sexy."[7] As someone who rejected the concept of heels early on in my explorations into my local BDSM scene, I remember attending a play party and being complimented on my clingy black wet-look dress, only to be criticized for the fact I was wearing flat-soled boots, *twice in the same night.* Apparently my failure to top off my kinky outfit with suitably crippling high heels meant my outfit failed at the last hurdle, which said a lot to me about preconditioned expectations of female sexiness within the BDSM scene.

The fact that supposedly dominant women do not escape these expectations either in real life or when they are portrayed in mainstream culture implies that full liberation when it comes to appearances still has some way to go. A quick Amazon search for reading material on how to be a dominant female will inevitably result in a swathe of book cover art portraying high heeled boots and corset-clad figures, even though dominatrix Claudia Varrin writes in her book *Female Dominance: Rituals and Practices* that when she truly wants to exhibit power over her sub, she wears jeans, combat boots and an old sweater, in order to deliberately convey that she is not dressed for his visual pleasure. In her extremely kinky video for her 2009 song "Alejandro" (dir. Steven Klein), Lady Gaga hints at this dynamic by sitting fully cloaked in black on a throne, watching her muscular male dancers perform for her pleasure. She is entirely covered, while the men wear nothing but fishnet stockings and black high heels as they grapple with rope on army-style beds. It is clear who the dominant figure is, because her clothing is not the focus of the scene; the only part of Gaga's outfit we really see are the steampunk spectacles through which she stares at the men.

Dressing Down

There is the odd character who turns up in pop culture without the standard uniform of corset, heels and PVC pencil skirt. In "Love Hurts," a 2005 episode of medical drama *House,* a young man named Harvey is admitted to the hospital with a stroke. The doctors fail to recognize that Annette, the woman who accompanies him, is his dominatrix until Dr. Chase admits he knows her. Dressed fairly casually in jeans, a blouse and a blazer, Annette looks more like a middle-class soccer mom than a dominatrix. Perhaps deliberately avoiding the typical BDSM colors of black and red, the program-makers dress Annette in inoffensive pale colors—more Laura Ashley, less dungeonwear. Of course, this may be as much due to the setting as anything else; few fetishists are brave or crazy enough to walk into a hospital in full BDSM regalia for fear of judgment, ridicule and possible trouble with law enforcement. Indeed, at one point the doctors tell Harvey he is lucky that Annette hasn't been arrested. There's no getting away from the fact that Annette is still a very conventionally attractive white woman, with long, blonde-highlighted hair, immaculate make-up (although subtle and nude—none of the standard dominatrix black eyeliner or blood-red lipstick); she is slim, feminine and young-ish, although still older than Harvey, her distinctly boyish sub. However, it's refreshing that it's her actions, rather than her appearance, are what gives away the fact she's a dominatrix: only when the doctors find her with a hand over Harvey's neck does the truth come out. This certainly makes a change from the crashingly obvious visual signposting that so many TV and movie producers feel compelled to use when dealing with a female dominant character.

However, most pop culture depictions of dominant women don't manage to avoid the clothing clichés. In *Charlie's Angels* (2000), when Lucy Liu's character Alex is masquerading as an "efficiency expert" at a company full of men, she does so in a tight leather suit jacket and matching leather pencil skirt. As she strides up to the front of the room, the camera focuses on her backside moving in the skirt. The song *Barracuda* plays as if to designate her ferocity, but for all that she is supposed to be the aggressor, Liu's body is still being served up as a spectacle for male consumption. As she stands at the front of the room she regularly uses a cane to make her point, slamming it on the desk and making the male crowd jump. She clutches a nervous young man's head to her bosom and grabs him by the hair and strokes another man's face, alternating gentle teasing with savage thwacks of the cane. She then breaks the cane over her knee, making the entire room wince (phallic symbolism, anyone?!). She is contrasted by a frumpy, overweight office administrator played by Melissa McCarthy, who wears an outsized blouse and cardigan, long skirt and flat shoes. The message seems to be that you can dominate a room of men so long as you're dressed right, and of course, are not overweight. High heels and leather pencil skirts, however restrictive one might find them, are apparently what dominant women must don in order to show their power.

Similarly, in *Secret Diary of a Call Girl*, dominatrix Sirona wears the standard uniform of all black, leather corset, leather pencil skirt,

Dragon lady: Alex (Lucy Liu) prepares to dominate a room full of men in *Charlie's Angels* (Movie Stills Database).

elbow length gloves and thigh-high boots. She is an older woman with long black hair and heavy, slightly gothic make-up—pale face powder, eyes ringed in thick black kohl. Granted, she is wearing many more clothes than her slave, who is only permitted to wear leather briefs, but her clothes still seem intended for the pleasure of a male voyeur. When Belle makes her own foray into domming, she wears a high-necked black latex dress with a pencil-style skirt, with a black PVC corset laced over it and high heeled black pumps. The effect is severe but sexy, and viewers can hear the latex creaking and squeaking over itself as Belle moves around the room.

Breathing Room

The fact that corsets regularly feature in pop culture depictions of the female dominant is also controversial, due to the association of corsetry with body modification and historical expectation of women to wear this item, even at the expense of their physical health. The return of corsetry as a fashion item has seen the item become more a fun piece of costuming and less an emblem of restriction. Gothic, steampunk and burlesque fashions have embraced the corset and brought it to generations who may be blissfully unaware that their great-great grandmothers had no choice but to lace themselves into potentially bone- and organ-crushing "stays" and wear them day in, day out, while modern women enjoy the choice to only don a corset for a fun night out.

However, the corset as a fun or sexy fashion item is less convincing when we consider the images of body modification associated with it. Corset training, tight lacing and waist size reduction are all fetishes with a considerable amount of followers, and the bodies being trained are, with very few exceptions, female. So why is burlesque performer Dita von Teese and her corset-induced 22-inch waist considered an object of admiration by many, while other female celebrities who show too many collarbones or ribs are condemned for encouraging anorexia? For those concerned that the female body is already under ridiculous pressures to conform to impossible standards of beauty, the practice of lacing oneself into a corset to reduce a waist which society already tells women can never be small enough seems at best unpleasant and at worst collusive with misogyny. An online commenter stated, "Now we don't reshape our bodies with garments as much as we do with dieting and plastic surgery, [but] the pressures to conform to the body type deemed 'desirable' (very thin, flat stomach, small hips and huge breasts) are no less restrictive than the stays of the past, only we're told to achieve that shape through 'discipline' and a little plastic surgery."[8] She echoes the views of feminist Laurie Penny, who writes that as women's social and economic power has grown, "we have been persuaded in greater and greater numbers to slim down, to take up less space, to shrink ourselves."[9]

Other commenters were not so quick to equate corsetry with sexism, claiming that waist reduction could be viewed as another form of body modification along with piercings (especially those involving plugs/piercing dilators), hair dyeing and tattoos, but this disregards the fact corsetry has a distinctly gendered bias. However, one thing I discovered in my research was the history of men wearing corsets, a fact of which I'd been previously unaware. As the above commenter also pointed out, "Being laced up in a corset can make you feel armored, untouchable and strong. Historically, corsets were worn as part of military garb by some men." Perhaps most relevant to the female dominant, the corset forces one to stand up straight, bringing a feeling of being upright, proud and commanding. There are also, still, today, men who enjoy corsetry, as I saw for myself out in the BDSM scene. One can read about men's taste for wearing corsets on the website of manufacturers Romantasy,[10] who make them especially for men. The blurb on Romantasy's homepage reads "Military men and 'dandies' too, were known in the eighteenth century, and even into this century, to wear corsets to achieve proper military stance and fit of the uniform, or to cut a fine figure. Our research and experience demonstrate that many modern men corset and perhaps for a wider variety of reasons than do women." To return to the "Alejandro" video again, Lady Gaga's beefy male dancers in military hats and boots are also seen sporting black waist cinchers, which a viewer may say enhances rather than suppresses their muscular torsos. So perhaps I was guilty of projecting my own bias on to the concept by assuming that corsets were solely a way to literally and metaphorically pressure women, and failing to appreciate that there are several alternative ways to read the tradition of corsetry.

Everyone Loves a Fascist

Outfits aside, there are other stereotypes applied to the character of the female dominant in popular culture, and a major one is racial. The association of a dominant female with foreignness occurs in several major comedy movies and betrays a tendency (especially in white, English-speaking countries) to reduce certain nationalities to deeply offensive caricatures. The dominatrices who close in on horny teenager Cooper in the 2004 comedy movie *Eurotrip*, despite being Dutch, have accents that sound distinctly Eastern European, to the point where the viewer wonders if the makers of the film confused The Netherlands with Germany or Russia. Milla Jovovich's character in *Zoolander*, the distinctly dommely "Katinka Ingabogavinanana" is clearly intended to be a caricature of severe, sharp-accented Eastern European womanhood, and there are no prizes for guessing from where leather-clad, whip-wielding baddie Frau Farbissner of the three *Austin Powers* movies is meant to hail.

Much like British people have had to endure the regular use of the British accent to denote a movie villain, one could simply say that the association of a Germanic accent with strictness, discipline and violence is a bit of fun. However, when one considers the origins of this assumption, it becomes a lot more offensive than any cat-stroking Bond villain could be to the British. The German reputation for humorless discipline comes, of course, from the stereotype of the Nazis and their leader Adolf Hitler (a stereotype itself perpetuated in various British comedies such as the 1980s sitcom *'Allo 'Allo*, set in 1940s France, where German soldiers were always stone-faced, immaculately groomed and dressed in leather), and it doesn't seem like too great a leap to say that movie makers feel a quick way to convey a dominant female is to give her a German accent. Comedy is often premised on irreverence, but I'm not sure this would be deemed an adequate excuse in a country where it is still illegal to say "Sieg Heil" or give the Nazi salute. Furthermore, the conflating of consensual BDSM with the violence and coercion of fascist regimes (Nazism, Stalinism) does little to disperse the public perception of kink as abusive, dark and twisted. Granted, the use of military uniforms and the accompanying imagery does find its way into some people's BDSM play, but it's by no means a kink held by many or even the majority of

BDSM practitioners (On the kinky social networking site FetLife 40 people report themselves as having the fetish "Girls in military uniform who can kick ass," whereas over 50,000 are into "schoolgirl uniform"). So why when pop culture producers want to depict a dominant female, do they always feel the need to resort to Nazi or Bolshevik stereotypes? Do they consider their audiences so unable to detect a dominant female without the obvious markers of an accent or outfit that implies a love of fascism, bullwhips and leather?

The dominatrix scene featuring Lucy Liu in *Charlie's Angels* also has some uncomfortable racialized overtones. Midori, a Japanese-born BDSM educator says that she works hard to break the stereotypes of Asian women "as either delicate flowers or dragon ladies."[11] One of Midori's more interesting solutions is to be "particularly sadistic while wearing a traditional kimono, thus mixing the 'delicate flower' image with hard-core sadism." Unfortunately, there were no such subtleties in the movie, which placed Liu firmly on the dragon lady side of the divide.

Some pop culture producers are capable of more subtlety when it comes to dominant women of Asian descent. In the second book of Stieg Larsson's Millennium Trilogy, *The Girl Who Played with Fire*, the BDSM scene between protagonist Lisbeth Salander and her sometimes lover Mimmi Wu is refreshingly free both of racial stereotypes and a typically a male gaze. The dialogue also acknowledges both that BDSM is theatre: "'I feel like playing. Are you up for it?' Mimmi said"; and that the female domme is simply a role, if sometimes a caricatured one—"Tonight I think I'll be a dominating bitch." Although there are nods elsewhere in the book to Mimmi Wu being a typical "dragon lady" dominatrix (the police discover "patent leather, corsets and fetishist whips" in her apartment), the actual BDSM scene is almost devoid of stereotypical paraphernalia. We don't even get a voyeuristic description of what the two women are wearing, beyond T-shirts (no yards of black PVC or spike heels for these two), nor is Wu's race present in Larsson's description of her as a dominant sexual partner. Perhaps most importantly, the scene focuses on the lust and pleasure of the two women, and the absence of tropes is what makes it one of the least sensationalized, and therefore enjoyable to read, depictions of kink in mainstream literature.

The 24/7 Domme

What Laarson's brief passage shows is that it's possible to portray BDSM and female dominance without restricting one's characters to being in kink mode 24/7. Other media producers seem to have trouble with this, perhaps reflecting a larger problem of pop culture producers struggling to portray women as multi-faceted characters in *any* situation. In the highly acclaimed BBC series *Sherlock*, beloved for its rich characters and head-spinning plot twists and turns, the character of dominatrix Irene Adler fails to shake many stereotypes about the female domme. Adler is a dark-haired, pale-skinned, slim young white woman fond of red lipstick and red nail polish, and throughout the episode "A Scandal in Belgravia" she is always either festooned with dominatrix clichés or spouting them. The first shot we see of her is her backside in a thong, barely concealed in a transparent black lace gown, brandishing a riding crop and swaying towards an unseen figure on a bed. She's supposed to be mysterious, but this certainly isn't synonymous with being concealed, as the audience still sees a perfect male-gaze-oriented view of her nearly naked behind. Later, we see her red nails stroking a photo of Sherlock then stroking a black leather riding crop, a sleeve of her black satin blouse the only part of her clothing we're party to. If the viewer suspects they are going to overload on black clothing by the end of the episode, they are correct.

Having gone through her wardrobe to decide what she will wear to meet Sherlock (and doing so in a slash-necked transparent robe, stockings and suspenders—apparently a dominatrix never just opts for sweatpants when she is off the clock, but is always in full-on sexy mode), the punchline is that Adler walks into the room completely naked. This is part of a ploy to disorientate Sherlock—it certainly works on Watson, who is barely able to speak—and also to withhold any clues from him that her clothes might give away. It's clever insofar as the audience has already seen Sherlock size up others in the episode and deduce numerous things from their shoes, trousers, haircuts and so on, but it's also undeniably part of a determination to constantly sexualize Adler.

Nudity aside, it seems that everything Adler does must be draped in BDSM symbolism—whether she is escaping from her apartment on a rope, sending Sherlock a Christmas gift tied with black rope, or remarking, "Look at those cheekbones. I could cut myself slapping that face..." about Sherlock, the audience learns nothing about Adler except the fact she is a dominatrix. She does show herself capable of wielding more than a flogger when she disables an attacker and pistol whips him, but when she turns on Sherlock himself, her weapon of choice to force him to hand over a cellphone seems more than a little unlikely. After disabling him with a tranquilizer and hitting him in the face, Adler then goes straight for the riding crop to get Sherlock to obey. I found myself wondering: of all the blunt heavy instruments Adler has to hand in her dressing room, would a riding crop *really* be the best instrument with which to disarm a grown man? Or could the program-makers just not resist the symbolism? After all, having Adler bludgeon Sherlock with a glass bottle or smash the mirror over his head would not then allow for the shot of Sherlock on the floor with Adler standing over him, stroking his face with the end of the crop and crooning, "This is how I want you to remember me—the woman who beat you."

If the power of the dominatrix comes from remaining aloof and mysterious then the BBC did its job, and in the context of a detective thriller show, that's understandable. However, in terms of avoiding clichés about the female domme, portraying a dominatrix outside of the male gaze, or adding any more facets to a limited public understanding of BDSM, *Sherlock* did not succeed.

As a concept, the female dominant holds potential to disrupt assumptions about gender, but rarely is this potential actually harnessed in popular culture. Dommes get to be sexy, sadistic or secretly vulnerable; rarely are they permitted to be all three. They don't get to be overweight, unattractive or comfortably dressed, they don't get to have lives outside what they do, and they don't get to exhibit genuine power or strength, but rather token outburst of viciousness that are draped in the symbolism of their role. Incidentally, my favorite scene of female dominance is in a film that's neither sexual or about BDSM; it's in *The Hunger Games*. I always found the force with which Katniss grabs Peeta by the back of his shirt and slams him up against a wall with her forearm against his throat (after he has confessed his love for her on national TV) a much more convincing show of violence than any amount of riding crops or handcuffs could convey. Of course, those who believe that what feminists want is actual female dominance would probably say I just enjoy seeing men getting beaten up. Speaking of which...

2

Brave or Pathetic?

*Masculinity's Troubled Relationship
with the Male Submissive*

"This pathologizing thing, 'Well, why would he want to do
this? Why would he want to crawl around on his hands and
knees and kiss the feet of this woman and have his dick
chained or something? What kind of man would want to do
that sort of thing?'"[1]—Interviewee "Stephanie," quoted in
Margot Weiss' *Techniques of Pleasure.*

The mainstream media relationship with men who decide to be
submissive is a decidedly uncomfortable one. As an anonymous commenter on *Bitch* wrote, "I am a submissive man. Outside the bedroom
I don't let people walk all over me, but neither do I have a lot of, or seek
out, power over others. I am extremely empathic, [and] sometimes I am
vulnerable."[2] It is perhaps this aspect of the male submissive that dis-
quiets those who subscribe to patriarchal narratives about male and
female roles the most. One conclusion I came to in my research was that
in mainstream Western culture, male sexual submission is only acceptable within extremely narrow parameters, and furthermore, is an act for
which the man in question is always expected to compensate.

When I examined "A Scandal in Belgravia," an episode of the popular BBC drama *Sherlock,* I noted the distaste with which other men
described the clients of dominatrix Irene Adler; Sherlock himself
describes Adler's work as "catering to the whims of the pathetic." This
need to denigrate men who submit to women implies a sense that these
men are "letting the side down" by seeking out a woman to humiliate
and overpower them, even if such activities are merely theatrical, or as
Mycroft describes it elsewhere in the episode, "recreational scolding."

Indeed, Mycroft's disdain for the rich and powerful men who seek out Adler's services belie his claims that domination and submission are merely a game—if he and the mainstream media who gleefully pounce on any emerging story of powerful man seeking to play the submissive really believe this, then why are they so vehement in their mocking and disapproval of such activities?

The social roles of the men involved tend to be what prompts the most scandal; when Formula 1 mogul Max Mosley was scrutinized in 2008 over claims that he had participated in a BDSM–themed party with several sex workers,[3] the worldwide media feigned concern over whether the party was Nazi-themed, but it was clear where their real fascination lay. The fact that an incredibly rich and influential man (the son of a UK politician who was known for his far-right leanings) paid a group of uniformed women to shave his backside, hurt and humiliate him, still has the power to fascinate a society ill-at-ease with unconventional male sexual tastes. Even though Mr. Justice Eady pointed out that the "'bondage, beating and domination' that did take place was 'typical of S&M behavior,'" the fact that this needed pointing out at all implies either genuine ignorance about what BDSM involves (something which seems unlikely in the West where a quick Google is all that it takes to shed some light on the matter), or a deliberate misreading of Mosley's activities in order to leverage the story into a legal issue, rather than merely a matter of prurient fascination.

Personally, I never quite believed that (alleged) Nazi aspect of the "F1 Boss's Sick Nazi Orgy with Five Hookers" story was actually of genuine concern, least of all to the now-defunct tabloid newspaper *News of the World*, which printed such a headline. The UK tabloids are renowned for being right-wing, xenophobic if not downright racist, and therefore pretty unlikely to be genuinely outraged at the prospect of a little theatrical fascism. They do, however, love a sex scandal, and their focus appeared to land squarely on Mosley's deviance. The idea of a powerful man in his 60s cavorting with sex workers, described in dismissive journalese slang, and his desire to be dominated by them, were what really fascinated the media, and were what those who disliked him saw as prime weapons with which to destroy his public image. Despite the tabloid media's own attitude to women being at best, reductive, and at worst, utterly dehumanizing, the editor of the *News of the World*,

Colin Myler, saw no irony in condemning Mosley's private and consensual activities as "depraved and brutal" and unfit behavior for "someone in his hugely influential position."

Power Is Such a Chore

However, although his High Court victory against said tabloid could be viewed as a victory for the right to privacy, Mosley's story does not actually fly in the face of stereotypes surrounding kink as much as one might hope. It still follows a very well-trodden storyline, namely that of the powerful man so exhausted by all his influence and responsibility that he wants to surrender it for a while. In this sense, kink functions as catharsis, a form of therapy, a temporary state of powerlessness which will be compensated for as soon as the man in question returns to his role of being a dominant male (in Mosley's case, that means being "head of the richest sport in the world, with 125 million members"). The *Sherlock* episode supports this narrative, with a policeman, a Ministry of Defense official and a forensic scientist being named among Adler's clients. So do some real-life anecdotes: rock photographer Bob Gruen describes Nancy Spungen (girlfriend of Sex Pistol Sid Vicious)'s work as a dominatrix: "Guys pay you to tie them up and hit them with whips?" We couldn't believe it. "Who does that?" we asked. According to Nancy, "mostly bankers, lawyers and German guys."[4] As for Mosley, the very fact that a man wanting to be submissive is still considered newsworthy shows how it is still viewed as a deeply unnatural state for a man. If male submission were viewed as an acceptable sexual behavior and acknowledged as one regularly chosen and enjoyed by many men, would such stories still gain such traction?

To normalize male sexual submission would involve acknowledging, like the anonymous man quoted at the beginning of the chapter, that all kinds of men do enjoy submission, and not necessarily because they are tired of being dominant in their everyday lives, or because they are too rich, too powerful, too physically strong and require a break from those pressures. Yet this is a narrative the media seems unwilling to grasp. A man who submits simply because he finds it sexually pleasurable, rather than to compensate for the exhaustion of a high-powered job or macho behavior elsewhere in the world, seems to be a nuance too far for mainstream media producers. Even in the recent Netflix series, *House of Cards* (a remake of a British political drama from the 1990s), a series praised for its slow-burning and intelligent portrayal of political manipulation, the only nod to BDSM is to show a multi-billionaire man playing the submissive. In Chapter 18 of Season 2, Xander Feng, a Chinese businessman who has gained asylum in the United States in return for his money-laundering services, enters the murky world of U.S. politics. The audience's first introduction to Feng is seeing him naked and restrained on a bed with a plastic bag over his head, being pleasured by a man and a woman sitting atop him; it later transpires they are being paid for their services. There is little to connect the scene with the rest of the series—I wondered if it was perhaps going to be brought up later for blackmail purposes, another standard storyline when it comes to kinky businessmen, but Feng's sexual preferences are never mentioned again. So the scene only seems to serve the purpose of establishing this well-tread dichotomy once again, namely that men who submit must be powerful in all other aspects of their lives, and that it is the pressure of being so powerful that leads them to seek release in BDSM.

There is also a sense that power warps these men's sexuality, meaning they can only find pleasure in twisted practices such as bondage and asphyxiation. The fact that Feng is Asian may be incidental, but one also wonders if there is a racialized stereotype at work, that of Oriental sexuality being particularly freaky—think of the sexual violence, bestiality and pedophilia portrayed in hentai, and the much mythologized vending machines selling Japanese schoolgirls' used underwear. In the episode of *House* mentioned in the previous chapter, Harvey, the male submissive who is admitted to hospital with a stroke as a result of his preference for asphyxiation is also Asian, and is referred to as a "perv" and "sick," although House defends him against his judgmental parents who complain that his proclivities have "humiliated" them in their community. In this case it's the parents rather than the kinky person himself who live into typical Oriental stereotypes, being emotionally cold and more concerned with losing face than about their ill son. However, other stereotypes about male subs are nonetheless still at work here, namely that the best they can hope for from the vanilla world is to be pitied and protected.

Not Every Sub Is an Alpha Elsewhere

In his book *Sex and the British*, Paul Ferris comments that there is something of a mythology at work when it comes to the belief that a high-flying job naturally equals a taste for submission. "Twentieth century folk wisdom made flagellation a vice of the upper classes, where powerful men—judges, bankers, indulged their infantile memories of helplessness by submitting to ladies with rolled-up sleeves."[5] However, this may be a skewing of the facts, since the acts of male submission most likely to reach the press were, of course, those for which men paid. "Prostitutes liked to say that their masochistic clients were top-drawer gents, though this was hardly surprising, since 'special services' were expensive." It would be interesting to know how many men enjoy masochism and submission despite not being rich or overwhelmed with corporate responsibility, yet it's unlikely we'll ever find out because the sexual preferences of a stay-at-home father or a male nurse don't generally hit the headlines, plus a sexist media usually assumes these men must automatically be emasculated anyway because they are already playing traditionally "female" roles. If changing diapers or working with small children already means a man must be "whipped," the assumption goes, then of course he probably gets bossed around in the bedroom too...

Looking, then, to the independent film market, where there are, generally speaking, more sensitive portrayals of sexual variation to be found, there might be a greater chance of finding a nuanced appreciation of male submission. In the 2006 indie film *Thumbsucker,* teen protagonist Justin enjoys some mildly BDSM–themed sex games with the object of his desire, Rebecca. Justin is physically slight, long-haired, fey, and while not overtly effeminate, he certainly does not fit the personality or appearance type of an alpha male (a video gamer friend of mine refers to himself and other non-alpha, stereotypically nerdy men as "gamma males," perhaps an appropriate term here). Rebecca only allows Justin to touch or kiss her while blindfolded, telling him, "Just touch, don't look," and when he asks why, she responds, "Because those are the rules." All the sexual contact they have is framed this way, with Justin blindfolded and Rebecca in control. After several instances of this, Justin says, "This thing bugs me. Why can't I see you?" Rebecca repeats, "Those are

Relinquishing male power: Justin (Lou Taylor Pucci) plays with submission in *Thumbsucker* **(Photofest).**

the rules," but this time Justin is not interested in being submissive, asking, "Why do *you* get to make up all the rules?," and taking off his blindfold.

Rebecca's need for a submissive male partner has an uncomfortable explanation behind it: "This was just a teenage experiment. I needed to educate myself ... so I decided to pick someone like you. Someone I'd never get hurt by." Although Justin is offended and hurt, and ends the relationship there and then, neither party is visibly scarred by the exchanges. Justin shows himself capable of assertive behavior when he finally questions and rejects the dynamic of the relationship, but until then, being submissive gains him things many "alpha" teen boys would envy him for; namely, the undivided sexual attentions of a very attractive girl. Justin isn't submitting because he's exhausted by power or masculinity—he's submitting because in this particular case, he finds it extremely pleasurable to do so.

Despite being somewhat insensitively expressed, Rebecca's actions do not seem implausible, especially taking into account the capacity for calculation that is the specialty of the teenage girl. Yet mainstream pop culture still seems hostile to portraying male submission (or the accompanying "girls on top") without sensationalism or recourse to simplistic gender binaries, or for that matter, simplistic depictions of power dynamics. The male may be the submissive in this case, but he has been specifically chosen due to an awareness of the corrosive power of other males. Rebecca is aware of her vulnerability as much as of her strength, and unlike Justin, does not have the luxury of letting that vulnerability out with a partner.

What troubles me, and appears to trouble a lot of feminists, about how BDSM is often read in popular culture, is the automatic association of the submissive role with femininity, and the corresponding treatment of male submission as an aberration. Even though, as Anne McClintock points out,[6] "S/M theatrically flouts the edict that manhood is synonymous with mastery, and submission a female fate," the need to treat male submissives as either disgusting or a joke implies a lot of pop culture producers are still uncomfortable with this transgression of traditional gender roles. The tendency to view a man being dominated by a woman as pathetic or deserving of mockery implies at best a discomfort with the idea of men willingly surrendering the power that is meant to be synonymous with masculinity, and at worst, such fear of women exerting any true power over men that all scenarios depicting this must be neutralized through comedy or other credulity stretches.

Instruments or Objects?

Another way of neutralizing the threat posed by the submissive man is to ensure that his physical strength is always apparent, even if he's in bondage, and that any power a woman exercises over him is clearly acted. A good example of this is the 2003 music video for the song "Too Lost in You" by British female 3-piece Sugababes, used on the soundtrack to the romantic comedy *Love Actually*. In the video, each band member is shown indulging her fantasy with a musclebound man she sees in an airport. Keisha is shown teasing and whispering to a muscular, baby-oiled young man who sit handcuffed in front of her, Mutya circles her similarly buff conquest while brandishing a fencing sword and slashing his T-shirt, and Heidi teases her member of ground staff with a bucket of ice. Although apparently in passive positions, the men's muscular physiques are displayed for maximum effect, making the flimsy handcuffs on Keisha's man seem little more than token efforts at restraint. Watching this, one can't help but think that given the man's size, a real dominatrix would surely have got out the ropes, chains and manacles (and a sturdier chair) to really have any chance of restraining him...

Two of the men are portrayed as manual workers, further reinforcing their physical strength (although it is troubling from a racial viewpoint that only the white man appears to have a white-collar job and wear a suit) and assuring the viewer that the physically slight, petite members of the Sugababes can only dominate these men in an entirely staged way. This in itself is not problematic in light of Anne McClintock's words—BDSM is not meant to be real, therefore why should it matter whether a 5'2" woman is actually genuinely capable of physically controlling her sub or not? However, it does matter when people equate male submission with female submission as if they carry the same risks. As Staci Newmahr points out in her analysis of Elizabeth Stanko's work, "women move through the world afraid for their physical and sexual safety and men do not."[7] This makes the parameters within which men are able to play the submissive much safer, less frightening ones. There are of course, other fears at play within this space—fear of being mocked, of seen as less of a man by women or outcast by other men, especially if the man in question is heterosexual and otherwise appears macho in his everyday life. However, as Newmahr writes, this fear is in no way equivalent to the fear that women live with every day, that they may be physically or sexually assaulted, and most likely by a man.[8] "Men move through their worlds with trust, if not that they will not be assaulted, then at least that they will emerge intact."

However, even putting the terminal unsubtlety of music videos to one side for a moment, demanding extreme realism in scenes of male submission is perhaps missing the point. For all the oiled chests and heaving muscles, the Sugababes video does depict the male surrender of power to women as pleasurable and erotic. The men's bodies may be instruments insofar as they are clearly physically strong, but they are objectified insofar as they do not get to use those instruments for anything except sitting and taking whatever their female partner chooses to dole out. For those who find imagery of male submission erotic, the strength of the restraints may come a decided second to the intensity of the mental power exchange between players, and this is portrayed convincingly by the actors in the video.

Another example of submission being more mental than physical is in the movie *Shortbus,* when icy dominatrix Severin is dominating Rob, the husband of sex therapist Sofia. When Rob says he does not want to be completely restrained, Severin says, "Good. Because I can't be bothered to tie you up. Turn round and hold the headboard. If you let go, I'll leave." Not only is Severin already beginning the domination by speaking to Rob contemptuously, as if he is a waste of her time, but she is restraining him without using any physical form of bondage. One of the nuances of BDSM that is often lost when it is portrayed in visual mediums such as TV, movies and music videos, is that domination and submission can be as intangible as it can be physical. Women may not, on average, have the same physical strength as men to call upon when it comes to dominating another person, but many BDSM practitioners will tell you that it is rarely actual physical strength which makes a great dominant (and it's certainly never *just* that quality alone). As anyone who can recall the fear of being spoken to in *that voice* by a parent, or the silencing power of *that look* from a certain schoolteacher, dominance is far more often asserted psychologically than just via the body. As Mollena Williams pointed out in a 2009 interview[9] on the issues involved in racialized BDSM, "There were millions of [black people] enslaved by a few hundred thousand people. Jews were systematically destroyed by Nazis in camps where there were many, many more prisoners than guards." Her interviewer, Andrea Plaid, chips in, "I remember someone saying the biggest damage the Nazis did to Jews was psychological."

Similarly, much of the domination Severin enacts is psychological, berating and screaming at her male submissives. Jesse, the young man who is her main client is constantly insulted for his bratty wealth—"Is your daddy paying for this? … you fucking hipster trust fund piece of fetus shit!" and her ultimate insult is one sure to land most harshly on a man in his late teens or early 20s—that his band is not very good. When dominating Rob, she screams, "Do you feel it now, you little faggot?" The use of homophobic insults seems jarring in the context of gay-friendly, pansexual safe haven Shortbus, but this may say less about Severin being politically incorrect and more about which insults are likely to have the deepest effect on a heterosexual male. Being financially powerful is associated with masculinity, ergo Severin abuses her young client for being a "fucking trust fund muppet." Being heterosexual is inextricably bound up with traditional views of male strength, hence the use of a homophobic slur to humiliate Rob.

Acting Like a Girl

"A submissive man risks his masculinity."—Margot Weiss[10]

In *Shortbus*, Severin also undermines her male clients by questioning their gender identity, again because heterosexual men's strength rests so strongly on defining themselves in opposition to the female sex. The suggestion that a man might not be a *real* man has a long history of being used as an insult, be it Dr. Cox in *Scrubs* constantly calling JD girls' names, or the terrible accusation of "running/throwing/fighting/crying like a girl" being flung at young boys who fail to fit prescribed gender roles. In the deleted scenes on the *Shortbus* DVD, the audience sees Severin tormenting Jesse during their scene by telling him, "When you were born, they couldn't tell if you were a boy or a girl ... they were going to make you a girl but they decided to go with a boy." Only in a society where being a girl is still viewed as such a terrible fate could this be viewed as a powerful insult.

In the 2012 movie *An Awkward Sexual Adventure,* shy, gentle protagonist Jordan takes some time away from his exasperated girlfriend, who bemoans his lack of sexual skills, and meets Julia, who agrees to teach him some much-need techniques. When Jordan threatens to leave, Julia shouts, "You're going back a bigger pussy than when you left!," and then says, "You need to stop letting people walk all over you." She then gives him a BDSM–themed lesson in how to "be the aggressor," but Jordan finds he is not a natural dom, so Julia tries to goad him in to flogging her by trotting out the insults that Jordan's female boss regularly flings at him—"Do you need a maxi pad? ... Is the little baby going to cry?" Again, expressing emotions and behaving in any way viewed as traditionally feminine is framed as shameful for a man—ones so shameful that in this case, they are effective tools in riling Jordan out of his submissive role and in to flogging Julia.

The sense of shame around men crying disregards an important aspect of BDSM; emotional catharsis. While assuming that men must want to play the submissive because they crave the offloading of suffocating power, few people ever consider that men may also want a safe space in which to release emotions. The belief that boys don't cry remains a pervasive narrative which dictates many men's lives and limits their self-expression. Men my age often tell me they can't remember when they last cried; I would put money on the fact that every woman in the same age group knows exactly when she last burst into tears, and furthermore, that it wouldn't be that long ago. Extremes of emotion are often what BDSM practitioners seek—humiliation, rage, grief, terror—in order to both process and release inner tension. Crying after an intense bottoming session is not uncommon; indeed, it's something for which tops are warned to prepare, as mopping up your submissive's tears may well be a key part of the aftercare you need to give them. Rather than subscribing to the standard belief that crying is bad because it represents not just a loss of control but the experience of pain, both processes we are generally taught to avoid in life, many BDSM practitioners believe that it's a healthy and necessary part of emotional growth too often denied to us. There aren't many places where it's still truly accepted for men to express emotion (unless their sports team loses, of course), and for some men, it may take some heavy beating or humiliation to break down the emotional walls that they have erected in their defense. Because crying means acting like a girl, and men are taught to avoid that at all costs.

As Madonna points out in her song *What It Feels Like for a Girl*, women wearing traditionally male clothing is not problematized in Western society, because being male is acceptable. However, for a man to wear women's clothes or behave effeminately is seen as degrading, which can only be so if we think that to be female is, in itself, degrading. As Anne McClintock writes, so much of traditionally constructed male identity comes from "the ritualized disavowal of the feminine ... boys are tasked with identifying *away* from women, that is, away from a founding dimension of their own identity."[11]

Much of how male submissives are portrayed in popular culture—being made to wear women's clothes or "sissified," perform female tasks, or assume the receptive role in sex—implies that in this supposedly liberated, gender-neutral society, there remains a belief that the best way to humiliate a man is to make him act like a woman. In the BDSM episode of *Secret Diary of a Call Girl* mentioned in the previous chapter, the humiliation of a male sub again comes from having his gender identity undermined. The man shown playing the submissive for call girl Belle is in his late 50s, and is made to kneel and do housework while wearing only a PVC thong and apron. While the humiliation factor of some of the acts comes from them simply being stomach-turning—e.g., cleaning the toilet bowl with one's tongue—it's still hard to deny that most of the degradation has its basis in the fact that the man is supposed to be playing typically feminine roles. In my own experiences in the BDSM scene, I saw forced feminization and being made to dress in women's underwear or high-heeled shoes as common preferences among men who chose to be dominated by women.

However, Anne McClintock suggests that the submissive male desire to cross-dress or be treated like a house servant doesn't necessarily support a sexist binary—rather, she suggests that it is a liberating breaking of taboo, whereby men reject their social conditioning and explore worlds which fascinate them, but which are forbidden to them by the cult of extreme masculinity. She writes, "By paying to do 'women's work' or by ritually worshipping dominas as socially powerful, the male 'slave' relishes the forbidden, feminine aspects of his own identity, furtively recalling the childhood image of female power and the memory of maternity."[12] While it is problematic that pop culture depictions of the male submissive regularly disregard this nuance in favor of caricatures, McClintock suggests that the humiliation of male subs via domestic work or female roles is not as clear-cut as simply an association of the feminine with degradation. In fact, she suggests that because men pay to perform these kind of roles—much like the man in *Secret Diary of a Call Girl,* "domestic S/M stages women's work as having both *exhibition* and *economic* value. The social disavowal and *undervaluation* of domestic work is reversed in the extravagant *overvaluation* of women's dirty work, and the remuneration of *women* for the supervision of *men's* labor."[13] The image of a grown man licking a toilet bowl has more value than just comedy, then.

40

The Male Submissive as a Figure of Fun

The very fact that the male submissive is often used as a vehicle for comedy in popular culture supports the theory that submission is associated with femininity, and therefore seen as a role worthy of mockery when a man chooses to adopt it. The male submissive as an inadequate, laughable character is a narrative that appears in several 20th century comedy films. In *Zoolander* (2001), the fleeting reference to BDSM features in a montage of vain, vapid model Derek Zoolander's work. The joke is that Derek will promote any product and appear in any commercial, no matter how embarrassing—he's shown pouring Diet Coke over his head and wiggling around sporting a CGI tail as a "mer-man." So the inevitable shot of him with a saddle on his back and a bit gag in his mouth, being ridden by an obese woman in a skimpy black leather harness, is just one of many shots to show how the male model will accept any amount of humiliation in his quest for money and fame. The shot is accompanied by the sound of neighing, just to drive home the point that pony play is a practice to be mocked (rather than one that many kinksters regularly indulge in and find deeply pleasurable).

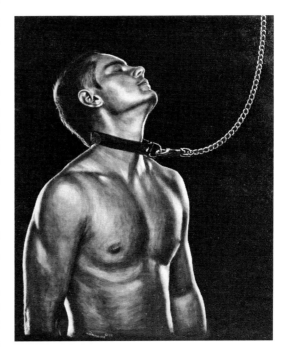

Similarly, in *American Pie: The Reunion* (2012), archetypal nerd Jim is portrayed as the submissive, being dominated by his wife Michelle. This is not entirely improbable, given that their first fumblings as teenagers (shown in the first movie *American Pie*,

Is male submission not taken seriously by popular media? "Serenity" (courtesy www.naughty art.co.uk).

1999) were directed by an aggressive Michelle shouting, "What's my name, bitch?!" as she sat astride the virginal Jim. Over a decade later, Jim and Michelle are married, exhausted by parenthood, and their sex life is in need of a boost. Cue Jim donning leather shorts and studded codpiece, plus leather suspenders and collar, and arranging himself alluringly on the bed while a house party takes place around him. The comedy element is already clear—how humiliating for a man to have to dress like that! What *does* he look like? The outfit leads to a misunderstanding with Jim's teenage neighbor Kara, whose jealous boyfriend AJ then attacks Jim, calling him a "gimp." When Jim says, "I'm not going to fight you, I'm an adult," AJ's response is, "Really? Because you look like a little bitch pussy." The feminine epithets and the assumption that submission equals weakness for a man (and also that being scantily clad and in leather equates submissive status) all fit into a sexist and mocking view of male submissives.

The scene descends into a brawl between the "class of 99" and the younger troublemakers. In keeping with the rest of their relationship, it is Michelle who comes to Jim's defense, appearing in a PVC catsuit and platform heels and attacking one of his teenage assailants with a riding crop. As a heterosexual male character who is regularly emasculated throughout the three *American Pie* films, it seems unsurprising that the makers chose to use BDSM as just another way to humiliate Jim.

Is Male Sexual Assault Funny?

In popular culture, men are not meant to be victims of sexual violence. Fist fights, gun fights, beatings and near-death misses are staples of the action movie, but rape threats (for men) are generally not. Give or take the odd predatory homosexual villain (e.g., Javier Bardem as Bond villain Raoul Silva in *Skyfall*) men's vulnerability is rarely situated in their potential to end up a victim of rape, certainly not to any extent comparable to the amount of times female characters are threatened with, or are victims of, sexual violence in movies, TV and books. The exception comes, it would appear, when a man is playing the submissive role, and when this, in turn, is being played for comedy.

In the 2004 movie *Eurotrip*, young male character Cooper visits an

Amsterdam brothel and is seduced by a group of Dutch sex workers into using their BDSM–themed services. He's happy to submit to being tied down, under the impression that it is the women who are going to pleasure him, and of course the punchline is that once he's restrained (with pink fluffy handcuffs, just to add that extra sense of masculine humiliation), a group of huge, muscular men wearing nothing but PVC aprons walk in, remove his trousers and begin brandishing testicle clamps. When he can't pronounce the Dutch safe word, a massive power-operated four-pronged dildo is brought out and aimed at his vulnerable buttocks. The movie scene ends on his agonized screams and the next scene begins with him limping towards his friends, clearly in massive discomfort after some unplanned anal penetration. When his friends ask him, "What did you do last night?," he mumbles, "I don't want to talk about it."

A scene like this in any other context would be massively disturbing; for example, if it was not placed in the context of a comedy film where sexual slapstick is a standard, or if the gender roles were reversed. Much like the *American Pie* franchise, the *Road Trip/Eurotrip* movies rely on the premise of clumsy, sexually desperate young men attempting to get some action, and instead ending up in one hugely embarrassing situation after another. One could almost view the movies' common message as a conservative one, as the young men are punished over and over again for their keenness to get laid, as if the makers are warning that desperation for sex will only result in humiliation. However, this is tempered by the fact that boy usually does end up getting girl, even if it's not quite the girl he envisioned or not quite the way he imagined ensnaring her. Regardless, the punishment meted out to young Cooper for his typical teenage attitude to women, sex workers and Amsterdam (like many British and American college-age teens, he sees it as nothing more naughty playground created for his amusement and satisfaction) seems unnecessarily harsh, and rests again on the tendency to mock men who voluntarily place themselves in a kinky and/or submissive position. Look what he gets for his wide-eyed, panting keenness to be dominated by four extremely conventionally attractive foreign women: testicle clamps and rotating dildos wielded by men! Presuming that an audience will find Cooper's terror at being approached by men wielding sex toys amusing begs the question—are we laughing at Cooper's homophobia, or are we just laughing at the fact he's about to be sexually assaulted? Considering how male rape is actually used as punitive justice in the book and movie *The Girl with the Dragon Tattoo,* when protagonist Lisbeth Salander violates Nils Bjurman with a dildo in revenge for him raping her (and tattoos his body with the declaration that he is a rapist), it is hard to see exactly what is supposed to be funny about Cooper being violated like this. Except, of course, that he's being submissive, and submissive men are fair game for mockery—he allowed himself to be tied up because he was so eager to have sex, and therefore he got what he deserved. This dehumanizing of male submissives is deeply problematic, not least because it implies men's sexual boundaries are unimportant or non-existent—a persistent patriarchal myth which already prevents male victims of sexual violence from speaking out.

Masochism as Macho?

What few pop culture depictions of the male submissive take into account is the possibility that submission, or more specifically masochism, can be an act of admirable endurance, and involve abilities and tolerances way beyond most people's pain thresholds. Men who seek pain in, or at least endure large quantities of it as a byproduct of sporting activities, are not seen as un-macho; quite the opposite. Boxing, rugby, soccer, American football, martial arts, ice hockey and countless other sports all entail pain and the risk of serious injury, and the men who participate in them are seen as making "a masculine commitment to victory through endurance."[14] Injuries as a result of these activities are worn with pride, and are not viewed as detracting from the male participants' masculinity. So why does the same not go for the man who has had his backside flogged bloody at his own request? Why is he viewed as a bitch, a pussy, a gimp, pathetic, freaky, sick, and most of all unmanly? Pepper Mint, a pseudonymous male blogger who writes about BDSM and alternative sexuality, says, "Strangely, my most clearly masculine S&M activity is masochism. I always feel very manly while taking pain."[15] This is not actually so strange in view of the fact masculinity is often associated with the ability to endure extreme pain—uncomplaining bravery and stoicism in the face of agony is a standard feature of war movies, action movies and thrillers, and as mentioned above, is also expected of sportsmen. However, what Pepper Mint has identified is that a man inviting and enduring pain as part of an act of submission or masochism, within the context of sexual, physical or psychological submission, is an act with which a heteronormative, gender-binary-obsessed Western culture struggles to reconcile itself.

The origin of the fear and disgust regarding the male submissive certainly seems to be a sexist one. Feminists have suggested that homophobia among straight men is really the fear that gay men will treat them the way they treat women. One wonders then, if the need to mock and dismiss the male submissive has similar roots. For a man to assume a position traditionally associated with femininity is deeply unsettling for those who still secretly hold the belief that a) being kind, gentle, passive, compliant, trusting, and meek are naturally female qualities and b) that holding those qualities renders one a second-class citizen. Why else would so much energy be put into mocking men whose actions harm no one, unless the roles they play are viewed as threatening some kind of societal order? Just as the very existence of gay men unsettles the heterosexual man who fears that he might be treated as an object of desire (rather than a sexual aggressor), and be harassed, groped or even raped by men—fears that heterosexual women are simply expected to live with on a daily basis—male submissives force men to confront the fact that their strength and masculinity could be undermined. Male submissives' willing surrender, often to female dominants, poses a conundrum to the heterosexual man who is brought up believing that a real man never gives in. "That *could* be me. And what if, God forbid, I *enjoyed* it? What would that *say* about me?"

With third and fourth wave feminism came the language of choice, especially when it came to defending women's right to express their sexuality. So much energy was expended on fighting for the right for women to simply be sexual, or have sex, without judgment, that the matter of actual bedroom roles are often dismissed as, "Well, as long as it's her choice." The same courtesy does not seem to have been extended to men. Although some branches of feminism assert that male sexual behavior always goes accepted and unquestioned, this is only actually true of the heterosexual dominant. The male submissive, as well as his brothers the gay, bi, trans and genderqueer submissives, doms and switches, are still viewed as decidedly suspect, if not downright aberrations, by a society still very much invested in the belief that masculinity equals power, and that to surrender is to be degraded. There is no suggestion that submission itself requires a strength of will all of its own, nor any acknowledgement that the dominant only has as much power as their submissive consents to give them. Even in the BDSM scene, this prejudice doesn't necessarily disappear. Once of Margot Weiss' interviewees, "Phil," a man who was a 24/7 bottom to his wife, said, "After I became known as a submissive, a lot of my male friends who were switches or tops didn't like me now.... I lost a lot of respect as soon as they found out I was a male bottom."[16]

The taboo around male submissives is borne out by the reports of women who encounter them. Two women in different areas of the U.S. said to me that submissive men outnumbered their female counterparts two to one in their local BDSM scene, and a woman in the UK complained of the numerous men who approach female submissives "and then want you to switch, and dom them." Although perhaps a little dated, Nancy Friday's *Men in Love* reports that men describing masochistic BDSM–themed fantasies outnumbered men wanting to play the dom by four to one, "totally at variance with our cultural edict that men must be tough and independent."[17] Submissive men are clearly out there, and they want to play—yet pop culture only seems to be able to pity or mock them, when it's not completely invisibilizing them in favor of the myth that since *that book* was released, the Western world has been suddenly and magically overrun by female submissives.

My experiences in my local BDSM scene certainly showed there were plenty of submissive males in existence, although this varied from event to event. Some play parties seemed to have many more male dom/female sub couples, and it was at one of these that a male dom actually admitted to me that he found it hard to see another man being dominated. His words were "I want to say to [the male sub], be a man!" He did, however, add that he was aware that this was down to his own personal prejudice and he respected that male submissives were doing what made them happy; however, there is certainly an echo of what Margot Weiss found in her research when a submissive woman told her that her husband (and other men) enjoyed being in a group of all male dominants and female submissives because "they feel uncomfortable" and "would rather not be around" couples that play differently. By this, she means "he would not want to be next to a woman topping a guy or a gay male couple."[18] Personally, I found being around a mix of different play dynamics comforting, as it demonstrated to me the multiple ways to do kink, rather than just ways that are sometimes uncomfortably close to real-life power dynamics. I attended several events that were exclusively for female sub/male dom couples, which had been organized precisely because of the discomfort described above, and I found them a little unsettling. I actually would have preferred the presence of female dom/male sub, male-male or female-female couples to balance things out, but apparently other couples viewed the presence of different gender combinations and power dynamics as, if not exactly threatening, then at least disruptive to their play. Weiss situates this viewpoint as embedded in a hegemonic viewpoint of masculinity and domination—"If proper masculinity is fundamentally about heterosexuality and the disavowal of homosexuality, then it makes sense that for some men (in a scene and in everyday life), gay male sexuality or female dominant sexuality are two related scenes of horror."

In risking his masculinity, then, the submissive male risks all the privileges that accompany this: the approval of his fellow men, the deference of women, the protection of safe spaces that most men take for granted. This is a high price to pay indeed, and yet there is a significant population of men sufficiently unintimidated by aggressive cultural demands that they always be the dominant or active partner in sexual exchanges. For a society that pays lip service to the idea that male sensitivity is now accepted, that it's OK for men to cry, to talk about their feelings, to bake cupcakes and change diapers, there is still intense discomfort at the idea of a man willingly surrendering his power. This shows just how fragile (heterosexual) male power must be, if pop culture producers still believe that it can be toppled by a depiction of a man happily choosing to be bound and gagged, flogged, feminized or penetrated.

3

Who's Vanilla, Who's Edgy and Why It Matters

The Mainstreaming of Kink

"Those of us who have different … notions of eroticism and sensuality are simply dismissed. The pejorative word [being] 'vanilla,' which is ironically, one of the most sensual aromas."—Andrea Dworkin[1]

"I'm often frustrated in my own local BDSM community by comments that people make mocking 'vanilla' folk (there is even a much-loved T-Shirt that reads 'Vanilla is boring')."—"K8," online commenter[2]

One of the most energetic discussions I came across in my research on BDSM and pop culture was the debate over the use of the term "vanilla." Some commenters felt that it had become a stick with which to beat non-kinky people, and that BDSM practitioners were being hypocritical by labeling—and implicitly pathologizing—those outside the kinky world, with a derogatory term. As an online commenter put it, "If you're making the case that everyone should be free to do what they like without being judged, why call non–BDSM people a derogatory name that implies they're all prudish bores?"[3] As a feminist who is highly aware of how the pendulum swung in the 20th century from women being expected to be chaste virgins to women being expected to perform every sexual trick in the book, it can be difficult to reconcile the demand for sexual freedom with the right of women to refuse sex or refuse certain acts. As Clarisse Thorn, author of *The S&M Feminist* and *BDSM and Culture: Fifty Shades of Stereotype*, told me, "Being a sex-positive feminist, I worry that other women will read my work and it will increase their performance anxiety … that it will lead other women to feel like,

48

'gosh, is this something liberated sex-positive women do? Is this something I *should* be doing?'"

I joined the BDSM social networking site (sometimes referred to as "Facebook for pervs") FetLife in May 2012, as part of my research for the blog series. During my time spent lurking in discussion groups I would see dismissive references to non-kinky people, and hear in the words of other kinksters a sense of superiority. Many kinksters seemed to believe it was automatically, and always, true that "there's more equality and consciousness brought to [the BDSM scene]."[4] My first forays into the scene implied there might be some truth to this—I was pleasantly surprised on walking into my first play party to see "House Rules" framed on the wall, clearly displayed in bullet points, with one of the key points being about respecting consent. When would you ever see that displayed in a vanilla heterosexual nightclub, I wondered, even though nearly every woman who has been to one can probably regale you with her experiences of gropes, sleazy comments and pestering by men with no respect for social, sexual and physical boundaries?

Yet the idea that the only place women can expect safety is in a place where extreme sexual tastes are catered to is not a satisfactory answer for those who do consider themselves "vanilla." There were several irritated responses to Cliff Pervocracy's defense of female submissives, where she stated, "I don't get on vanilla women's cases about how maybe they're only vanilla because society discourages women from unconventional sexual choices."[5] In context, she was trying to make the general point that judging *any* sexual taste is unhelpful and hypocritical, but the binary clearly got people's backs up, not least because of the implication is that one group is more enlightened than the other. Which Pervocracy had actually said, earlier in the same interview, was not her belief—"I don't want to pretend super-specialness. Our community is better at consent and communication than the general world, but we've got no monopoly on it." In an interview for the blog series, Canadian feminist writer Stacey May Fowles also condemned "this ugly thread deeming people who make more mainstream choices as somehow less progressive.... I want my choice to be acknowledged as healthy and valid, not celebrated as 'cooler.'"

The unwelcome limitations of the "vanilla" label have the potential to leave people feeling hemmed in—when I did finally enter the kink scene, I noted that one of the reasons I myself hadn't dared to join a fetish website, or go to a play party, until years after I first felt curious about BDSM, was a subconscious sense that I was probably *too vanilla*. I did not dress head-to-toe in latex or own any shoes with 7-inch spike heels, and I didn't take my partner down to the local shops on a dog leash. My realization that there was much more to the BDSM scene than just stereotyped clothing, beatings and sex (and furthermore that BDSM can occur without any of those things) certainly involved rejecting a prevalent media stereotype that tells us the boundaries between kinky and non-kinky are clear-cut and instantly identifiable. As Dossie Easton and Janet Hardy write, "Both of us have had experience with people who have brusquely said, 'Naah, I'm not into any of that weird S/M stuff' then gone on to behave in a way we would see as outrageously toppy or bottom."[6]

What constitutes "normal" sexual behavior is anyone's guess in a world where, if reports of the effect of pornography on men's sexual expectations can be credited as accurate, women are expected to perform a variety of explicit and extreme acts as standard without anyone ever mentioning BDSM. Whether we agree with the analysis of some feminists (and also some conservatives) that women are expected to be "up for anything," and that this is necessarily as a result of increased patriarchal attempts to undermine women's contentment with their sexuality, research does imply that, for whatever reason, sexual goalposts have shifted. After surveying thousands of women about their sexual preferences, Shere Hite wrote in 2000, "Whereas twenty-five years ago, it was perfectly acceptable for a woman not to like fellatio and not to do it, today it 'must be part of every girl's repertoire.' Some women in the UK report they feel more pressure into man-pleasing than ever, though no longer in terms of baking cakes or 'feeding him a hearty breakfast' but rather by being an exciting sex playmate, at whatever age."[7] Now that previously 'exotic' acts such as oral and anal sex are seen as increasingly mainstream, the pattern of keeping people in a constant state of paranoia that their sex lives are still "too vanilla" dictates that something—which may well be BDSM—must take their place as the ultimately transgressive act.

"Vanilla" as a Concept in Popular Media

Popular media contains several astute examples of the increasing expectation of sexual exoticism in 21st century Western society. In an episode of the British cult comedy *Peep Show*,[8] one of the main characters Jez is discussing fantasies with his girlfriend Michelle. He unenthusiastically reveals his fantasy of a threesome to her, and then worriedly asks, "Is that too much?," placing Michelle in the role of sexual gatekeeper (a position traditionally occupied by women, as it is taken as read that men will always want sex) and assuming that she will refuse any act too extreme. The punchline is, of course, that Michelle laughs, "Are you kidding? That's *vanilla!*," implying that the benchmark for judging which sexual acts are "edgy" has shifted so significantly that *ménage à trois* is now a standard, expected, even slightly boring activity in which to participate. In keeping with the show's theme of perpetual disappointment, the threesome with Michelle and another rather hostile woman turns out to be nowhere near as erotic or exotic as Jez hopes, perhaps making a point about how the constant imperative to be spicing up our sex lives with more and more alternative acts is fated to leave us dissatisfied.

Another example of how the term "vanilla" seems to have become a byword for "sexually pedestrian" came in the long-running and much-loved comedy of the late '90s and early 2000s, *Friends*. At the time of airing (1995–2005), the show was seen as a barometer of sexual and social relations between Western men and women in their 20s and 30s, and by the many fans who remember it fondly, it often is still viewed as such. It's therefore telling that this show got in on the act of using "vanilla" as a pejorative, in the episode The One with Rachel's Big Kiss.[9] When Rachel's old friend Melissa (played by Winona Ryder) appears, Phoebe refuses to believe that Rachel and Melissa shared a drunken kiss at a college party, saying, "It just seems pretty wild, and you're so … y'know, so vanilla," an accusation Rachel receives with indignation, spluttering, "I am NOT vanilla! I've done lots of crazy things!"

Being sexually unadventurous is now apparently the most grievous character flaws which a person (especially a woman) can be accused of displaying. Again, the alterations in expectation (but not in degrees of pressure) upon women's sexual behavior is clear—only decades previously, women would be expected to vociferously and disgustedly defend themselves against accusations of lesbianism, whereas now it is presumed that they will detail any bi-curious behavior with pride, and probably for the satisfaction of a male audience (indeed, when Rachel describes the kiss, Phoebe notes how aggrieved their male friend will be to miss such a salacious tale—"Somewhere, Joey's head is exploding..."). However, the conflict pivots less on the particular act in question, and more on Rachel's general determination to be seen as sexually wild and adventurous. When Melissa denies the kiss ever took place, Rachel protests, "Look, that night was the *one* wild thing I have ever done in my entire life, and I'm *not* gonna let you take that away from me!" This answers any questions as to why exactly it is so important to Rachel that she has her brief, decade-old experience validated—because it was the only time she has behaved in a sexually unconventional manner.

However, the fact that the experience is framed as singular and has, to the audience's knowledge, never been repeated with Melissa or any other woman, could be read as evidence that far from encouraging sexual experimentation, popular media actually depicts it as something to be carried out only within strictly limited parameters. Women may dabble in exotic acts, but must ultimately always move on from them. Having had her one wild experience, Rachel's sexual trajectory throughout the ten seasons of *Friends* is otherwise depicted as heterosexual and monogamous, and the final series concludes with her forming a traditional family structure with a male partner and baby. Although Phoebe (who, probably not coincidentally, is the character portrayed as most bohemian and anti-establishment) may dismiss Rachel as sexually unadventurous, it is Rachel who remains the alpha female character for whom the audience roots; her vanilla nature does not ultimately detract from her popularity. By allowing Rachel one past act of sexual experimentation and no more, the writers may be implying that, while it's acceptable for women to have their bit of fun in their youth, the ultimate aspiration for every woman remains a very vanilla one—a monogamous heterosexual partnership and family life.

Vanilla and the BDSM Community

In 2012, there was a definite sense that lines between the kinky and vanilla worlds had been blurred to an unhelpful extent, as a new media outlet seemed to run a story on *that book* every day in spring 2012 and a new bondage range was added to, and subsequently flew off the shelves of female-friendly British sex shop Ann Summers. Indeed, the retailer credited said book with the fact their sales went through the roof[10] during 2012. Then there was the sudden influx of curious people to the BDSM scene, resulting in sneering discussions on FetLife about "vanillas" who had the nerve to consider themselves kinksters just because they had read one (very mildly) kinky piece of Twilight fan-fiction. I vividly remember one particular discussion thread where a submissive female complained that she arranged a play date with a new male partner, who in the event ending up bursting into tears and confessed he felt unable to hurt a woman. The woman blamed the mainstreaming of kink as a major factor in causing "anyone to think they can be a dom."

This trend clearly did not sit well with some people in the BDSM scene, as participants often report that the kink scene has provided a refuge for them from a mainstream model of sexuality that they find

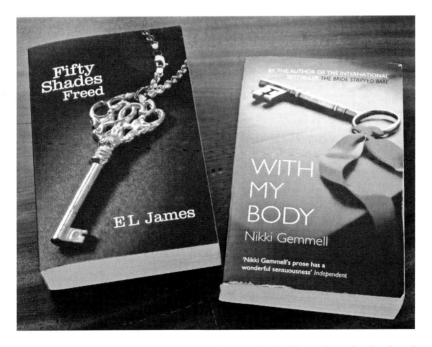

The year 2012 saw the lines between vanilla and kinky blurred, as *that book* and its imitators became popular (courtesy Thomas Bliss).

constraining and alienating. In Staci Newmahr's study of a BDSM community, *Playing on the Edge*, she writes, "Members of the scene readily share the perspective that they did not belong anywhere prior to finding the SM scene. They frequently assert that 'people here *get* it.'"[11] It stands to reason then, that to those for whom BDSM provides a safe space for them to express socially troublesome desires, the influx of "casual players," or "gawkers" as Newmahr's interviewees label curious visitors to their local dungeon, may feel invasive. Newmahr also writes of her interviewees being united by a sense of outsiderness—an identity that is difficult to maintain if the very people by whom one considers oneself to be alienated are starting to buy floggers and attend play parties. Yet, this determination to reject vanilla folk while maintaining the reputation of the BDSM scene as a safe haven involves a certain degree of self-contradiction. As one of Margot Weiss' interviewees, "Jezzie," put it, "You can't have it both ways. You can't be totally open and accepting and accessible and [also] be dangerous and edgy and forbidden."[12]

Of course, sniffiness over who is authentically kinky and who is just a pretender dipping a toe in the BDSM world from the safety of their vanilla life is not a new debate. In a speech given in 1997, Gayle Rubin complained, "At some time in the mid–1980s ... people began to care more about what the audience saw than what their partners experienced. Leather had become trendy and popular rather than despised and stigmatized."[13] I myself received a message on FetLife suggesting that the kink scene had become much more safe since the good old days of the '70s and '80s—which the male (cross-dressing, dominant) writer did not see as a good things—and blaming this on the influx of heterosexual women into the scene. Increased demands for rules, safe words, consent and negotiation seemed, to this person, to be a negative sign that the scene had lost its edge, and one for which the audacity of females wanting to feel safe was apparently to blame. However, the complaints during the 2012 influx of curious "nillas" into the BDSM scene did not seem to be so much about the mainstreaming of the scene making it boring, but rather about clueless individuals playing with potentially deeply dangerous practices they did not understand or respect. In this spirit, one of Margot Weiss' interviewees complains about a woman who "decided she was a pervert one day and she [snap] had the pants, had the jacket.... I think, 'This doesn't mean anything spiritual to you! ... I think, OK, you've been a perv for 8 hours.'"[14]

The Race to Be Edgy

The use of kink as a portable, easily discarded way of providing excitement to a vanilla public is particularly evident in visual mediums such as music videos. Having pushed sexualized imagery to such extremes that it seems that music videos can go no further without actually becoming pornographic (and many would argue that they already are), it seems that directors of mainstream music videos have recently begun to pick up on kink as an attractive way of adding edge to already heavily sexualized videos. An example of this is Rihanna's "S&M" video,[15] which seemed to me little more than an attempt to shoehorn every kink cliché into the space of a few minutes without any context, aim or significance. The ball-gagged reporters sitting nodding as Rihanna sings from behind a sheet of clear latex could be viewed as a dig at the press, depicting them as silenced, slavishly following their celebrity of choice, and implying that celebrities exist behind a transparent wall, which renders them visible but still cut off from their public. However, in the context of the rest of the video—Rihanna in a latex outfit, Rihanna leading Perez Hilton on a leash and spanking him with a riding crop, Rihanna tied up with rope—it ended up coming across as simply another tick on a checklist of kinky paraphernalia and imagery. Director Melina Matsoukas admitted, "When I make something, I kind of go out with the intention to get it banned,"[16] strongly implying that her sole aim in including kinky imagery in the video was to be "provocative," rather than demystifying kink for a vanilla public, or examining it in any kind of nuanced or normalizing way.

When Madonna appeared clad in black PVC with a host of similarly-attired dancers and played with chains, riding crops, blindfolds and restraints in her 1995 music video for the song "Human Nature,"[17] there was at least a sense of kink being used to send a message. Often viewed as Madonna's defiant riposte to her critics, especially in the American and British press, the lyrics and especially the refrain about self-expression versus repression, mocks the prudish media with lines about what can and cannot be mentioned in public. There is a clear sense of challenge to a hypocritical, sexist media in Madonna's snarled lines, even if she is having her body manipulated and being chained to a chair by a troupe of muscular men as she sings them. Indeed, much of the song's and video's power comes from Madonna's unwavering confidence regardless of whether she is playing dominant or submissive roles, demonstrating to a sexist, reductive and largely male media world that she, not they, is in charge of framing her sexuality however she chooses.

Yet for modern directors, kink appears to be just one of an increasingly reduced toolkit available to them to try and grab their audience's attention—the chances of it being used intelligently or politically seem slim. I spent a blog post considering the BDSM imagery used in 30 Seconds to Mars' overly long and often tedious "Hurricane" music video from 2011,[18] and didn't find anything particularly edgy about it. As I wrote at the time, despite basing the video around imagery from an incredibly diverse subculture which frequently challenges hegemonies of sexual identity, it apparently did not occur to director Bartholomew Cubbins to use kink as an opportunity to depict more varied bodies, gender identities and sexualities than is normally seen in mainstream media. Instead, Cubbins largely used the music video to reinforce every clichéd heteronormative image possible—submissive, feminine, slim, white cisgendered women either being dominated by men or grappling with each other for a predictably male gaze. Butch or dominant women are almost entirely absent from the video, making it hard to argue that it is not simply trying to eroticize the control of women.

In one sense, the video was distinctly non-vanilla, with its various blindfolds, hoods, sledgehammers, chains and brief shots of pony play. However, in terms of its failure to depict any physical or sexual diversity and therefore any scenario that resembled one you might actually find in a real-life play party or bedroom (as opposed to a porn set or a modeling shoot), plus its failure to abandon a totally heterosexual male gaze, the video actually aligned itself with the vanilla mainstream much more closely than its makers might like to admit.

Another more recent BDSM–themed music video, Britney Spears' "Work Bitch,"[19] released in 2013, was a further example of the same problems. It was hardly surprising that, having filled every one of her music videos with provocative dances, bare flesh and suggestive moans, Britney (or her marketing team) would run out of tricks and feel the need to do something new—enter the whips and chains. Yet the video did not come across as subversive, but rather felt entirely safe. Indeed, the only difference between Spears' other videos—which tend to show the singer, often accompanied by a troupe of slim, largely white, young, feminine, cisgendered dancers, wearing little and performing in a sexually provocative manner—and this particular video is the presence of black PVC corsets, whips, riding crops and a truly cringeworthy bit gag constructed out of a "Beats by Dre" pill speaker.

Subversive readings of the video are possible, of course—the title and chorus of the song owe much to drag queen culture and echo the arch, camp style of RuPaul's 1992 hit "Supermodel." Also, whether intentional or not, the song and video say much about how show business is the ultimate capitalist empire, always guaranteed a workforce willing to sing, dance and model for a consumer audience, in order to fulfill their own hopes of attaining fast cars, designer clothes and a life of luxury. This issue—especially in light of the speaker bit gag!—in turn feeds into the question of how the BDSM lifestyle, far from being counter-cultural, often supports capitalist narratives, an issue to which I'll return later in this book.

Ultimately, if kink is being used in the "Work, Bitch" video to express anything more complex than the desire for hits on Vevo, it's very hard to find the evidence. It certainly doesn't appear to be expressing a desire on the part of Britney Spears to suddenly become a dominatrix—her evident discomfort when asked to comically pretend to whip studio staff on an episode of chat show *The Alan Carr Show* (and, some singletail enthusiasts might add, lack of skill when she attempted it) implied that the dancer-whipping mistress of the video was a two-dimensional persona adopted for a day's filming. This in itself should not be problematic, seeing as music artists take on many different roles in their videos in order to create fantasies in which their audiences can immerse themselves. We all know Michael Jackson would never have made a very good gangster, but whose breath still isn't taken away by his sharp-suited dancing in the "Smooth Criminal" video? Yet the hijacking of kink, a way of life which is central, spiritual and involves great risk-taking for many in the BDSM community, as a disposable method for film-makers with which to get quick hits for their work has begun to rankle with some.

The Reality of Rejecting Vanilla

The outsider status nurtured by many participants in the BDSM scene means that some kinksters feel indifferent to the way they are portrayed in popular culture, viewing it as a world that is simply irrelevant to them. Others take a humorous view, as evidenced by Cliff Pervocracy's sardonic comment to video makers, "If you could make some directorial choices other than 'black shiny clothing, dark bare room, grindy industrial music...' that would be *super spiffy*, thanks." However, there are also BDSM practitioners who feel that there is a high price to pay for the media's failure to depict kink in the form of anything other than predictable stereotypes. In 2000, Pat Califia wrote, "We are supposed to be content with existing as two-dimensional caricatures of vanilla people's erotic paranoia, emerging from our warrens only after dark, always clad in body-hugging fetish gear, having no real lives outside of public dungeon clubs and 'violent' pornography."[20] This, Califia went on to say, leads kinky people to isolation, self-loathing and sometimes even suicide. Califia clearly feels that the reduction of kink to clothing, props and an entirely superficial sense of "edginess"—precisely what the three videos above exemplify—is not merely evidence of how, like any subculture, BDSM must necessarily be simplified and reduced to obvious symbols in order to function in a visual medium. Instead, it is a dangerous example of how the vanilla mainstream dehumanizes kinky people, reducing them to nothing but their outfits and sexual practices. This, in turn, makes it easier to demonize and discriminate against such people, as they are not viewed as full members of society with lives, jobs, relationships and finances, but rather as black PVC-clad perverts.

This is where I found the debate over the term "vanilla" became most heated. Not only were some commenters unconcerned that non-kinky people objected to the term, they were actively annoyed that the latter even dared to protest. As online commenter K. Kelly Meine wrote, "Kinky folk have been jailed as abusers, they have lost custody of their children, and they've lost their job [sic], just because they were outed as being kinky. When we can move beyond this kind of thing happening, just because of a sexual preference, then I might be more sympathetic about whether someone's feelings are hurt because they were called 'vanilla.' But, sorry, it's just not important to me right now."[21]

Indeed, while writing the series in summer 2012 I became aware of a legal case involving a member of the UK BDSM scene. The woman (who goes under the pseudonym Legally Bland) was the subject of malicious allegations from an ex-partner, who told police that she had partaken in BDSM. She was arrested, and because she was a social worker whose responsibilities included domestic violence, the police felt it appropriate under the Notifiable Occupations Scheme[22] to report the allegations and damaging photographs to her employers. Legally Bland's employers then fired her—even though the police had decided to take no further action. After a lengthy and self-funded legal battle to be reinstated in her job, on the grounds that the European Declaration of Human Rights enshrines the right to privacy, and that participation in BDSM in her personal life did not impact upon her work in any way, Legally Bland won her case.[23] This could be taken as a sign that British society, and as a result the UK judiciary, has moved on and become more accepting of BDSM—a decade previously Laurence Pay, a probation officer, was dismissed after it was revealed that he had taken part in consensual BDSM activities in his private life, a decision upheld even after appeal to the European Court of Human Rights.[24] The fact that Legally Bland did not meet the same fate is in one way a sign of progress, but unfortunately, the fact that her case occurred at all also speaks volumes. At the same time that British popular culture was saturated with one popular BDSM–themed book, and couples were being encouraged to try bondage and corporal punishment in the bedroom, an actual member of the BDSM community was fighting for the right to keep her job. It seems that there is still a line between the "vanilla" and BDSM worlds that can be crossed, and one that can carry with it a great cost.

During the same time, a former aide to the Mayor of London was cleared in court of possessing "extreme pornography," as defined under the British 2008 Criminal Justice & Immigration law which defines such material as "grossly offensive, disgusting or otherwise of an obscene character,"[25] which "portray[s], in an explicit and realistic way" any act "which results in, or is likely to result, in serious injury to a person's anus, breasts or genitals."[26] The acts in question were urethral sounding and anal fisting, depicted in attachments which Simon Walsh kept in a personal email account, unconnected with his work. Yet upon his arrest, he was immediately fired from his position in the London Fire Authority, the taint of suspicion being enough to condemn him before his court case had even begun. Much as the case apparently hinged upon whether the practices of sounding and fisting were likely to cause serious injury, to the average BDSM practitioner this might seem like spurious grounds for both firing and charging someone. Neither act is illegal in the UK, and both are standard parts of sexual practice for many in the BDSM lifestyle, especially among gay and bisexual men. As anyone who performs these acts will attest, there are safe and unsafe ways to practice them, and any conscientious participant in the BDSM scene will have taken extreme care to make sure they know the difference. A casual observer to the case might suggest that the safety of the acts was actually much less a concern than the nature of them, something which remains shocking and distasteful to a vanilla public, and the fact they were carried out among gay men. If the sex hierarchy that Gayle Rubin proposed in her 1982 essay *Thinking Sex*[27]—with married, procreative heterosexuals at the top and BDSM practitioners, promiscuous homosexuals, transsexuals and sex workers at the bottom—exists, and many in the latter categories would firmly agree that it does, then Simon Walsh was paying the price for transgressing double boundaries, with both his homosexuality and his BDSM preferences being used to demonize him. While the 21st century British public was happy to hear jokes about spanking on morning television, and walk past Ann Summers shops in shopping precincts offering ranges of handcuffs, whips, floggers and blindfolds, gay men inserting metal into their urethras was still apparently a bridge too far.

Walsh's acquittal on all charges implies that liberal attitudes ultimately prevailed, but again it is significant that Walsh's case made it to court at all, considering, as *Guardian* writer Myles Jackman pointed out, "While some defendants have hundreds of thousands of allegedly extreme or indecent images on their computers, Simon had five images of consensual adult sexual activity and a single unrequested picture unopened on his email server."[28] Rather than issues of safety, the trial really seemed to pivot on the twin conflations of male homosexuality with pedophilia (the unopened picture, sent to Walsh without his request, was said to be of a 14-year-old: the man actually turned out to be in his twenties) and BDSM with violence, two misconceptions which still pervade our supposedly sexually liberal culture. Interestingly, prosecution counsel suggested, "If the fisting pictures were of women they must be degrading and objectifying," a statement with which expert defense witness Dr. Clarissa Smith disagreed. Yet Smith's evidence was labeled "disingenuous, self-serving and dishonest" by the prosecution, further contributing to a sense that practitioners of BDSM are neither respected nor credited with agency by influential members of the British legal system.

Perhaps, then, kinksters can be forgiven a tendency to homogenize and even mock the vanilla community in light of the fact that, as Prof Breanne Fahs, author of *Performing Sex*,[29] said in an interview with me, "BDSM practitioners have had to defend their choices for a long time and this has taken a toll." However, Fahs did go on to note a degree of hypocrisy in the scene, one which I myself sometimes noticed: "I have found the BDSM community to be one of the most vocal and ardent critical voices when dealing with 'mainstream sexuality' but I also find that the BDSM community often resists self-criticism." During my time spent observing the scene both online and in real life, I witnessed more than once a sense of that people were competing to be the most kinky (and ergo the least vanilla). The never-ending march of pictures uploaded onto FetLife proudly displaying rope burns, bruises, welts and blood contributed to a culture of competitive domming, or indeed competitive masochism. Often, play appeared to be much less about pleasure than about sending the self-satisfied message to others "look how hard I can hit" or "look how much pain I can take." Our increasingly visual society, where events gain validation via Likes on Instagram, may be partly to blame for this, but to me, this preoccupation with *looking* kinkiest rather than *experiencing* kink seemed to be supremely missing the point of a supposedly liberating sexual subculture.

The irony was, of course, that some of these same people, who considered themselves edgy, sexual outlaws, still subscribed to their own hierarchy of acceptable kinks in mind (unconsciously mimicking Rubin's hierarchy described above). In my local fetish scene, I noticed that adult babies, diaper play and scat play were regularly condemned and mocked in conversation; sometimes, as I've discussed earlier, male submissives too. Edgy play was all well and good if it made a good story, or a sexy photograph, and allowed the dom or sub involved to draw the admiration of others, but it was still apparent to me that in most BDSM practitioners, there lived more of a vanilla soul than they might like to admit. They might have rolled their eyes at clueless "'nillas" buying bad-quality floggers from Ann Summers because they didn't know of the exquisite hand-crafted items available at kink fairs, but they were equally ready to grimace or laugh at the idea of a grown man wearing a nappy.

And so another apparent binary—kinky/vanilla, edgy/safe, wild/boring—became much more blurred around the edges than popular culture's treatment of kink might imply. If I learned that simplistic assumptions that everyone must fit into categories of dom/sub, gay/straight, empowered/disempowered, etc., are far too blunt instruments with which to tease out the multiple nuances that inform sexual identity, then I also learned that few people are as vanilla, or as kinky, as they might believe.

4

Billionaires, Bullies and Lost Boys

The Male Dominant

> "Without power over others, particularly over women, men are supposed to crumble, to lash out, to collapse.... If this really is the case, then men must be fragile creatures indeed."—Laurie Penny, *Unspeakable Things*[1]

The disproportionate focus on submissive women that followed the intense media spotlight on *that book* in summer 2012 meant that her counterpart, the dominant male, was largely forgotten. While so many people were analyzing and worrying about what the (alleged) explosion in women's desire to be sexually submissive *meant,* little attention was paid to her real or imagined play partner. Part of this may be due to the fact that in a sexist society, female sexual behavior (or even just erotic reading habits) remains under much greater scrutiny than male behavior does. Perhaps it also came from the assumption that dominance is a naturally male state and therefore it merits no further discussion, whereas argument over what is the natural female state is continues to rage.

Whenever the figure of the male dominant was mentioned, it was usually in concerned terms by feminists who assumed that men who play the dominant role in BDSM must necessarily represent masculinity gone wild. Even though it is feminism which challenges the very belief that nature slots male and female into neat dom/sub roles, there still seemed to be an unease among feminists who felt that there exists a base instinct in men to dominate women, which if allowed free rein via kink, would become dangerous. Freud wrote that sadism "correspond[s] to an aggressive component of the sexual instinct which has become ... exaggerated and has been brought to the foreground"[2]: anti–BDSM feminists, and those such as the creators of the website and Twitter account Fifty Shades is Domestic Abuse[3] seemed to feel similarly.

Yet, as more than one commentator has pointed out, the BDSM in *that book* is pretty mild—some spanking, some restraints, no canes, whips, no broken skin, no fisting. Although the character of Christian Grey has been highlighted as cause for concern, again by feminists who feel his behavior outside the bedroom is borderline stalker-ish at times, there is significant evidence to suggest that he is a character not created by a male conspiracy to render women submissive, but rather a melding together of female desires to have a man who is ridiculously rich and successful at a young age, good looking, meticulously organized, and adventurous in the bedroom.

If the female sub/male dom pairing really is such a patriarchal fantasy, then why is it women who were seeking out erotic literature with this theme in their droves, but not men? A quick look at the back cover of one of the many copycat erotic novels that emerged in 2012, *This Man* by Jodi Ellen Malpas, doesn't exactly sound like it's describing a male fantasy with its "devastatingly handsome, utterly confident, pleasure-seeking playboy who knows no boundaries." I suspected that if I investigated more of these bandwagon-jumping imitators of *that book*, I would find male protagonists who were very much a female ideal, not a figure most men were interested in emulating. A world where men are expected to be muscular and toned yet not too beefy, well-groomed, intelligent and articulate, exquisitely dressed, extremely rich, sexually aggressive yet also sensitive and sensual, and able to both spank a woman and cuddle her when she's upset does not strike me as giving men the easy ride. Rather, it seems to provide a world where men do all the work and women lay back and get all the orgasms.

Indeed, 27-year-old billionaire Christian Grey seems like the kind of figure most men would snort with derision over—a handsome, confident, sexually talented man who has it all to such a ridiculous extent that no human male could ever hope to come close. I doubt reading about the hugely rich Grey and his ability to pick up his dates by helicopter would give many men much of a kick; if anything, they're likely to view him as a threat, since women find him so attractive. Margot Weiss quotes one of her heterosexual male dominants complaining that too much is asked of dominant men, and went on to add, "SM forms of white heterosexual male dominance promise the deep satisfaction of ... dashing men, strong men ... while simultaneously producing fantasies of masculinity that many—or even all—men could never embody."[4] So, it seems that construct of the dominant male is not necessarily the friend of patriarchy that anti–BDSM commentators believe him to be.

The Sensitive Dom

The sensitive male dominant who gives a woman spankings but also expensive gifts and cuddles is quite a world away from the much harder sadism of the male characters portrayed in Marquis de Sade's *Juliette*, or Pauline Réage's *The Story of O*. Those who believe that the 21st century female fascination with male doms is evidence of failed feminism would do well to look a little closer. In Sophie Morgan's real-life memoir *Diary of a Submissive* there may be plenty of kneeling and addressing her partners as "Sir," but when the protagonist begins to cry during a play session, her partner immediately "undid my wrists and ankles, pulled the blindfold from my eyes, grabbed a blanket ... he gently draped the blanket over my nakedness, making sure not to touch my arse as he did so.... I cried, and through all of it he just stroked my hair and waited."[5] Surely a real sadist would just laugh, kick her into a corner and then turn on the TV? This attentive, considerate male dominant hardly seems to be enacting the "humiliation and savage domination" of women that feminist writer Yasmin Alibhai-Brown[6] is convinced that fem sub/male dom fiction encourages.

As blogger Karen Gordon writes,[7] "Women who read about men who work at staying in shape, know how to dress and have a working knowledge of female sexual anatomy and desires, often do start wanting some of that in their own lives." How many women achieve pleasure, let alone orgasm, in their first sexual experiences? Yet that is precisely what Christian Grey provides the virginal Anastasia when they first have sex. So much for the belief that dominant men must be selfish alpha males who are necessarily indifferent to women's sexual needs.

In her erotic memoir, *The Surrender*,[8] author Toni Bentley suggests there is a misconception about what domination truly means. "If a man can possess a woman sexually—really possess—he won't need to control her ideas, her opinions, her friends, even her other lovers." This does run counter to the controlling, demanding Christian Grey, who indeed wants to micromanage every aspect of Ana's life, down to her diet, exercise and the other men she sees. However, I would suggest that this extreme demonstration of control is E. L. James' clumsy way of depicting what she sees as a BDSM relationship (there was much to suggest that James herself had not had much, if any, experience in the kink scene, not least the fact that she writes about the particulars of BDSM in a manner that could have been copied and pasted from Wikipedia). And of course, there are plenty of happy couples in 24/7 dom/sub scenarios. Nevertheless, the media's determination to interpret this one book as the sole guide to kink shows the dangers of assuming that any piece of pop culture can provide the very definition of BDSM. Bentley writes that, in her case, power exchange in the bedroom negates the need for it elsewhere: "He fucks my ass for hours with a dick an inch too big for the job: that is possession. After a round like that he doesn't need to infiltrate my life, my psyche, my time or my wardrobe, because he has infiltrated the core of my being."

Dominant but Not Alpha

Much of Bentley's memoir centers around anal sex and her preference for it with one particular man. She certainly sees their interactions as having a distinctly dom/sub dynamic, writing, "Ass-fucking a woman is clearly about authority. The man's authority; the woman's complete acceptance of it. A man must have this confidence, in himself and his cock, to fuck a woman in the ass." However, she goes on to say that the stereotypical view of male authority is not what she is referring to; indeed, any aggressive, typical Alpha-male behavior will only ruin the experience. "Contrary to easy supposition, I do not believe that it is the arrogant, macho man who is the great ass-fucker: he is the asshole. That guy probably doesn't even like women, he's too busy competing with other men."

Far from the feminist assumption that male dominance equals sadistic, aggressive men, Bentley adds, "The great ass-fucker is the patient, gentle man, the one who knows how to listen to a woman, how to be with a woman … he is the one who can imaginatively experience her submission.… He is a kind man." Rather than constituting an image of the male dominant that reinforces patriarchy, this type of dominant man sounds distinctly like a female fantasy to me. Patient, gentle, kind? This doesn't match the profile of the violent misogynist too often let off the hook by mainstream society, but definitely sounds like the kind of man women often say they want.

In her essay "Of the Flesh Fancy: Spanking and the Single Girl,"[9] Chris Daley writes how her partner "assumes the role of dominating top with breathtaking mastery in bed despite being decidedly untoppish in real life, a delightful combination." She also notes that mimicking traditional gender roles in BDSM play is not the same as endorsing those roles in reality; the power she consents to give her partner over her in kink is a "power over me he'll never experience in any other realm of the relationship." Toni Bentley goes even further, suggesting that her sexual partner is happy to even be inferior in other areas of their relationship: "He's a doer, not a thinker, and he openly admits that he wants a woman to be smarter than he is." These men sound distinctly like the sensitive, reconstructed "New Man" who was much-discussed in the '90s and 2000s—one at ease with himself, not constantly trying to prove himself via macho pissing contests or by degrading women, and one unthreatened by intelligent, strong women. Perhaps it is only when a man has abandoned the toxic demands of patriarchy-shaped masculinity that he can truly be dominant.

The Other Mr. Grey

There is another dominant Mr. Grey whose fans have indignantly reminded the world that he existed 10 years before *that book* caused such a furor, in a film many say depict the nuances of a BDSM relationship (and one between a dominant male and submissive female) much better than its later counterpart ever managed. *Secretary* (2002), which shows the burgeoning of Lee (Maggie Gyllenhaal)'s sexuality through a dom/sub relationship with her boss, E. Edward Grey (James Spader), is often cited by kinksters as a great introduction to the lifestyle, or indeed as their gateway to coming out as kinky. However, not everyone was impressed by it. Feminist and BDSM blogger Cliff Pervocracy said in her interview with me, "It shows a boss abusing and harassing a vulnerable subordinate, but that's okay and romantic because this develops into a BDSM relationship? Screw that." Indeed, E. Edward Grey does initially come across as the archetypal controlling, bullying male dominant. In Lee's first days at work he subjects her to multiple minor humiliations—making her go through the trash, making her clean mousetraps and rejecting her thoughtful gift. When he sees her outside of work with another man, he becomes jealous and takes it out on her by harassing her about her typing errors, nearly reducing her to tears. He criticizes her personal habits, the smell of her feet. His questions to her become invasive, and in a normal workplace would be considered downright harassment: "Do you have a boyfriend? Did you have sex?"

However, where Grey becomes less of a bully and more of a human is when he intervenes over Lee's self-harm. He orders her to never cut herself again, an act of control, but this time one with caring intent. Lee describes feeling liberated by his taking control of her life like this:

The Other Mr. Grey: James Spader as domineering boss E. Edward Grey in the BDSM-themed film *Secretary* (Movie Stills Database).

"Because he had given me permission [not to cut myself], because he had insisted on it, I felt *held* by him as I walked along." It seems that, for all the bad press they may receive, a dominant man might actually benefit some women's mental health; Grey certainly helps steer Lee away from self-destructive tendencies.

The dynamic continues to walk a fine line between sexual tension and simple bullying—Grey is extremely irate and aggressive with Lee in the run-up to her first punishment for typing errors. The spanking he gives her is brutal, but significantly, it leads Lee to tell her mother she has given up self-harm and throw her self-harm "kit" off a bridge. Then the BDSM starts in full-flow: we see shots of a closed door with the sound of spanking and moans emanating from behind it, a shot of Lee working in the office wearing a yoke, one of her crawling on all fours towards Grey with an envelope in her mouth, eating out of his hand, and having a saddle put on her. In an unwitting precursor to Christian Grey's demands that Anastasia is only allowed to eat "from a prescribed list of foods ... not snack between meals, with the exception of fruit"[10] and furthermore be provided with a personal trainer, E. Edward Grey instructs Lee on what she is allowed to eat—four peas, a scoop of mashed potatoes and, "all the ice cream you want." No prizes for guessing which diet women would prefer their male dominant to put them on...

However, E. Edward Grey's need for control does have its downsides. He is emotionally repressed; when Lee seeks him out for emotional support after a run-in with her alcoholic father, he fails to respond and just leaves her standing, visibly upset, on his doorstep. This is the point at which "he put me back at my old desk and he just stopped doing it ... he just treated me like I was a regular old secretary," implying that Lee reaching out emotionally is a bridge too far for him, and that Grey feels compelled to stop their relationship before it gets any more involved. He still watches her and is unsettled by how erotic he still finds her, apparently dealing with arousal through his exercise routine. The audience sees Grey doing pull ups, sit ups and jogging—what Freud would probably label the sublimation of sexual energy. This is further implied after the scene where Grey masturbates over Lee's naked backside, as he is clearly distressed and unsettled by the fact he has let go of himself like this, and in front of Lee too. He frantically scrubs at his clothes as if he feels dirty, and later goes on to burn Lee's letters and smash pictures of her. We then see him typing awkwardly, one finger at a time, in a poignant reversal of the secretary/boss roles, a letter to Lee that says, "This is disgusting. I'm sorry. I don't know why I'm like this."

Although Grey ultimately shreds the letter and attempts to be forceful by firing Lee, he is still the more vulnerable party in the exchange. He says to her, "You have to go, or I won't stop," implying that he sees their relationship as an unhealthy addiction on his part. When Lee says tearfully, "But I want to know you," and caresses his hair, he is clearly affected and struggling to maintain his authoritative air. He also accepts a massive slap in the face from Lee with no fight. Grey is the reluctant partner who views their BDSM leanings as warped, whereas it is Lee who ends up as the driving force, who believes their partnership is worth fighting for. When Grey tries to inject some logic by saying, "We can't do this 24/7," it is Lee who retorts, "Why not?"

Far from the assumption that submission is something women are pressured into by men, the exchanges in *Secretary* show that there is little a man can do to influence a woman once her mind is made up. E. Edward Grey's role shifts from being the boss to being a victim of his own obsession, and the changes undergone in the power dynamic between Grey and Lee are palpable as she grows in strength and certainty, while he is diminished. When the two are reconciled, the scenes between them are of tenderness, as Grey tends to Lee, bathing her and lying her down softly. Some might see this scene as a reversal of dom/sub roles, others might view this as an example of aftercare, seeing as Lee has just completed a marathon of sitting at the same desk for days on end in order to prove her love for Grey. What is absent, however, is the aggression, haranguing or coercion that is often assumed to be part of dominance, especially male dominance. Lee's choices are her own, as emphasized by the final shot in the film where Lee sits on her porch, having made the bed and kissed her husband goodbye for the day, and stares into the camera, challenging the viewer to judge her.

In this case, then the figure of the male dominant may start out as a bully, but in order to have any successful interactions with his female submissive, he ends up having to cede a great deal of ground and demonstrate far more sensitivity than a patriarchal context would ever allow.

Real Sadists

There are less sensitive, more sadistic male dominants in modern popular culture, of course. In Belle de Jour's bestselling *Secret Diary of a Call Girl*, a book adapted from the real life blog of an anonymous London sex worker, it is the men Belle encounters in her private life whose behavior is perhaps more shocking to the reader, than that of her clients. She writes, "I've always been attracted to strong, tall men. And they have not ever forced anything on me. Except for one. But I begged him to do it."[11] The man in question, known only as W, has the typical dom physique: "tall and nicely built, the result of a career in sport … long thick limbs and large hands." So far, so alpha male. Belle writes how W's strength and his potential to physically harm her is a turn-on, and their first kinky act is her biting him, an act of submissive brattishness to egg him on. Soon, W is hitting her regularly: "No pretense of romance. Just us, anywhere we could be together alone, and his open palm." An element of sadism is certainly present—"On cold days in parks where the biting weather would make it sting all the more, he'd stop the car suddenly, and we'd get out and he'd smack me one." And just to make it clear to the reader that W is no secret softie, Belle quotes him saying, "I've never made a woman cry before…. I liked that."

Belle's description of her relationship with W is disquieting, not least because of the way some of it echoes the excuses made by domestic abuse victims: "I couldn't explain the bruises. I didn't. 'Ran into the door,' said with a shrug." However, her enjoyment of the relationship is also always apparent—"My knickers were always sopping wet after." The reader learns less about W than they do about Belle's pleasure in submitting to whippings, watersports, forced deep throating and facials. As is often the case in pornography, the male in this story is something of a peripheral figure, while the pleasure of the woman in question is center stage. W is sensitive enough to be "as mystified by the attraction as I was" and to ask Belle what she thinks about when he's hitting her, and if it makes her angry. Her responses are simply "nothing" and "no." Later, when explaining why she won't do degradation scenarios with clients, only in her private life, Belle also writes, "I know it sounds odd, but even when W was treating me worst, I knew it was because he cared." Many BDSM practitioners do describe their relationships as loving and caring, and this description of a dom/sub relationship which is not lacking in violence yet is still founded on mutuality and tenderness does much to dispel the misconception that BDSM is done out of hate or viciousness. Although W is clearly at home with his sadistic side, to call him a misogynist would be a stretch. After all, he does nothing Belle has not asked him, nay *begged* him, to do.

The reasons for their relationship ending are similar to those given by E. Edward Grey in *Secretary*: "The relationship felt too tightly wound to survive." However, unlike in *Secretary* (or indeed, the ending of *that book*), the couple refuse to entertain the possibility of their relationship ending up "a suburban marriage," and so "we engineered, on the flimsiest excuse, the demise of our affair." Belle ends by writing "That never stopped me wanting him. Two weeks later I sent a note. 'There are still marks on my left breast from your fingernails. I miss you.'"

Were Male Doms Harsher in the Past?

When *that book* was at the height of its popularity in 2012, more than one lover of erotic literature pointed out that in terms of satisfying BDSM novels depicting male dominance and female submission, Pauline Réage's *The Story of O* is a far superior book. Indeed, it was on my own bookshelves more than half a decade previous to the panic about women enjoying erotica about male dominance and I would agree that it's a much better written, better edited and generally sexier book than its— by comparison extremely tame—21st century counterpart.

It's also noticeable, and perhaps not coincidental, that the male dominants depicted in the book are much colder, much more aloof and much more sadistic than the modern male dom. First appearing in France in 1954, the book depicts a young woman agreeing to submit to the desires of a chateau full of men out of her love for her partner, Rene. Later, Rene hands O over to Sir Stephen, whose attentions are even more savage than those of the anonymous men at Roissy who have repeatedly used her for their sexual pleasure. Despite being the man for whom she is willing to endure whippings, floggings, branding, piercing and orifice widenings, Rene is a fairly shadowy figure of whom we learn little, except that if O has been placed in role of whore, then, "I am the pimp who's furnishing you."[12] Reage writes that Rene takes "pleasure in wresting or in having others wrest from her decisive proofs of his power over her," and describes his sadistic leanings early on in the book, when Rene notices because one whip marks O the least, it can be therefore used for the longest period of time and "asked that they use only that first whip." However, as with the other examples described above, there are still moments of tenderness that mitigate the savagery of the treatment Rene subjects O to. "Gently, he caressed her hair ... said that he loved her.... He pressed her to him and said, 'My love, my darling.'"

"Love makes it all OK" is a theme that could be applied to a surprising number of BDSM–themed stories in popular culture. While some feminists would argue this is simply the language of abuse, used to coerce people, especially women, into acts under the guise of loving relationships, others (including myself) might suggest that this is actually what makes many BDSM–themed stories quite female friendly. If we do buy into the stereotype that women are more concerned with romance than men, then there are certainly enough plenty of kisses and caresses, deep stares and whispered sweet nothings to satisfy the average female reader in *The Story of O*. Whether they could also stomach the tales of anal stretching or labia piercing remains up for debate, but the point remains that there are few male dominants depicted without some degree of romance.

Sir Stephen initially appears to be the exception to the "love rule," stating when O is first given to him, "You're going to obey me without loving me and without me loving you."[13] He treats her savagely, penetrating her anus so roughly she bleeds—"it pleased him to force her to scream"[14]—yet O believes Sir Stephen cannot "avoid becoming enamored of his work and end up loving her a little." Again, those outside the BDSM scene may condemn these as the words of a victim attempting to justify the abuse they are receiving, or perhaps use that term sometimes used by certain feminists who believe sex workers or kinky women are simply brainwashed by the patriarchy—"Stockholm Syndrome" (even though the latter concept may actually be nothing but a media-friendly myth).[15] However, those who have engaged in dom/sub play, whether casually, in a long-term relationship or 24/7, would argue that the sense of winning or earning a dominant's love is not some kind of survival response, but instead constitutes a big part of the satisfaction experienced by submissives. After his violent treatment of her, Sir Stephen "did deign to touch his lips to her fingertips," a small act of tenderness which communicates to O that her submission has not gone unappreciated. Later, after another session of forceful anal sex, Sir Stephen "kissed O upon the lips, and tenderly." Even the rough and remorseless male dominant here shows a chink in his armor, giving in to the need for a little romance. It's also important to remember that the real life submissives, bottoms or masochists who enjoy forceful and painful anal penetration, or other wince-inducing acts, may argue that they don't need to be kissed or romanced afterwards to make up for the savagery of the act, because the savagery is *exactly what they want anyway*.

According to the standards of traditional romance, Sir Stephen's most savage act is not any of the rough sex, whipping, branding, piercing or manacling he subjects O to, but the fact that (in the alternative ending to the book), he leaves her. As anyone, be they kinky or not, who has ever struggled with unrequited love will know, the greatest pain comes not from the object of one's desire being cruel or aggressive, but from their indifference. This perhaps doubly goes for dom/sub relationships, where the sub strives to please and serve their dominant, and will happily endure punishment in order to do so, but still relies on a reciprocation of their devotion in order to motivate this endurance (albeit expressed somewhat asymmetrically to theirs). The cruelest male dominant therefore is not the one who whips a woman bloody, but rather one who no longer cares enough to hurt her any more. In O's case, the devastation is too great and she asks Sir Stephen's permission to commit suicide. The book ends with the chilling line "To which he gave his consent." Of course, there are those who find an erotic charge in experiencing indifference from their lover—there must be, otherwise why would so many men list "cuckolding" as a fetish of theirs?—however, this is mostly in the context of role play. I imagine that most kinksters would draw the line at playing with a partner who genuinely did not care whether their submissive killed themselves or not. I would also imagine, for all the frightmongering about the apparent misogyny of male doms, there are very few men, kinky or not, who could ever be as cold to their female partners as Sir Stephen is to O.

Assumptions About Male Sexuality

The feminist concern about what heterosexual BDSM, especially that between dominant men and submissive women, says about relations between the genders usually seems founded on an assumption that male sexuality always automatically tends towards the dominant, and that BDSM "runs the risk of unleashing 'the dark side' of human nature, 'with particular danger for women'"[16] This is a familiar view of sexuality, held by conservatives and feminists who are opposed to porn, sex work and BDSM alike; that sexual aggression and desire is the preserve of men, who foist their wicked urges upon unwilling women. As Heather Corinna writes, "We've long idealized or enabled the romance-novel script of ravishment: reluctant women and passive girls seduced by strong partners."[17] The male dom is, in many ways, that stereotype taken to extremes, except with an important exception; in the BDSM world, such a man is actively sought out by women who have consciously chosen to play the submissive to him. This disrupts the assumption that male domination within BDSM is merely patriarchal power run rampage. It also highlights a difference between BDSM and actual sexual violence that is too often forgotten—the ability to choose one's partner, stage a scene both partners find erotic, and stop that scene whenever either partner wishes to. Yet as the editor quoted by McClintock above shows, men who play the dominant role as part of BDSM with a consenting partner are still too often lumped in with rapists, abusers and murderers.

In his book *Perv*, Jesse Bering writes, "Males are more likely to be 'true' sexual sadists, especially of the criminal variety."[18] This is a stunningly casual assertion to make, considering that the "criminal variety" of sadists Bering is referring to includes cannibals! While most of us would probably be happy to accept that, given the evidence of the world around us, men are the gender more prone to violence, including that with a sexual element, it is important not to confuse this with a predilection for BDSM. As other chapters in this book demonstrate, the safe and consensual expression of sadistic or dominant sexual leanings requires a level of civilized organization often unseen in the vanilla mainstream sexual culture, not to mention "a safety record most sports teams would envy."[19] Lumping every dominant male in with serial killers, cannibals, mutilators and those considered sufficiently dangerous to society that they have either been executed, imprisoned for life or committed to mental institutions isn't just inaccurate and unhelpful—it also implies male sexuality is forever a few steps away from psychopathy, and furthermore, that the men who choose to unleash their dominant or sadistic side (always assumed to be their "true nature," despite the existence of male submissives as discussed in Chapter 2) must be edging ever closer to it.

That book can certainly be accused of perpetuating this myth, by following a storyline in which the (young, naïve) female is shocked and disgusted by her partner's sadistic leanings and therefore must reform him so that in the end it is *he* who submits, albeit to a normal marriage, monogamy and parenthood. This depiction of the man as a wild, uncivilized force who must be tamed by the love of a good woman (whose job it always is to be the sexual gatekeeper and tamp down her man's savage desires) is a story as old as literature itself, although it's worth noting that Christian Grey is portrayed less as an uncontrollable sadist and more as a damaged, vulnerable man masking his issues with a fetish for control. Still, it does little to address the dynamics at work for the many couples who enjoy male dom/female sub dynamics without anyone being asked to change or visit a psychiatrist.

The Self-Scrutinizing Dom

Most of the heterosexual male dominants I spoke to or became personally intimate with had experienced conflict about their desires to dominate women. Guilt, shame and fear that they were psychologically warped or a danger to others were commonly mentioned. Most said to me that their desires felt at odds with their culture and upbringing, where they were taught to respect and never harm women. Although this is not to say they were all brought up as feminists, it certainly runs counter to the assumption upon which some feminists seem to operate; namely that all men are bombarded with messages that tell them to hurt, degrade and discard women, and are so easily conditioned that they cannot ignore such influences when they do encounter them. Most of these men I spoke with had attempted at some point to squash their kinky desires; several had deliberately tried to submerge them by going into relationships with a non-kinky partner, which always ended unhappily. For all that they claimed to have come to terms with their urges by the point when I encountered these men, I still sensed a residual guilt in most male doms. I remember reducing one (with whom I played) to tears by voicing my concerns that maybe male dom/fem sub BDSM was just the replication of horrendous abuse and none of us could admit it to ourselves. He sobbed, "I left someone I've really loved because of kink, and now you're telling me it's abuse?" It was such a defining part of his identity, yet he was never truly at ease with it.

It's also worth adding that, in case it's not obvious already, that particular man was not particularly domly outside of the bedroom. Nor were any of the guys I played with, really. However savage things got behind closed doors, and not counting the odd erotic game I subtly played in public with one special playmate, all was normal in everyday life. We'd go to pubs, restaurants and the cinema, splitting the bill or taking it in turns to pay. We'd go for coffee, chat about our lives and careers. Those who believe that BDSM relationships are a cover for power abuses might be interested in the findings of Dancer, Kleinplatz and Moser's 2006 survey[20] of 146 individuals who were in 24/7 kink relationships. Even in these cases of BDSM dominant/submissive roles extended to their extremes, 98 percent of slaves still had bank accounts in their own names. Perhaps even more interestingly, when BDSM relationships ended, two-thirds of the times it was at the slaves' behest. This tallied with my own personal experiences with male dominants; outside of our BDSM play, they were not interested in trying to control me. Contrary to the media depiction of dominant men as emotionless and cold, I often found fairly soft centers to these men, and on more occasions than one was the less emotionally attached party.

Much like the assumption that submissives (and submissive women in particular) must necessarily be doormats, the assumption that dominant men are misogynistic sadists devoid of empathy is at best an irritant, and at worst, enables genuine abusers to go undetected, as the conflating of violence against women with consensual male dom/fem sub play leaves many unable to tell the difference. As demonstrated by the attitude of prosecutors in court cases where BDSM is assumed to be so dangerous that those participating can't possibly have truly consented to it (see previous chapter), failing to distinguish between the consensual expression of sexuality and savage violation leaves innocent BDSM practitioners open to prosecution, while rapists, wife batterers and murderers are walking the streets unmolested. This topsy-turvy state of affairs implies a queasiness at confronting male sexuality unless it has clear strains of deviance, hence the high-profile news stories about cannibalism, fisting, sounding and men banging nails into each other's scrotums. However, because most rapes, beatings and other violations of women by men take place in fairly un-kinky surroundings, they're unfortunately not different enough from the narratives we still believe in to be addressed seriously: "Well, it's just in men's true nature to be a bit forceful. Well, some women don't know they're in the mood until you pressure them a bit. Well, men are just biologically programmed to fuck, what do you expect?"

It's no wonder men with dominant fantasies feel self-disgust and want to distance themselves from such apologism for male violence. Jay Wiseman even wrote in *SM 101* that he considered suicide if his desires did not subside. It's understandable that it's hard to stomach the replication of some of our culture's most troubling crimes against women, and as a female submissive myself I experienced the converse questions—What does it *say* about this individual man that he wants to do these things to me? *Is* he a really a closet misogynist? Yet all of the men I have played with have had their limits, and sometimes these have been considerably more conservative than my own. One guy said he didn't ask women to lick his boots, and the implication seemed to be that he considered it too degrading. Given the caring, sexy, trusting and communicative relationship we have, I would happily have done it (although not right at that moment, as he had just visited the shoe-shine guy, prompting the conversation, and the chemical taste didn't appeal to me...), but I found it interesting that he drew a line there. I wondered if he suffered from a bit of conditioning; not the impulse that made him want to tie me up and flog me (an impulse which too many people assume could only have been borne from misogyny), but rather the viewing of women as delicate flowers whose virtue is so easily shattered. How else to explain his distinction between certain acts? Some he saw as sexy, others just simply a bridge too far, a bridge too degrading. Yet I, the woman in front of him, would've happily done them. I also remember being extremely disappointed when another guy said he wanted to give the ropes and gags a miss one night and "make love" to me. He'd had enough of the kink, whereas I was the one who wasn't really interested in sex without it. Even men who identify as dominant aren't in 24/7 aggressive mode, and it's often forgotten that the sub desires savage activity just as much as, sometimes more than, the dom.

Ultimately, non-kinksters and anti-kink feminists can and will wring their hands over what they perceive as terrible men who've brain-washed women into thinking they want such awful things done to them. What they fail to realize is that plenty of dominant men are already prac-ticing self-analysis and agonizing over their desires, and that what is most liberating for these men is the realization that their female partners desire and enjoy kink play—it is the perpetuation of the myth that women are passive, easily brainwashable idiots with no agency or sexual identity of their own which hinders that. And it is precisely that myth that anti-kink feminists are spreading, hardly much of a victory for women.

Male Dominance as Desperation

> "Anyone who thinks legal prostitution is a clear case of men exploiting women hasn't watched a 60-year-old investment banker offer $40,000 for a weekend of back-rubs and cud-dling."—Mrs. White[21]

The feminist objection to BDSM, especially that which depicts male domination and female submission, is that it's too close to reality, that men already have all the power in our society, so why should they get to take even more in the bedroom? While resting upon an already much-discussed misconception of what BDSM is, this also fails to take into account the multiple vulnerabilities of heterosexual male sexuality. As Lesley Hall wrote in her study of male sexuality in the first half of the early 20th century, a time when men wielded even more power than they currently do, "Whatever the social potency of men, their actual sexual potency is always dubious and open to question."[22]

This statement is borne out by the social standing and behavior of the men who feature in the 2012 Australian movie *Sleeping Beauty.* In the movie, Emily Browning plays Lucy, an attractive young student who is struggling to make ends meet. Demoralized by tedious office work and waitressing, she answers an advert for a job where she's required to waitress in lingerie. It soon becomes apparent, however, that this isn't your average strip joint—it's an elite, private club where old men in tuxedos are waited upon by women in stockings, suspenders and peephole bras, where the waitresses are told to match their lipstick to the color of their labia, and where the furniture in the after-dinner lounge includes two naked women, kneeling at the fireplace with their heads to the floor.

So far, so patriarchal. Scantily clad young women serving food to older, powerful, and (we assume) wealthy men, and then sitting draped over them, stroking them and hanging off their every word. Yet Lucy finds the work preferable to waitressing or office work, and agrees to more involved assignments. These involve taking a drug which renders her unconscious, and then spending the night with a paying client. However, as Clara, the older woman who runs the club assures Lucy, no penetration is allowed. The sleeping drug may render her an object, but not quite the sex doll that some assume a female submissive must resemble, or that some assume all male dominants must desire.

The men who do share Lucy's bed are all older, but are hardly powerful physical presences. When each man undresses to get into bed with her, their nakedness shows their age and hence their vulnerability. The first man hints to Clara that he is suffering from extreme ill health, and does nothing more to Lucy than look at her and stroke her skin, before laying his head on her resting back and going to sleep. The second man is more savage, calling Lucy a bitch, a whore and talking aggressively dirty to her. He burns her with his cigarette, grasps her face and claims he is going to fuck her. However, the audience already knows that this is all just talk. He has already told Clara that he is impotent, and can't get an erection without "a fuckload of Viagra." This is an important point—that some men feel the need to be in a dominant position precisely because they experience a *lack* of sexual power, *not* a surfeit of it. He has also told Clara that he needs anal stimulation in order to get aroused, and actually admits, "*I'm* the one that needs the penetration," inverting the assumption that it always the female whose body is entered. (Having had a male partner myself who identified as a dom yet found the idea of me using a strap-on on him very erotic, I can attest that this man was very embarrassed about his desire to be penetrated, seeing it as at odds with his dominant persona, and dreaded the thought of anyone among his kinky friends finding out about his fantasy.) Although we still may question what drives a man to want to lie in bed with an unconscious woman under half his age, snarl obscenities at her and burn her, it does not seem to be the total sexual entitlement that some assume must be at the root of men's desire to be in a sexually dominant position. Rather, it's a need for safety (indeed, Clara assures all her clients, "You are safe here"), protection from expectations of male virility and from exposure of one's sexual failings. As Lynne Segal says in her refutation that pornography necessarily expresses male power over women, scenes like this "suggest male sexualities which are both anxious and defensive, in need of reassurance through fantasies of control over others."[23] The very important word to note here is "fantasies."

Indeed, Lucy's interactions with men in her private life are always on her terms. In complete contrast to her experiences at the Sleeping Beauty club, she is always the one doing the propositioning, her partners are young, handsome men, and she does have full sex with them. The chaste nights spent unconscious in the arms of the old men who pay for the pleasure seem rather tame by comparison. It raises the question of who is really in the weak position—Lucy certainly seems to be having her cake and eating it, while the men who pay to (literally) sleep with her come across as pretty sad. While their age (and presumed seniority in whatever jobs they do) has given these men the financial power to have an unconscious woman at their mercy, the trade-off is that it has robbed them of the good looks and energy to have sexual relationships in any organic way. The parameters of what they are allowed to do with young, beautiful Lucy is firmly set by Clara, an older woman. The assumption that the men must have all the power in this situation certainly seems a flawed and oversimplistic one.

Don the Dom

No discussion of dominant males in 20th and 21st century pop culture could possibly be complete without a mention of the sharp-suited '60s ad man, Don Draper. Feminists and pop culture commentators alike went mad for Matthew Weiner's *Mad Men* when it premiered in 2007, providing as it did a chance for viewers to smugly look back at the cringe-worthy gender and racial politics of the USA in the 1960s, while secretly enjoying the outfits, music and lava lamps. Renowned for its slow-burning, underplayed style, it made sense that such a show would pivot around the adventures of a mysterious, powerful alpha male.

The obvious manifestations of Don's power can be ticked off like a list: he's in control at work, whether with his colleagues or his clients, and at home, whether with his wife or his children. However, as the show progresses across its multiple seasons and other characters grow in power, Don sees himself increasingly challenged. His wife refuses to accept his constant infidelity any longer and divorces him, his secretary-turned-copywriter protégé Peggy begins to stand up to him, and his young daughter Sally begins to act out. His murky, shifting past and deeply poor upbringing are also shown in flashbacks which crack his mask of strength whenever he remembers them. In Season 4, after separating from his wife Betty, Don hires a sex worker but is not interested in playing the dominant partner—instead he asks her to slap him in the face during sex, whispering "Harder … again…" when she does.

By Season 6, Don has restored some of his social power by marrying his much younger secretary, Megan. Much of the suspense surrounding Season 5 entailed wondering when and if Don was going to subject Megan to the same infidelity to which he constantly subjected his first wife, Betty. By the start of the next season, the viewer has their answer, as Don has begun an affair with Sylvia Rosen, who lives in the same building and is married to a doctor. Sylvia is much closer to Don in age, possibly older, and seems streetwise, inured to the risk of becoming sentimental. However, as their relationship intensifies, and she tells him "I need you—and nothing else will do," Don takes advantage of this show of emotion to start behaving sadistically and testing Sylvia's devotion to him. In the episode "A Man with a Plan," Don tells Sylvia to crawl on her hands and knees to find his shoes. She does so, and puts them on for him. He then tells her to get undressed and get back into bed, and leaves her waiting in the hotel room, not knowing when he'll come back. He calls, then orders her not to answer the phone any more (when he does ring again to test her, she obeys and instead lies masturbating in time to the rings). He sends her a dress to wear but when she puts it on and asks if they're going out, he says, "Why would you think you're going anywhere? You are for me. You exist in this room only for my pleasure." Later when they're in bed together he demands, "Who told you were allowed to think?"

However, when he returns the next time she is dressed and ready to leave, and says, "I think this is over." Don responds, "It's over when I say it's over." But Sylvia stands firm. "This is over. And not just 'this'" she adds, indicating the sub/dom play they've been indulging in in the hotel room. Realizing that a relationship he has come to treasure is about to end, and all because he felt the need to torment Sylvia for showing emotion, Don starts to beg. "Please."

The ultimate dominant male? Jon Hamm as troubled 60s ad man Don Draper in *Mad Men* (Movie Stills Database).

What started as a game of erotic power play has come to an abrupt end, and again it is the supposedly dominant partner who ends up as the vulnerable party. Don's dealings with women throughout the series are distinctly uneven, swerving from callous to surprisingly restrained without warning. It's too simplistic to write him off as an old-fashioned sexist, a product of his time; even when we see him reprimanding Betty like a child for letting a salesman in the house, or see him having affairs with anything in a pencil skirt, we are aware that there's more to the story than just basic chauvinism. Much of this doesn't come out until the latter seasons of the show—while we are aware that Don's conflicted relationship with women may have something to do with being the child of a prostitute who died in childbirth, it's not until season 6 that we see how his adolescence spent in a whorehouse may have truly warped his sexual attitudes. His loss of virginity is an unwilling one, at the hands of a much older prostitute, and when his stepmother finds out, she hits him. Don Draper the man may be a confident sexual operator, but his adolescent experiences with sex represented fear and coercion, and undoubtedly left their mark.

Contrary to the assumption that dominant men must be so due to a loathing of women or a need to control them, Don Draper comes across as someone who simply likes power full stop; but there is a human behind the suit, and one able to transgress the sexism of the era at that. He supports Peggy's career trajectory from secretary to copywriter, unlike the other men in the office who make cracks about her appearance and question her ability. He is one of the few people who knows that Peggy has secretly given birth to an illegitimate child, and passes no judgment on her for it, simply telling her to move on from the experience and not let it define her. When Don dismisses Jane, his secretary, for having an affair with Roger Sterling, the viewer is tempted to gasp at Don's hypocrisy; he is clearly still a subscriber to the double standard that allows men to have affairs while their female partners shoulder all the blame. However, in mitigation, it is apparent that Don acts at least partly out of loyalty to Roger Sterling's wife, Mona. Far from condoning the dumping of the faithful middle-aged wife for a younger model, Don is outraged on Mona's behalf.

Perhaps it is the character of Mr. Draper who best sums up the contradictions present in the pop culture depictions of the male dominant. In control on the outside while conflicted on the inside, a loner with an insatiable need for female company, sometimes sexist but with a secret feminist side, the template of the male dom could, really, be stepped into by any one of a million 21st century men.

Apart from in *that book*, of course, where he's supposed to be a billionaire.

5

Safe Words
BDSM and the Concept
of Consent

In a *Daily Beast* online article, somewhat misleadingly titled "My 'Kink' Nightmare: James Franco's BDSM Porn Documentary 'Kink' Only Tells Part of the Story,"[1] adult movie performer Aurora Snow describes her uncomfortable first foray into the world of BDSM porn. Snow writes that despite her ample experience acting in mainstream porn, "I'd shied away from the BDSM culture. It scared me. Despite signing paperwork and a checklist of dos and don'ts, I was in way over my head. What I thought I was agreeing to felt a lot different in reality."

Although Snow's naïveté might not ring very true (surely it's not that difficult to investigate the BDSM world online and in real life before agreeing to participate in it—indeed, that's the path most of those curious about kink find themselves following), there are perhaps truths in her words which will speak to some people. The quickest defense of BDSM from accusations of abuse is the existence of prior negotiation, and the all-important safe word. In the BDSM–themed episode of *Secret Diary of a Call Girl*,[2] call girl Belle takes the audience through her first attempt at being a dominatrix. She turns to the camera after demanding her submissive strip and kneel, and reminds us, "Everything's worked out in advance: the script, the scenario, even the insults I'm going to use." This is reassuring for those who fear that BDSM has the power to unleash aspects of human nature that may be too dark; they are reminded that there are still boundaries, there are still get-out clauses.

For all the things that those in the BDSM community felt *that book* got wrong in its depiction of kink, one area in which it did attempt to accurately educate a mainstream audience was in the area of negotiations and safe words. The book includes a contract, lengthy to the point of tedium, which states, "The Dominant may make demands of the Submissive that cannot be met without ... harm" and therefore "the Submissive may make use of a Safe word." It also helpfully details the difference between "yellow" and "red" as safe words, a distinction that is not always made apparent. Viewing safe words as a binary between "Stop everything" and "Go ahead and do anything" often fails to account for the variations of experience between those two poles—a submissive may well want their dominant to ease up, change their pace or intensity or choose another activity, without stopping the scene and breaking the spell altogether. A midpoint safe word, denoted in the "traffic light system" by "yellow," allows for these adjustments to happen mid-scene without dom or sub having to break role. By contrast, there are no explicit references made to safe words in other erotic fiction such as *The Story of O* or *Sleeping Beauty,* and references to consent in *The Story of O* are decidedly ambiguous. O's lover, Rene, who is the driving force behind her sexual enslavement, says to her, "It's because it's so easy for you to consent that I want from you something you can't possibly consent to, *even if you say yes in advance,* even if you say yes now and suppose that you are actually capable of submitting to it. You won't be able to prevent yourself from saying no when the time comes [and] when the time comes, *it won't matter what you say,* you'll be *made* to submit."[3]

The idea that consent in advance is not necessarily enough protection if a scene begins to spin out of control and terror sets in is one that Aurora Snow illustrates, and raises the question: Is having a safe word always enough? As Snow identifies in her article, knowing that you *can* use a safe word, and actually feeling able to do it when you're tied up and being beaten bloody, can be two very different things. Snow writes in her article that using a safe word is not just a skill one can pick up immediately; rather, it's something people need to train themselves into doing: "I'd never used a safe word before (and forgot to), so when things became too much to bear and I began protesting, no one listened." She does, however, go on to contradict her claim that no one noticed her distress by later stating, "Halfway through, I had to be untied and calmed down."

Whether we agree that what Snow experienced is actually "nightmarish" or whether it just constituted a kink scene gone awry—something which does happen, but which BDSM practitioners can be unwilling to acknowledge, so high is the price of admitting that BDSM *does* entail certain risks—the response to her words is telling. The first two comments after the article place the blame squarely on Snow for her decisions. One says, "So I guess the lesson here is, if you're not kinky, you shouldn't do fetish porn. Most people don't voluntarily sign contracts consenting to 'nightmares,'" implying Snow should have known her limits, and what she was getting into, better before she participated in BDSM porn. The second is, unfortunately, a comment I have seen and heard several times too many for comfort: "you didn't use your safe word so that puts this all on you." As a feminist highly attuned to the language of victim-blaming, I've definitely been unsettled by the willingness of people in the BDSM community to blame traumatized people for not being the ones to put a stop to their unpleasant kink experiences.

If You Didn't Safe Word, I Don't Care

I witnessed an example of this reductionist attitude in my local BDSM scene. After a play party, a female submissive complained in a FetLife discussion that while she had been semi-suspended, someone began caning her feet without having asked first. Responses were mixed, but the (female, submissive) host of the event's first response was, "Why on earth didn't you say something at the time?" By expecting the complainant to be able to process, verbalize and have the nerve to say something in the middle of an intense BDSM scene, the host placed all the responsibility for this non-consensual behavior on the complainant's shoulders. This is not, unfortunately, dissimilar to the attitudes we witness in mainstream sexual cultures where victims of sexual harassment, sexual assault, rape and domestic violence are chastised if they do not report their assaults to police straight away (or at all), while their abusers' behavior goes unscrutinized.

This attitude also seems disingenuous considering the amount of discussions in the BDSM scene that go on about subspace and dissociation. There seems to be little doubt among kink practitioners that subspace (the experience of "spacing out" and dissociating from reality, often accompanied by inability to communicate) is real, and happens a lot, especially during intense scenes with a lot of impact, pain, or psychological torture. Dissociation is the human body and brain's natural response to extreme pain or fear, and in extreme cases people can pass out from an overload of either. Yet there seems to be a disconnect between acknowledging this, and admitting that a safe word alone is not going to be much help if someone is so disorientated from a scene they can barely speak.

Experienced BDSM practitioners can testify to this. Author and BDSM educator Mollena Williams wrote in her book *The Toybag Guide to Playing with Taboo*: "I have a hard time safe wording,"[4] something she learned the hard way from participating in an intense hostage scene which involved racial abuse and murder threats being made against her. She writes, "As this particular scene progressed, the funny thing was: *I forgot I could safe word. I forgot* there was a way out. And the more I forgot, the rougher the scene became, the more afraid I was for my safety...." By the climax of the scene, the threat became so real that Williams says she actually wished for her own death. She writes that the experience was ultimately an opportunity for learning about her own tendencies, valuable information which she can take to her next play scene. "I learnt that I am, reflexively, obedient ... that I am capable of disassociating." However, genuinely believing one is about to be killed does seem a high price to pay for a learning experience, and begs the question: if even a very experienced and self-aware BDSM player, a kink educator who was named International Ms. Leather 2010, admits that safe words are not always adequate for protecting her or her mental health during a scene, what else can people use to keep themselves safe?

Is Negotiation Boring?

It was reassuring to encounter people in the BDSM scene who didn't place all the onus on the submissive to set boundaries. I talked to dominants who believed that they had as much responsibility as their submissive to keep the scene within safe boundaries: the dom should be constantly observing their sub, especially their physical reactions (e.g., flushed face, dilated pupils, weak grip) and should be able to tell when the sub is getting close to their limits, without forcing the scene to such a limit that the safe word is necessary. For obvious reasons, these dominants tended to be popular with female subs, but were sometimes referred to disdainfully by others doms for this brand of "sensual domming," as if taking into account a submissive's feelings prevented a person from being a *real* dominant. This echoed some of the complaints I read in Margot Weiss's *Techniques of Pleasure,* where older kinksters were dismissive of the new generation's insistence on negotiation and safe words. "These critics of both safe words and negotiation argue that by codifying very specific ways of doing SM, the intense connection that SM can create between partners is destroyed, that excessive negotiation will diminish interpersonal intimacy."[5] This is confirmed by a couple she interviews, Vince and Pam, who "play without safe words or negotiation," because, as she explains, "He just knows where I am at every moment, and plus if something does happen that he's not aware of, I can just say it, I don't have to go 'beige' or 'yellow' or 'green' or whatever the hell they're all doing."[6] Pam's sniffy tone implies that she sees safe words as a fashion bandwagon that the younger generation of BDSM practitioners have all jumped on, rather than appreciating why they may be necessary. Safe words were designed as unconnected, neutral words which allow the submissive (or perhaps the dominant—people tend to forget that doms may want to use safe words too) to convey their needs without breaking the scene. If a kink relationship doesn't involve any scenes of consensual non-consent (rape play, fighting, hostage taking, interrogation, etc.), then it may be safe to assume that the words "no" and "stop" mean exactly what they should. However, once role play is involved, lines become distinctly blurred. Part of the attraction of BDSM for many is the sense of struggle, of being overpowered, and it seems practical that both parties know beforehand that "No, no, please stop" is just part of an erotic game (whereas "red" means STOP NOW), so that the sub does not leave feeling violated, and the dom is not unwittingly being made into abuser. Yet the pragmatism of having a safe word is still looked down upon by those who claim not to need them.

Another of Weiss' interviewees is unequivocal in her defense of safe words. Monique Alexandra, a submissive (who, possibly significantly, is 20 years younger than Pam), says, "I want things that are exciting, but I want to know that I decided to have that done, and at any point I can say whatever the codeword is and it will stop.... I would not play with anyone who has the attitude 'I won't negotiate because it's bor-ing.'"[7] This taps into an aspect of the vanilla sexual mainstream often highlighted by feminists as flawed and dangerous—the belief that com-munication in the bedroom is a turn-off. Feminist kinkster Cliff Per-vocracy said in her interview with me, "I wish we could teach [the vanilla community] that guessing what your partner wants to do in bed is diffi-cult and over-rated; there's nothing unsexy about asking, 'so, what do you want to do?'" Yet romance novels and movies often teach us that kisses, touches and sex happen pretty wordlessly, without planning or negotiation, or any uncomfortable conversations (for example, there are few sex scenes in mainstream movies or TV shows—apart from in movies like *Knocked Up* where contraception is key to the storyline—where anyone stops to find or put on a condom). Combine this with toxic myths taught to us about male and female sexuality—the unstop-pable, aggressive, perpetually ready male sex drive, and the teasing, inconsistent female who says no when she really means yes—and we have some of the worst pillars of rape culture standing strong. So when Vince, Pam's partner, says, "I think we can *think about* sex or we can *have* sex" [my italics], as if the options are mutually exclusive, he's imply-ing that to stop and make sure both partners are comfortable with the activities is some kind of unsalvageable boner killer. He goes on to say, "My questions and my process has always been 'Is this someone that I can connect with? Can I sense you? Can I feel you?...' If that's possible, then I don't really need to negotiate because all I really need to do is pay attention."

Although in Vince and Pam's case, the bond of a long-term rela-tionship has hopefully provided them with enough knowledge about each other that they can indeed enjoy their master/slave relationship without the need for safe words or negotiation (or at least, explicitly stated versions of either—many might argue that any relationship involves constant negotiation whether we're aware of it or not), Vince's words carry with them an uncomfortable undercurrent. In an episode of *Sex and The City*, when Carrie is trying to decide whether her ex-boyfriend Aidan wants to get back together, she tells Miranda "His words said, 'No' but his kiss said, 'Yes.'" Miranda sardonically shoots back, "That's the defense invoked by date rapists." It's funny, but it's also hor-ribly true. How many times have we heard the toxic phrases "she was sending mixed signals" or "she led him on" used as excuses for sexual violence, or at least for presuming that women are constantly available for sex? Expecting that all one needs to do in order to understand what their submissive wants is "pay attention" to them seems at best naïve and oversimplistic, and at worst downright dangerous. Is anyone really so well attuned to their partner that they can always tell the difference between frightened gasping and aroused panting? How can you say for sure that your partner is flushed because they're turned on, when they actually could be experiencing breathing difficulties? It can go both ways, of course—a shriek may sound bloodcurdling, but may simply be a sign of euphoric release. Some kinksters enjoy being pushed to their emotional limits, and tears are not necessarily a sign of a scene gone wrong. The point is; without prior negotiation, and safe words/safe signals or equivalent, *how is your partner going to know for sure* they are not doing something absolutely terrible (or just absolutely boring or unarousing!) to you?

However, at least Vince acknowledges that the dominant plays a part in engaging with and responding to their submissive's physical and mental state during play. Not everyone I encountered in the BDSM scene seemed to think that the dom had even that much responsibility. Some took the simple binary approach of "If they don't safe word, then they consented and it's fine." I subscribed to this theory less and less the more I saw how submissives' senses were compromised by play, and it was disappointing to see, as with the example of the woman who complained of having her feet caned without permission, that several people wrote her complaint off as "You didn't safe word at the time, ergo you have no right to complain." Taking the line that the absence of a safe word = blanket consent seemed unnervingly close to the standard excuse for vanilla sexual coercion, i.e., the belief that the absence of a no = a yes. In her essay "Beyond Yes or No: Consent as Sexual Process," Rachel Kramer Bussel writes, "It's not enough to just assume that if she (or he) doesn't say no, they want it.... The burden is not on the woman to say no, but on the person pursuing the sexual act to get an active yes."[8] Bussell was referring to the tiresome concept of "gray rape," where sexual violence is excused via apparent failure of the victim to make their resistance clear, but her rebuttal to it applies in BDSM too. Consent isn't something that just happens once and is then irrevocable, all-encompassing and non-negotiable—because then pretty soon it no longer is consent, but simply a matter of one person pushing to see what they can get away with, a model of sexual behavior still too often accepted as the default interaction between men and women.

The Safe Word in Pop Culture

As I've written in other chapters, the failure of pop culture producers to distinguish between non-consensual violence and BDSM, and the resulting tendency to conflate the two, can be troubling. Defenders of kink spend so much time pointing out the myriad ways in which BDSM is different from abuse, that it can be disheartening to see media producers with so much influence constantly associating the two with each other. In Season 2 of the hugely popular Netflix series *Orange Is the New Black*, protagonist Piper is struggling with guilt after having savagely attacked a fellow inmate at the end of the previous season. She confides this to sassy fellow inmate Nicky, who responds, "What, you gonna beat the shit out of me now too?" and with a teasing grin adds, "Just tell me the safe word." Bearing in mind that Piper's savage beating of Pennsatuckey, a woman considerably shorter and slighter than her, has left Pennsatuckey bloodied, unconscious, and needing a set of new teeth, this humor seems decidedly black.

However, when we consider that Nicky is Piper's friend (the next two lines in the dialogue are the women telling each other they have missed each other while Piper has been in another prison), and that Nicky's interactions with most of the people she likes have a teasing sexual undertone, her invitation to some sexy violence does seem—in a strange way—to be a friendly gesture. By addressing the act of violence with which Piper is tormenting herself, and turning it into a joke, Nicky is telling Piper to lighten up. She's telling her to stop wallowing, stop attacking those who are trying to help her, and in her trademark style, adding a little of her predatory sexuality in (jokingly) for good mix. She is also, perhaps, showing love through submission. Yes, Nicky is saying to Piper—I will put up with your crap, metaphorically if not physically, because that's what friends do. However, she's also reminding Piper that she's not there to be an emotional punching bag, hence the mention of the safe word may actually function as an important reminder that even friends have their limits.

Consent as Comedy?

> "The cost of violation [in BDSM] is high: most obviously, SM play can result in death or severe psycho-emotional trauma induced not only be the physical experience, but from the betrayal of trust itself."—Staci Newmahr[9]

The very fact that the term "safe word" turns up in comedy shows on more than one occasion could imply that a serious tool to determine consent is viewed as nothing more than a joke (although this could also simply indicate pop culture's juvenile tendency to play any and all sexual references for laughs). It's referred to in *Scrubs* (Season 1, Episode 8) when Dr. Cox's new girlfriend teases him with her plans for the evening—"It involves wine, an amazing dinner and a safety word we've agreed upon in advance." However, comedy or no, you can't fault the program-makers for an incorrect description of how safe words should function—this short exchange refers both to mutual consent *and* advance negotiation, keeping the most ethical of kinksters happy. Even *Family Guy* manages a similar trick, where a kink scene is included presumably for the comic opportunity to portray overweight slob Peter Griffin in a PVC suit. Peter and his wife Lois chat amiably about unrelated topics while zipping themselves into their kinky outfits, then Lois says, "The safety word is banana" before the lights go out and the sound of a firm impact and Peter groaning is all that's left.

However, the inclusion of safe words as comic tools becomes less easy to condone when what is actually being mocked is the violation of them. In an episode of *The Office* (U.S.) Season 3, "Women's Appreciation," bumbling boss Michael Scott (Steve Carell) tells the camera that he and ice queen partner Jan "have a safe word in case things go too far: foliage." After a pause for the audience to have a snicker at Jan and Michael's leafy green safe word, Michael drops the punchline—"although last time she pretended she didn't hear me."

The comedy is presumably meant to originate in the idea of a woman forcing a man to participate in a sexual exchange, when the familiar social narrative is that of course, no man ever refuses sexual advances from a woman. Unfortunately, this presumption leads to the trivializing of male sexual assault and the belief that men cannot be raped—or at least, that *real* men don't get raped. As I mention in more depth in Chapter 2, there is a tendency to assume that men who get violated by women somehow deserve what happens to them, and deserve to be mocked for it. As a character, Michael Scott is deluded, ignorant, desperate to be liked and an incompetent boss. Much of the comedy in *The Office* is derived from how much his intelligent, authoritative partner Jan bosses him around. Yet it seems to be pushing the joke a little far to imply a man deserves sexual violation just because he's a bit of an idiot. Some might speculate that the joke lies in the fact there's only so much damage a woman could do to a man, and he gets to have sex anyway, so he really should just man up and stop complaining (something referred to in an episode of *Friends* where Chandler complains of having been tricked into having sex, and then when Joey points out "So? You got to have sex, right?" despairs, "What's the matter with me? Why am I such a girl?"). Safe words, according to this logic, are more of a female concern and are only a necessity for women. A *real man* doesn't need protecting from a woman because (as I mentioned in Chapter 1) women just aren't physically capable of harming a man the way a man is capable of harming a woman.

In the case of BDSM, however, where the right restraints and the right instruments can compensate for any difference in physical strength, this may be a dangerous position to take. As Jay Wiseman points out, if someone genuinely thinks their partner might not listen when they use the safe word during a BDSM scene, "they may quietly conclude they are in danger of being tortured to death."[10] He goes on to tell the precautionary tale of a female dominant who teased her partner with this possibility, and found that her male submissive unfortunately took her at her word. The man squeezed himself out of his restraints and was ready to attack his domme with an iron bar in his defense; a pretty serious consequence for what was meant to be a joke. This is definitely not how safe words are meant to function, and demonstrates precisely why there can be no lack of clarity over what's consensual nonconsent, and what's just nonconsent.

No Laughing Matter

This is something pop culture producers often fail to take into account, using the idea of a misunderstanding over safe words as merely another opportunity for slapstick humor. As I wrote about in "The Male Submissive," the (implied) violent penetration of a frantically resisting Cooper in the BDSM scene from 2004 comedy *Eurotrip* apparently occurs because he's unable to pronounce the long, tongue-twisting Dutch safe word that the dominatrices present him with before the scene begins. One explains in a heavy Dutch accent "Sometimes we find with our clients, they are so overwhelmed with the pleasure that they sometimes scream out 'no' when really they mean 'yes,'" and her colleague adds, "That's why we have a safe word." Considering that many pop culture depictions of BDSM leave out any reference to negotiation or safe words at all, this brief dialogue does a pretty good job of succinctly explaining the need for them. However, the punchline is that the horny Cooper is so overwhelmed by the thrilling prospect of three women

An experience in an Amsterdam brothel in *Eurotrip* goes from fun to frightening when the safe word fails (Photofest).

attending to him at once, that he doesn't bother to look at the slip of paper on which the safe word is written. When he's about to have testicle clamps administered by three beefy men, he panics and whips out the piece of paper, only to realize it's a long, unpronounceable (and in real life, utterly nonsensical) European word. When he does attempt to say it, he pronounces it wrong and it is interpreted as a request for the men to bring out a four-pronged rotating vibrator and aim it towards his backside. It's not exactly a plausible scenario, but in light of the fact that being unable to safe word (or unable to make oneself understood) in the middle of a BDSM scenario is a terrifying prospect for many submissives or bottoms, one wonders why exactly this is meant to be humorous.

Still, one might suggest that the idea of someone using a long, foreign-sounding, polysyllabic word as a safe word is pretty silly; and that furthermore, it's not as if kink sessions never go wrong or involve misunderstandings, however well-intentioned all parties are. A satirical book, *Fifty Sheds of Grey*, was released in the UK following the success of *that trilogy*, and contained pages of innuendo which actually mostly refer to gardening. One page states, "As we were discharged from the casualty department for the third time that month, we began to wonder whether we should change the safe word from Llanfairpwllgwyngyllgogerychwyrndrobwllllantysiliogogogoch [the longest place name in the UK]." However strongly some feminists and BDSM practitioners may feel that we should not be joking about an important tool for both establishing and withdrawing consent when we're already living in a culture which respects consent too little, others may point out that it's a sign of considerable progress that the term "safe word" has even managed to enter mainstream media discourse. Not only does it contribute to a norming of BDSM, positive insofar as it removes some of the stigma from BDSM being seen as a freaky, shameful activity, but it also creates opportunities for discussions about consent, and whether the vanilla mainstream model could take some valuable lessons from the kink model. When safe words are being talked about on prime time television, at least a mainstream audience is being exposed to the concept of an unassailable right to withdraw consent *at any time* in a sexual exchange. In a society where there still seems to be far too much confusion about what constitutes "blanket consent" to certain acts (many of us would say there is no such thing, yet rape apologists insist otherwise), the concept of safe words is pretty unconfusing.

A Poignant Reminder

You can't please all of the people all of the time, and my previous writing about BDSM has shown me this, although—unlike, say, when I wrote about why breast cancer advertising shouldn't be so sexualized for a UK newspaper and had such a barrage of four letter words flung at me on Twitter that I had to go offline for the weekend—it was largely constructive disagreement rather than foul abuse. Ironic, really, that a community of people viewed by the media as savage, violent and psychologically warped, were polite and thoughtful in disagreeing with me, whereas whenever I've written about feminism for other major media outlets, dismissive sexism always appears in the comments section, often couched in pretty obnoxious language. Still, when I wrote about kink there was always someone who wanted to point out that the way I'd defined dominant or submissive or top or bottom or BDSM or kink was not the way *they* would define it, or that they didn't like a particular label I'd used, or didn't like labels at all, or that in their particular style of play, they negotiated but didn't use a safe word and therefore I should be careful about implying everyone should use a safe word.

As a writer, you often find yourself in the position of having to generalize for the sake of brevity, while also knowing it's your job to blow blithe generalizations out of the water, and you're also constantly trying to speak to a multitude while being all too aware that you can only ever really speak for yourself. Realistically speaking, demanding that the subtleties of 24/7 master/slave interactions without safe words (but with the consent of all involved) were accurately portrayed in popular culture was likely to be a bit of a big ask. It also wasn't something I had room to stop and address in an 800 word blog post, nor even in the 19,000 words to which the "Thinking Kink" series added up. I felt instead that I addressed what was really a priority; the fact that our culture's belief in people (especially women)'s right to refuse sexual acts at any time, and at any point in the act, is still so very much in its infancy (if, indeed, it's been birthed at all) means that safe words need to be central to any discussion about BDSM, even if there are a segment of players who don't believe in their necessity. If kink is going mainstream, then the edgier players may have to accept that they won't always see themselves represented (although logically, they shouldn't care anyway, because being accepted into the mainstream would presumably render their edginess void) because the most important secret about kink to reveal to vanilla audiences isn't one about fisting, scat play, blood, dead animals or incest fantasies; it's one about consent.

The value of writing about safe words was truly shown to me after I received one of the most poignant comments out of the whole series. As well as discussing some of the above topics and references, I included links to two articles where women spoke about having their safe words violated. These were brave and upsetting pieces, and I wanted to put them out there as a contrast to the treatment of safe words as a comedic concept. In a blog post entitled "Why I Didn't Just Call the Cops,"[11] Cliff Pervocracy wrote about being sexually and physically assaulted by a play partner during BDSM, how he disregarded her safe word, and how being part of a BDSM community adds extra obstacles to reporting an abuser, in addition to the ones all women already face (victim blaming, police skepticism/inefficiency, ostracism from friends and family). It was a deeply sobering read:

> I said "red" and he didn't stop. I said "red, safe word, stop, ow" and he didn't stop. Like when he was holding me down, this was going to end on *his* time. He kept going and I kept saying, "no, really, fucking *red*, fucking *stop*." I wasn't screaming or yelling … but I was definitely not unclear.

As was the other article I mentioned, "When Safe Words Are Ignored,"[12] written by Tracey Clark Flory for Salon.com. It details both the violation of safe words experienced by prominent BDSM educators such as Maggie Mayhem and Kitty Stryker, and the indifferent or minimizing responses of other kinksters:

> The scene that they negotiated was "fantastic," Mayhem says, but then things took a turn. "I found myself tied up and unable to get away when that individual decided that he was going to have sex with me," she says, tears welling in her eyes, "even though we'd specifically negotiated against it, even though I was saying that it needed to stop, and even though he was not wearing a condom at the time."
>
> For the most part, she kept the experience to herself, but on the rare occasions when she did tell people in the community about it, she says, "I got

one response … which was people saying [things like], 'I don't do drama. This is a respected person in the community. I'm very sorry that you had a miscommunication during your scene that made it not very fun for you, but I don't want to hear about it.'"

The victim-blaming here echoes the type I saw during the afore-mentioned incident in my local scene, and is also echoed in the simplistic construction of safe words as a) a simple binary and b) a foolproof method of self-protection. The idea that the disregarding of negotiated terms and a request to stop the scene can be interpreted as a "miscom-munication" demonstrates at best, an unwillingness to acknowledge that abuse goes on in the BDSM scene (understandable, given the stigma that still exists around the community, but still not condonable) and at worst a flagrant attempt to stonewall any reporting of what the listener knows is sexual assault.

As Kitty Stryker says in the same article, "[There's] this belief that if I make sure I get references, have a safe call [a scheduled check-in with a friend to make sure things haven't gone awry] and negotiate using a checklist, I'll be safe," Stryker tells me. "But then you find out that you can do those three things and not be safe anyway, and that's terrifying. You realize how vulnerable you are." The frightening truth is that a safe word is no protection at all if a top or dominant doesn't give a shit about your boundaries.

I was glad to have publicized the issue in my piece of safe words, not least when I received the following (anonymous) comment on my post:

> Thank you for all of the information provided in this post. I am so relieved (and horrified) to now know that there are many people who have been raped and assaulted during BDSM. I felt like I was at fault for what happened to me even though I repeatedly said, "no" and "stop."

The horrible thought of a person blaming themselves for their assault in BDSM showed me just how important discourse on safety in BDSM remains, and how fear of stigma, our knowledge of the hostility with which rape victims are still treated, plus our culture's tendency to snigger like teenagers at the mention of kink or sex, stops that discourse from happening.

The comment was titled "On the Road to Recovery," and went on to say, "Your information, Pervocracy's experiences, and Clark-Flory's article have affected me so deeply. To know that I am not alone, to know that I have a right to be angry, and to have my self-doubting thoughts disproved has helped me move towards healing."

Even if it took a picture of Peter Griffin in PVC to achieve it, I was very glad to be able to help.

6

A Heavy Load to Bear

Feminism and the Submissive Female

"Women are bombarded with messages about how they should comply with and accommodate male sexual desires and needs so submission fantasies map onto this."—Professor Breanne Fahs, author of *Performing Sex: The Making and Unmaking of Women's Erotic Lives*

I make no secret of the fact that my writing and research on kink was originally prompted by the uninformed speculation surrounding heterosexual woman who enjoys playing the submissive to men. Such a woman finds herself stuck between the rock of a sexist society which tells her she's just exemplifying women's true nature, and the hard place of a feminist community which considers her brainwashed by the patriarchy. I saw so much kink-shaming visited upon heterosexual submissive woman after *that book* became so popular, both by those one would expect to condemn her (sexists looking for an opportunity to say that women just want to be dominated, conservatives, religious fundamentalists) and sadly, those who one would expect to be fighting her corner; namely, other feminists. The need to pathologize female submissives also seems to be continuing even as I write this book, over two years later. Just the other day, a story popped up in my Facebook newsfeed. Apparently a study found that women aged 18–24 who had read *that book* were more likely to suffer from disordered eating, and more likely to have been in abusive relationships.

It was hard to say which was more annoying, the fact that the study had been conducted in the first place, or the lazy suppositions pulled from it. As Clarisse Thorn, feminist writer and sex educator points out in her book *The S&M Feminist*,[1] disproportionate scrutiny of women's behavior is where sexism starts. Why does it matter what women like to read or what they like to do in their bedrooms, unless someone is looking to use that information as an excuse to disempower them? The obsession with finding out what female submission might *mean* comes from the assumption that it must mean something bad, and as Thorn puts it "If we weren't constantly forced to deal with the broken assumptions of a broken misogynist culture, this question would never occur to anyone!"[2] Or, to put it another way, while male submissives may encounter certain obstacles to having their kinks accepted, men's submission is not generally used to make an argument that men don't *really* want equality. No one suggested that the fact racing mogul Max Mosley enjoyed being spanked meant he actually wanted to hand back his Formula One millions, or be subservient to women in his everyday life. The fact that woman are not free to even read erotic literature without their particular choices being given political weight shows how the unexamined life is a privilege not yet extended to the female gender. It also implies that we're still living in a media culture that is looking for any excuse to dismiss the concept of female agency.

From Stats to Blanket Statements

This can easily be seen in studies like the one mentioned above, which claims women who read *that book* were 25 percent more likely to have a partner who had been verbally abusive, 34 percent more likely to have a partner who displayed stalking tendencies, and 75 percent more likely to have used diet aids or fasted for 24 hours. Media outlets have picked up on this information and are reporting it with fascination, but thankfully snarky online commenters also began to cut through the nonsense straight away. For one, are there many 18 to 24-year-old women who *haven't* used diet aids or indulged in unsafe eating practices to try and lose weight? I've known a lot of women in that age bracket (and I've been in it myself!) and I can report that sadly, a messed-up relationship with food is almost a standard feature of young female life in the 21st century. Secondly, the "study did not distinguish whether women experienced the negative emotional and health behaviors before or after reading Fifty Shades"[3]; a pretty damn crucial distinction to make, one would think. Anyone with a basic understanding of how causality works can see the problem here: by the logic of this study, someone who suffered an eating disorder two years ago can blame it on a book they read this summer. Furthermore, even if there is a link between being more accepting of unhealthy relationships and choosing to read that book, correlation is not the same as causation. One book does not a generation of damaged women make. Does it occur to those conducting the study that a major factor in abusive relationships is low self-esteem, a condition possibly caused by growing up in a society that constantly scrutinizes, criticizes and condemns women's behavior as failing to adhere to this or that particular standard? Is it any wonder young women may feel lousy about themselves when every day there seems to be a new study out telling them that they're doing life, love or relationships wrong?

Perhaps young women in bad relationships were more likely to read *that book* as a form of escapism. Perhaps those concerned about their partner's stalkerish tendencies read *that book* because they'd heard that the guy in it displays similar tendencies, but ultimately turns out to be a good guy, and that fact gave them hope. Perhaps reading about a guy who was charming, attentive and concerned for his partner's every need was a nice fantasy if you're dating a guy who is verbally abusive. So why are none of these explanations ever offered? Why, instead, does our media jump straight to the idea that women are so easily influenced that one book has brainwashed a whole generation of them into accepting abusive relationships?

I've mentioned it so many times elsewhere in this book I hope I don't even need to get started on how dangerous and lazy it is for the media to conflate consensual BDSM with abuse. While the journalists reporting on the study aren't explicitly making the connection, by saying that women who like to read about a woman who consents to be tied up and spanked by a controlling man are more likely to have bad relationships, they're pretty much placing one image next to the other and waiting for the public to put two and two together. Furthermore, not every correlation between women liking BDSM fiction and accepting abuse is even that subtle. Whole webpages and Twitter accounts are dedicated to saying that *that book* actually is a tale of domestic abuse, a statement offensive to BDSM practitioners, genuine victims of domestic violence, and anyone who simply found the book erotic and enjoyable. There seems to be little common ground between those who understand BDSM and those who want to clutch their pearls over the apparent romanticizing of an abusive relationship.

The only ground I'll cede is to say that, yes, the fictional character Christian Grey's attempts to control fictional character Anastasia by buying her extravagant gifts, criticizing her friends, following her movements and telling her what to wear may indeed echo the textbook signs of a controlling partner whose next move is often control through physical violence. But my next phrase is going to be simply: so what? Have any of those so worried about the effects of *that trilogy* read *Titus Andronicus* recently? Funnily enough, most Shakespeare lovers have never indulged in cannibalism, rape or mutilation as a result of it. Do feminists next need to burn *Wuthering Heights,* a story often considered a great romance when in fact it is about two people exacting psychological torment on each other, the spouses they marry to torment each other and their children? I wonder when there will be a study on what women's fondness for *Jane Eyre* might really mean, given how Jane slavishly devotes herself to liar and bigamist Mr. Rochester despite his frequent cruelty and indifference (interestingly, *that trilogy* is described as having "a narrative arc reminiscent of Jane Eyre" by Julie Clawson in her paper "Fifty Shades of Hope: Finding Healing Power in a Cultural Phenomenon")?[4] Or when *A Streetcar Named Desire* will be pulled off Broadway for eroticizing domestic violence with Stella's willingness to put up with Stanley's abuse due to their sexual passion, and that's before we even get to Stanley raping Blanche and then committing her to a mental institution with the complicity of her sister? Finally, if we're worried about idealizing controlling relationships, why was no one objecting to the teen worship of moody, controlling Edward Cullen from the Twilight series a few years ago? We all know what *that book* was originally based on, after all.

Yet the heterosexual feminist woman who enjoys playing a submissive role in BDSM—or even just reading about it—gets criticism on both sides. Conservatives and the religious right wing tell her that "women are drawn to the books because they know deep down that equality is wrong and that they need a man to dominate them."[5] Feminists tell her that she's in league with the patriarchy and a sexist media, with Laurie

Penny recently writing "Sexual submission is the acceptable face of female perversion: pliable, obedient and about pleasing your man"[6] but at least deigning to tell submissive women that "in a culture where women who express sexual agency are punished … that sort of fantasy is entirely comprehensible." The best response the submissive woman can hope for from feminists seems therefore to be along the lines of, "your sexuality does nothing but contribute to a media fantasy of female passivity, but at least it's understandable because it must simply be a survival response to cultural shame regarding sexually active females." There's no suggestion that the submissive female may actively and consciously choose her behavior in the first place.

Talk to Me, Not About Me

Speaking in 2012, Stacey May Fowles said to me, "So often I see conjecture about why a submissive woman might want to be dominated and grow increasingly frustrated that no one took the time to actually ask even one submissive what her personal wants or needs are." There certainly seems to be a lot of talking *about* submissive women rather than with them, and never more so when female submission is being used as evidence that society or gender relations are going to hell in a handcart. When I watched the 2005 movie *The Notorious Bettie Page* as part of my research, a scene where Bettie sits outside a courtroom while a roomful of men debate the ethics of the bondage depicted in her photoshoots reminded me of this tendency to deny the subject of a controversy the right to participate in the actual discourse surrounding them. Much like the tendency of some feminists to assume that they know better than themselves what sex workers, porn actresses or transgender women really want/need, the failure to actually engage with female submissives seemed to imply that if anything was stifling women's voices, it wasn't ball gags. It was the fact that those who wanted to wag their fingers at female submissives weren't interested in hearing whether such women wanted their pity in the first place.

There also seemed to be no acknowledgment that *that trilogy* ends with the submissive character, Anastasia, "realizing that the BDSM elements can be pleasurable, but only when mutually chosen for equitable pleasure."[7] This is an important distinction, and one too often neglected in discourse around the book and what it supposedly signifies about female sexuality. Instead, as Julie Clawson points out "the backlash against the *Fifty Shades* books focuses solely on the domination aspects of the story ... ignoring the complete narrative arc towards mutuality." Look for critiques of the book online and you'll find plenty of comments that start with "I haven't read it, but from what I've heard...." Feminists were by no means innocent of such laziness during the 2012 shitstorm over the alleged explosion on the population of female subs (a deeply questionable myth that needs looking at in light of how often the male sub is invisibilized, as mentioned in Chapter 2), and as current writing implies, they're still unfortunately at it.

All Eyes on You

> "A family's honour is carried by its daughters. Maybe because the strongest of men would break their backs under its weight."—Meera Syal, *Life Isn't All Ha Ha Hee Hee*[8]

The disproportionate focus on female sexual behavior, while men's often goes unexamined, showed no signs of abating when BDSM suddenly went mainstream in 2012. For every woman who said to me, "We don't get to impose our PC values on what makes us hot,"[9] there were others who told me, "We live in a culture that is deeply threatened by women with intense sexual desire, so it makes sense that women may internalize a need to distance themselves from their own desire by having [submission] fantasies."[10] The way submissive women were written off as brainwashed by the patriarchy irritated me intensely, so I went in search of pop culture examples of empowered female submissives. It was a tricky journey.

Lee, the protagonist in the movie *Secretary,* is a young woman who finds the courage to stop self-harming and explore her sexuality through a dom/sub relationship with her boss, E. Edward Grey. Although she is initially intimidated by Grey, she grows in strength and assertiveness as they begin to explore spanking, restraints, pony play and other erotic power games in their office. The movie is very popular with BDSM practitioners; I remember showing it to a vanilla friend and her being utterly

An empowered submissive: the movie *Secretary* sees Lee (Maggie Gyllenhaal) find fulfilment in a BDSM relationship (Movie Stills Database).

baffled by it. I knew I couldn't ask for perfection from a movie, but I felt that there was too much ambiguity about Lee's mental state. Did she only get into kink because she was mentally ill, an assumption kinksters spend a great deal of time fighting against? Is submitting to E. E. Grey simply a substitute for self-harm, getting the euphoria of pain from BDSM without having to inflict it upon oneself? As Clarisse Thorn points out above, perhaps our answers to these questions should be "Who cares? What does it matter?" but it feels like the stakes are particularly high when defending the female submissive in popular culture. If she isn't strong, mentally healthy and able to confidently state that her submission is freely chosen rather than the result of an abusive background or sexist conditioning, she risks her sexual fantasies being written off as "a direct correlate to disempowered experiences they have in the rest of their life, in work, family, and sexual dynamics."[11] Yet, as Cliff Pervocracy pointed out in her interview with me, "We're all subject to harmful social influences. Why single out kinky women?"

Wherever I looked, I found excuses for female submission, as if it's something that always needs justifying, rather than something one might practice simply because it brings a woman erotic delight. In Anne Rice's *Sleeping Beauty* trilogy (written under the pen name A. N. Roquelaure), Beauty submits to the attentions of a palace-full of perverts out of her love for the prince. *The Story of O* is a great example of art imitating life, as it not only portrays a woman submitting to extreme sexual torture out of love for her partner, but was also apparently written by Anne Desclos (under pen name Pauline Réage) to please her partner, who was a fan of De Sade. As I've written about further in the chapter on the male dominant, other writers mitigate the savage attentions of a dominant partner by describing him as tender elsewhere. This is a storyline not limited to BDSM, but rather any tormented romance—as I've said elsewhere, love apparently excuses all. As Cliff Pervocracy said in her interview with me "the biggest misconception about female submission is that they do it because of psychodrama, they do it to find themselves, they do it for love—it's never a woman just plain getting her rocks off." Cliff echoed my own thoughts perfectly; why was it so difficult to show a happy, mentally healthy female submissive asking a man to restrain, slap or flog her without having to "excuse" it via love, mental ill-health or an abusive dynamic? However, when I thought of how few mainstream books, movies or TV shows were willing to portray a woman doing *anything* sexually for herself, rather than for her partner, the male gaze or for love, I realized I probably had my answer.

The 2012 Australian film *Sleeping Beauty* didn't tick any new boxes in terms of portraying women in submissive sexual roles, as it showed broke student Lucy working at a secret erotic club in order to pay her bills. Like Belle de Jour agreeing to a client urinating on her in *Secret Diary of a Call Girl*, or professional courtesan Phaedra submitting to floggings as part of her job in the *Kushiel's Dart* fantasy trilogy, women playing a submissive or masochistic role as part of their profession isn't a new trope. It also doesn't help advance the argument of women submitting out of choice, although some sex workers would be annoyed by the assumption that it's impossible to enjoy sexual activity just because you've been paid for it. In *Sleeping Beauty*, Lucy does seem largely indifferent to her work at the secret club, but as her finances grow more desperate, and her other jobs (office work and waitressing) become increasingly demoralizing, she goes from waitressing in lingerie to agreeing to be drugged and spend the night unconscious with older men who pay for the pleasure.

Avoiding the usual narratives of exploitation and victimized women that films and TV shows about sex work often opt for, director Julia Leigh instead encourages us to ask who is really exploited. Lucy makes so much money from her secret job that in one scene we see her set fire to a $100 bill. Soon after her first night at the club, we see her lying on the floor at her despised office job, waiting for the photocopier to finish. It's a noticeable echo of the submissive pose assumed by two naked women on the floor of the secret club the night before, yet even though Lucy is fully clothed, she seems far more defeated at her office job than the two kneeling women. She's also tormented by her spiteful boss at the office, an older female who has no sympathy for her family problems and ultimately fires her. By contrast, Lucy's work at the club is hardly taxing (used to the drudgery of waitressing, she's surprised to be told she doesn't even have to wash up, that the cleaners will take care of that for her), and incredibly well paid. By also making Lucy white, middle class and extremely conventionally attractive, Leigh ensures that the audience doesn't feel too sorry for her—indeed, as I discuss more in the chapter on the male dominant, it is the men who pay to sleep with her who often come across as much more pitiable.

It's also worth mentioning that, while the blurb on the DVD cover describes Lucy's work at the club as "an erotic experience that requires Lucy's absolute submission," counter to the assumption that the ultimate submission must involve sex, no penetration is actually allowed. In fact, Clara, the older woman who runs the organization, tells Lucy, "Your vagina is a temple." Lucy snorts and responds her vagina definitely is *not* a temple. Regardless, the supposed submission still involves Lucy's body being designated as inviolable. Refuting the idea that the ultimate surrender must involve penetration—a phallocentric belief that has its flipside in male fears of castration and vagina dentata—*Sleeping Beauty* does not endorse the belief that men who desire a pliant woman necessarily want to commit rape. There are other scenes where Lucy helps a medical student friend of hers with his research, presumably in return for money, and has a probe put down her throat. Her gagging and obvious discomfort has echoes of forceful oral sex/deep throating, and makes this ordeal appear a much more unpleasant one to undergo than falling asleep for money. Leigh appears to be encouraging the audience to question where the artificial submission that Lucy undertakes at the club is really any more unpleasant or degrading than the countless unpleasant things to which every working person must submit to in order to make money. Although the film stops short of endorsing the neoliberal belief that the activity which makes you the most money is automatically the most acceptable one, it does demand a more nuanced approach to sex work, work, submission and female agency than many portrayals of submissive women do.

Objectification: What If You Want to Be a Feminist AND a Footstool?

The feminist tradition of condemning all images which appear to objectify women runs into difficulty when applied to the BDSM community. There are few areas of BDSM where women don't appear to be objectified to a greater or lesser extent, regardless of whether they are playing dominant or submissive roles (see the chapter on the Female Dominant for further discussion of how, despite supposedly being in a position of power, female dominants in popular culture are still regularly constructed for the male gaze in terms of outfit, appearance and actions). A glance at FetLife's "Kinky and Popular" page invariably throws up images that are either solely or predominantly populated by women (if men are depicted, they may well only be present via a disembodied penis). The popular images of rope work always feature female subjects. Every so often, a FetLife member will write a post bemoaning the lack of male bodies and the lack of pictures depicting kink any more varied than heterosexual male dom/female sub pairing, and the post will attract many supportive comments, yet despite the apparent appetite for this, little seems to change.

Those who defend the status quo often trot out the "Men are just more visual creatures than women..." line, or the "Women's bodies are just nicer to look at" excuse. These are both inadequate responses for so many reasons, but the main one is that it is impossible to separate any biological truth out of these claims because they are so bound up with sexist cultural bias. A 2006 study showed that women "are no less visually engaged than men when viewing erotic images,"[12] but because of the social shame surrounding female desire and fantasy, were much

What's even more absurd is that her $110 dress is only $29.99.

DAFFY'S

daffys.com

No comment? Ms magazine criticized this advertisement as sexist, but a BDSM reading may suggest otherwise (Daffy's).

less open about their levels of arousal when self-reporting. As for whose body is "nicer to look at," this is an entirely subjective issue, but one which a patriarchal society frames as objective in order to legitimize men's objectification of the female form. Women, well aware of all the unattractive aspects of the female body which the media conveniently pretends doesn't exist (when did you last see a model with thread veins, moles, visible scars cellulite, stretch marks, large labia, a visible mons pubis or even so much as a laughter line?), know that there is little truth to the matter than either gender has the monopoly on pretty bodies, but a sexist society attempts to flatter us into believing that women are there to look pretty and to be looked at, while men are the ones meant to do the looking.

Until this changes, say feminists, nothing will improve for women—we will always be considered passive objects and will always be judged on our looks rather than our deeds. This means anything that appears to be objectifying the female form is, by default, seen as deeply negative for women. So how do women who want to practice BDSM, especially that which explicitly and literally practices objectification of the human body, reconcile their desires with these objections? And do pop culture depictions of BDSM deserve any more of a "pass" when it comes to objectification, or are they necessarily just as sexist as any other picture or film which renders women as decorative rather than active?

Ms. magazine, the original U.S. feminist magazine founded in 1972, regularly critiques aspects of popular culture for anti-feminist content. Its "No Comment" segment at the end of each issue takes to task sexist advertisements, and gives contact details of the offending publisher so that readers can complain to them. In its winter 2012 issue, it featured an advert for Daffy's, a fashion label, which depicted a woman in a tight black dress, elbow-length gloves and knee-high spiked boots on all fours, posing as a human table under a sheet of glass. The tagline read "What's even more absurd is that her dress is only $29.99." Kinksters may be more bothered by the idea that human furniture play is necessarily viewed as absurd, but it was clear what the grounds for feminist complaint were meant to be—the woman was being sexualized and objectified in a world where women are already too easily treated as discardable objects, all in order to sell a thirty dollar dress.

I agree that as advertisements go, this one certainly deserves to be entered in the Fail column. I'm of the belief that if a product is good, it shouldn't need sex to sell it. Even from a hard-eyed capitalist viewpoint, the mantra "sex sells" no longer even washes, as studies[13] have shown that viewers have no greater product recall after watching adverts that use sexual content than after watching those that don't, and that using sexualized imagery to sell a product that has nothing to do with sex can actually decrease product recall by 10 percent.[14] The female form is far too readily used as window dressing to sell products, and the insincerity present in labeling the woman/table as absurd while still using her to push your fashion label shows to me the high level of contempt advertisers still hold for women. Add to that the fact the woman in the advert is young, white, slim, able-bodied and cisgendered, as nearly every woman in fashion advertising is, and you have pretty much everything that is wrong with the advertising industry. So, I'm with *Ms.* so far on that point.

Where I can't fully condemn the advert, however, is the notion that objectification is necessarily sexist. It's certainly misplaced and inappropriate in this context (what has BDSM got to do with selling a pretty average, non-kinky dress?), but to imagine that all contexts in which a person voluntarily acts as an object is a victory for sexism is to take an extremely simplistic view of sexuality and desire. The dogma that all instances of objectification are wrong and misogynistic appears to demand that sexual desire always be cerebral, profound and pure. In her essay "A Cock of One's Own: Getting a Firm Grip on Feminist Sexual Power,"[15] Sarah Smith bemoans the idea "that there must be a way to have sex that is 'feminist,'" feeling that it results in " laundry list of must-nots that would hold our libidos hostage." She notes that the directive that she must not objectify her (female) partner is one of these frustrating restrictions, and practitioners of BDSM would no doubt agree. Whether enacting a straightforward dom/sub dynamic, role-playing with costumes or engaging in animal play, BDSM practitioners often find themselves in scenarios where one party is the object to be looked at, to inspire arousal, and the other party is the aggressor, to enjoy looking at, touching and manipulating the other person's body. Both parties gain great pleasure from enacting their chosen roles, and usually a great deal of pleasure is gained from the perceived enjoyment that the other person (or persons) is experiencing, whether they are the voyeur or the looked-at.

Any sexual interaction concerned with mutual pleasure is already far away from the vision of patriarchal, misogynistic sex that some feminists assume must accompany all objectification. The objectified woman is assumed to have no voice, no feelings, just as the man (or possibly woman) visually consuming her is assumed to be incapable of caring about either of those things. So how on earth can the man who uses a woman as a human footstool not be a horrendous misogynist, or the woman in question a brainwashed idiot?

Katherine Martinez, an academic at the Metropolitan State College of Denver, conducted a study into self-objectification among consensual sadomasochists, and found that contrary to the accepted belief, especially among feminists, that objectification leads to reduced self-esteem and increased anxiety, BDSM practitioners who self-objectify actually report better mental health and greater happiness.[16] Reporting on her findings,

Martinez states, "The data presented suggest that self-objectification theory fails to adequately address the CS (consensual sadomasochist) context, where sexual objectification is often desired and even requested." Martinez found that contrary to existing studies which found a positive correlation between self-objectification and body shame,[17] her research among the CS community found the opposite, *especially* for women. Martinez comments, "correlations between self-objectification and self-surveillance were significantly negative for women and men, while the correlation between self-objectification and body-shame was significantly negative only for women." It appears that for some women, not only is consensual objectification not the terrible anti-feminist activity which it has previously been seen to be, but it's actually a positive reinforcement of body confidence and sexual autonomy. This implies that the simplistic feminist argument that all objectification of the female body contributes to a hostile sexual culture does not stand up, at least when it comes to the BDSM community. Martinez goes on to comment that perhaps "something unique is happening in the CS context to guard against some negative effects of sexual objectification."

Having taken part in such play myself, I can certainly understand the outcome of Martinez' study. Without consent, mutual respect and mutual pleasure, a person acting as a table, chair or indeed any object of voyeurism, would be not just one of sexism, but one of assault and coercion. But then, *so would all sex.* There is little to separate many acts from pure violence (leg waxing, boxing, rugby, roller derby, the latter which I myself play) except consent and willingness. Why then, do we seem to make sex and sexually charged acts (because of course, not all BDSM involves sex) a special case, unless we believe that to have any interaction with a man is to constantly run the risk of unleashing the closet misogynist some feminists assume lives in every male? We may say there is a difference between private play and using BDSM in advertisements, but again this presupposes the existence of an uninformed and automatically sexist public, and still presumes that the default position for BDSM, both its imagery and play, is negative and harmful for women.

In response to this, I would pose the question: who is truly objectifying the woman who consensually plays the footstool to her male partner: the partner with whom she's choosing to play, or the feminist who assumes she must be disempowered without bothering to actually ask her, who reduces her to a voiceless body when in fact she's a happily thinking, feeling, fully engaged human having fun with role play? I would also suggest that it is at least partly the tension between the way practices such as human furniture make objectification almost comically explicit, and the more subtle ways women can be objectified, which gives such play its taboo and therefore thrilling edge. The man with the woman under his feet knows he's not actually resting on a real footstool; he knows there is still a living, breathing woman there, but the erotic charge comes from the forbidden nature of treating another human being this way. So does the erotic charge in many forms of sexual play. Any insistence on focusing on the (artificially) dehumanizing aspect of such play, rather than keeping in mind that it's being participated in by full human beings (yes, even when it's being used in yet another tacky advert), says more to me about how these critics regard women in the first place, than the women and men participating in it.

Between a Rock and a Hard Place

All this said, I do understand the frustration of encountering yet another glossy magazine page where the female body is yet again used a tool to sell products. I regularly feel it myself, and so I appreciate that feminists feel the stakes are sometimes simply too high for women to give up any ground. We worry that as soon as we admit to enjoying anything that does not perfectly fit the template of "What a strong, independent woman should be doing," a sexist society will jump on it and use it to take away the few hard-won rights that we have barely even had time to enjoy. However, it is worth mentioning that generally speaking, the only people who have made me feel bad about being feminist and practicing BDSM and submission are not upholders of the patriarchy—they are, sadly, other feminists. Yes, there are the likes of Katie Roiphe who are just looking for any excuse to say that feminism is dead/broken/fatally flawed, and who will sink to hijacking BDSM and even rates of college campus rape in order to elevate their own name by causing some cheap controversy. However, when other feminists begin condemning other women's consensual pursuit of pleasure, it begins to feel very much like Sarah Smith's aforementioned laundry list of must-nots. By the same token, refusing to entertain that there are alternative readings of images like the above risks pushing BDSM back into a closet of shame by conflating it with sexism. The ad's *tactics* may be tired and predictable: that is not the same as saying the ad's *contents* is offensive.

In an article condemning the popularity of *that book* as signifying a terrible defeat for feminism and titled "Do Women Really Want to Be So Submissive?" British feminist writer Yasmin Alibhai-Brown writes, "When young women become instinctively assertive and free of gender constrictions, their liberty threatens the 'natural order.'[18] So they have to be reminded of their place, taught that they can never be good enough and must relearn submission." Exactly how Alibhai-Brown thinks that erotic fiction functions as a patriarchal tool to reprogram women's brain is not explained, but it is clear she has added a sexist society to (some women's) taste for submission and made five. Earlier in the article, Alibhai-Brown condemns "middle-class female singletons who are clueless about [the book's] implications." One wonders why it's considered feminist to criticize other women's literary and sexual tastes and presume that they are "clueless," but anti-feminist to enjoy whatever books you wish and, if you choose (and I don't believe for a second that everyone, or even the majority, of people who have read that book has even re-enacted any part of it in their bedrooms!), participate in BDSM.

Author of *The S&M Feminist*,[19] Clarisse Thorn said in her interview with me, "Such unsubstantiated allegations can have a negative impact on feminists BDSMers ... who spend years untangling our anxieties about our sexuality." It certainly seems to run counter to a movement which was intended to free women's sexuality from the narrow boxes patriarchy wished to place it in to tell women that the way they behave in the bedroom is letting the sisterhood down. Thorn adds, "I'm tired of such lazy so-called critiques. They're almost always leveled by people who have done zero research and have very little experience in actual BDSM communities." Alibhai-Brown's conflation of drug rape at UK universities with the popularity of a book about some (very mild) consensual BDSM implies she certainly does not understand the difference between kink and abuse, and would therefore be better off not condemning it in the name of feminism.

The Female Sub(versive)

"What pussy wants is fucked up stuff, really dark scenarios that test the boundaries and cut with an exhilarating level of danger."—Mollena Williams[20]

Strength and bravery are rarely terms used about submissives in general, but are particularly absent in discussions of female submissives. This is despite the fact that, as discussed in the chapter on the male submissive, it takes powers of endurance beyond most people's capacity to take a flogging, a caning, a whipping, to be restrained without panicking, or to go through an intense role play without breaking down psychologically. Yet this is conveniently forgotten in the rush to assume that the term submissive is synonymous with being a doormat. The conservative belief that femininity equals weakness (and therefore submission is just women's true nature taken to its logical conclusion) falls apart once people are forced to acknowledge the bravery possessed by a woman actively seeking out a man to hurt her.

Society teaches women to be afraid not just of male aggression, but masculinity in general. Men's physical strength, their sex drive—always portrayed as insatiable, domineering and predatory—and their capacity for violence are all the things women are conditioned to both fear and avoid. The little girl learns quickly that what poses the greatest threat to her is male; the mythical child abuser hiding in the bushes, who later in her life will morph into the lurking rapist in the alleyway. This constant murky presence of potential male violence both dictates and limits women's movements in the world.

What women also learn is that failure to take every step to avoid this violence will be punished, and that if the worst happens, they will be blamed for their own violation. While *Buffy The Vampire Slayer* may have had a complicated relationship with feminism in some ways, it was unequivocal in its statement that women can reclaim the spaces they are taught to fear; dark, deserted streets, graveyards, alleyways, basically all the places women are taught rape is most likely to happen, even though statistics do not bear this out at all. Buffy not only went to all these places, she deliberately sought them out, and patrolled them, protecting both men and women from the predatory violence of vampires (usually portrayed as male). In terms of inverting the fetishistic horror movie portrayal of the helpless female victim running around panicking in the dark, *Buffy* was extremely effective. It took a young, slim, traditionally attractive teen girl who in many other genres would end up gorily mutilated and murdered (and possibly sexually assaulted beforehand), and made her the warrior against nighttime attacks.

So why aren't submissive women seen as equally transgressive? Like Buffy, they actively seek out scenarios they are taught to fear—being alone with a man who is able to physically overpower and harm them—and they ratchet the odds up even further. They *ask* men to do those things. It's taboo, and perhaps it's taboo for a different reason than the one we are given to believe. Not because female submission is shameful, or anti-feminist, but because it actually requires *some serious guts*. A society which still discourages women from making active sexual choices, indeed from being anything other than passive and pretty, does not like admitting that. So instead it opts for simplistic narratives about equality being too much of a strain, or porn and pop videos conditioning women into passivity. But that obscures the reality of subbing in BDSM, as any bottom will tell you—you don't just wait for a dom to come along and start beating you. You make a conscious choice and you seek out the situation you find erotic. Often, you might have a list of demands that you present as part of negotiation; pleasurable things that you want done to you. As Anne McClintock puts it, "By scripting and controlling the circus of signs, the fetishist stages the delirious loss of control *within a situation of extreme control.*"[21]

In the 2011 movie *A Dangerous Method*, it is not Carl Jung, the supposed male aggressor, who dictates the pace and content of his sexual and kinky encounters with his patient Sabina, but Sabina herself. Having admitted she has a masochistic streak and is aroused by humiliation, Sabina tells Jung "I want you to be ferocious. I want you to punish me." These articulate demands for her needs to be met are hardly aligned with patriarchy's indifference to, or desire to eliminate, active female desire. Yet, again and again female submissives are told that they only like what they like because "we live in a culture that eroticizes power imbalances."[22] Yet how powerful is Jung's "ferocity" (presumed to be a natural part of every male) if he's only permitted to unleash it in controlled circumstances at Sabina's choosing? Can it even be viewed as real aggression, if all it actually does is arouse Sabina rather than frighten her? This goes to the heart of the issue—the response of the female submissive to male aggression disrupts, rather than supports, heteronormative and patriarchal narratives about male and female sexuality. Yes, patriarchy demands that women submit to men, but unwillingly and under coercion, with no regard for their pleasure and safety—not in artificial circumstances that they themselves have engineered, in which they are aroused rather than afraid, and in which their pleasure is paramount to the scene.

As Staci Newmahr writes, "Through bottoming, women confront and withstand and symbolically survive male violence…. These women are not celebrating violation, but actively defying the cultural proscription to live in fear of it."[23] The stereotype that women like "bad boys" because it gives them a thrill may feed into this—there is a dizzying high in "trusting men whom [women] 'should' not trust to take advantage of them." This is seen in an episode of the teen drama *Skins*,[24] where misfit Franky becomes involved with Luke, a shady character whose life of drugs and violence appeals to her when her middle-class friends have dropped her. Grieving over the death of her friend Grace, Franky tells Luke, "I'm fucking sick of it. I just feel like…" and he finishes the sentence for her "…exploding." Franky finds Luke's participation in brawls with rival gangs intoxicating, and starts to join the fighting herself, even though Luke previously describes these scenarios as "a bit of a girl-free zone." Like Buffy before her, another young woman is shown reclaiming space considered too dangerous for women.

The two have a frenetic physical relationship from the outset—their first kiss occurs in the middle of a bloody pub brawl, and their sex life moves from intense to distinctly d/s as Luke gets rougher and rougher with Franky, grabbing her by the hair and slapping her in the face. Yet Franky genuinely seems to find the violence pleasurable and continues to go back for more; their sex scenes are intercut with shots of Luke showing her how to box. Having previously found relationships boring, Franky retains her spirit of independence—when clean-cut Nick tries to rescue her from a pool hall fight, she screams, "I don't need fucking saving!" at him. Franky is asserting her own right to seek danger and thrills just like men do, as echoed in Staci Newmahr's words that BDSM play "is a space in which *women* can insist 'I will not be hurt … even if I put myself in harm's way.' It is a path to feelings of invincibility to which only men have historically been privy, in a particular and deeply gendered context."[25]

Unfortunately, as pop culture representations of girls going off the rails tend to, *Skins* ultimately implies Franky is in over her head, as Luke becomes increasingly controlling and violent. The status quo is re-established by the end of the episode, with Franky needing her father to protect her from his influence. Before this, though, there are distinctive parallels with Newmahr's theory that female submission can be an act of subversion to the patriarchal insistence that women should never seek out danger, especially not from or with men.

Sexism and the Scene: When Patriarchy Comes Knocking

> "I observed several instances of policing submissive identity [in the BDSM scene], a practice that I interpreted (and continue to interpret) as profoundly misogynistic, particularly since they have been most often initiated by dominant-identified men."—Staci Newmahr[26]

For all the vociferous defenses of the right of women to submit, however, it is important not to be blinded either to the faults of the BDSM scene, nor the wider world within which it exists. Kink takes place not in a vacuum but against the background of a world still riven with inequality: walking into a play party does not, unfortunately, mean that sexism, homophobia, transphobia, racism or classism suddenly fall away. Kinksters may consciously attempt to subvert those hateful trends, or mimic them in a way they find pleasurably challenging, but it is as simplistic to pretend that the real world does not infect kinky play as it is to write off all BDSM as being nothing more than the enactment of hatred and violence.

The language of choice will only take any of us so far, when we are aware that a level playing field (pun perhaps intended) is impossible to find in a society still a long way from dismantling the hierarchy that places the straight, white, cisgender male at the top. As "Paul," a white male top said to Margot Weiss,[27] "I think people in the scene are much too fast to … say, 'Well, you know as long as everybody consents … then it's all OK....' I think it's just crazy for people to try and pretend that sexuality is this magical realm that is somehow natural and is unaffected by anything social, economic or political." The neoliberal belief that choice renders any scenario unproblematic often functions to reinforce a status quo which keeps the privileged in their position. In their interview with me, BDSM and feminism blogger Charlie Hale said that they found the kink scene to be organized in a patriarchal way, with cisgender heterosexual men still being the majority of scene leaders (event organizers, workshop runners, vendors, etc.), and tropes of male dominance still being the most prevalent in much of the discourse and narrative in kink.

I too found that, although events in my local scene seemed to be more equally organized by men and women alike (although the women were more often subs or switches), the majority of workshop organizers and demonstrators were men, and pretty much every rope rigger I ever encountered was male. Pictures on FetLife suggest that this is the case elsewhere in the world too—either that, or female riggers just aren't so interested in photographing their work and displaying it online. Some events did seem to have a surfeit of male doms and female subs, although others were incredibly mixed, with plenty of fem dom/male sub, male-male and female-female pairings, plus a fair bit of group activity and solo players—I'll always remember a very military-fashioned young man happily tying himself up at a play party. I did encounter cis het male doms whose behavior bordered on the misogynistic ("kick her in the cunt" was the charming comment of a self-proclaimed sadist watching a friend of mine get tied up, which I found incredibly inappropriate not for the language or the sentiment, but for the fact he was not part of the scene and at no point had my friend consented to his involvement, much less him hurling obscenities at her. When I frowned at him he laughed) but most were well-behaved and polite.

However, as Kitty Stryker writes, "Just because someone is a community leader does not mean that they're actually safe. When gathering stories for Consent Culture's blog carnival, over 50 percent of the stories [of abuse] were [about] people who were community leaders, who taught workshops and were dungeon monitors."[28] I found the truth of this statement for myself, when I discovered that going to a kink event did not automatically mean freedom from the leering and gropes of a typical night out in vanilla world. At one play party, the older, male, white dominant host groped my backside while giving me the welcoming hug that he insisted on giving to everyone who attended. It was so sly that his hand had gone by the time I had realized what had happened, and I felt unable to raise the issue without making a scene. I told the person I was with but didn't feel empowered to tell anyone else, because I suspected the man would deny it, make me out to be a troublemaker and hide behind his friends in the scene—I was a relative newbie, he was established. This is a prime example of rape culture; where abusers go unconfronted and their victims end up feeling like the ones who have to change their behavior instead.

Whenever I went to that event in future, I asked the male dominant I was playing with at the time to keep the groper away from me (and also the charming gentleman mentioned above, in case he felt the need to come and give some of his verbose commentary on any scene of ours). The feminist in me, and also the person who simply does not shy away from confrontation, disliked taking what I saw as the coward's way out, i.e., getting someone else to fight my battles for me. However, pragmatism won out. If a man had little enough respect for women that he thought it was OK to grope them in a space where all touching was meant to be expressly negotiated and consensual (he was the *host* of the event, for Christ's sake—he had *written* the very rules pinned up on the wall), then I did not have much to gain by trying to educate him, and much to lose in terms of risking an unpleasant confrontation with an unwilling listener and the ruining of what was meant to be a pleasurable night of kinky play. The person he might listen to, however, was likely to be another male dom. In this instance, fighting every feminist (and kink-related) battle had to give way to the real world. It does, however, make one wonder how many other BDSM players are having to adjust their behavior in the scene because of sexism, racism or homophobia.

The fact Staci Newmahr says it only took her three weeks to stop using the term "submissive" to identify herself in the BDSM community in which she was carrying out her research, precisely because it seemed to bring with it such a slew of sexist assumptions, implies it wasn't just me who met with gender-based harassment in the kink scene (the example above is one of three instances where I was touched in the BDSM scene without my consent, every time by a cis het man). Newmahr writes that a mere three weeks as a submissive had left her "angry about my interactions with many dominant-identified men and deeply troubled by the misogynistic overtones."[29] Margot Weiss writes of similarly disappointing sexism in the kink community she studied: "Rather than reporting a scene free of gendered assumptions, many practitioners complained about sexism in the scene.... Women of all SM orientations reported that some men assume they must submissive." Somewhat stunningly, one subject Weiss interviewed even complained of "people brushing me off because I happen to be female."[30]

This is where the feminist female submissive walks a delicate tightrope—between wanting to confront sexism and fight sexism wherever she sees it, while also enjoying sexual acts and kinky play that many condemn as replicating patriarchal power dynamics, and finding a safe space in a community not immune to sexism in which she can enjoy those acts. It can sometimes seem like a lot to ask.

What Sisterhood for the Kinky Woman?

> "[Some feminists believe] that our society is so patriarchal that women cannot validly participate in S/M ... I don't suppose these authors would say that our society is so patriarchal that a woman cannot validly consent to have an abortion."—Jay Wiseman, *SM 101*

Pop culture images depicting female submission to male dominants remains provocative and unsettling, and that is part of their erotic charge. I think Stacey May Fowles best sums up exactly why submission is a guilty pleasure for women whose strength, intelligence and feminism have never been in question—"sexual submission and rape fantasy can only be acceptable in a culture that doesn't condone them. On a simplistic level, a fetish is only a fetish when it falls outside the realm of the real."[31] That's why there's a particular extra level of guilt for the feminist who enjoys subbing as part of BDSM—they feel that they are inadvertently aligning themselves with a culture that already doesn't care about genuine violations of women enough, while deserting their feminist sisters who fight for sexual violence to be taken seriously. Yet causing discomfort to those who often have not interrogated BDSM anywhere near deeply enough is no reason to demand that pop culture producers censor depictions of BDSM, nor that women deliberately prohibit themselves from practicing scenarios they find pleasurable.

My search for the perfect depiction of the female submissive in pop culture never actually landed upon that elusive creature, but the very fact I felt obliged to look for her in the first place probably says a lot more about the expectations thrown at women from both sides of the sexism fence. Feminism is accepting of women as full and flawed creatures in so many ways—it encourages us to love our bodies, faces, brains, abilities, talents and idiosyncracies in the face of a monolithic media culture that constantly tells us we're not good enough. Yet, should we find an erotic charge in play that may (however loosely) replicate patriarchal power dynamics, we're suddenly told to feel ashamed and pipe down, lest we muddy the waters of what feminism is supposed to mean, or somehow betray the movement. As recently as 1994, Norma Ramos said she believed that any woman who enjoyed sadomasochistic sex should rewire her sexuality—"I'm getting sexual pleasure from this, so what do I do about this? You work to change that. You have to challenge it."[32]

I could understand this confusion, to an extent, coming from older feminists such as Ramos and Yasmin Alibhai Brown, women who I assumed had no experience with BDSM, or who perhaps had experienced actual male violence in their lives and went on to assume that BDSM was merely an attractive disguise for the same thing. However, the discomfort with women who consensually play the submissive does seem to have trickled down to my generation of feminists (I was born in 1983) and those younger still. When I gave my talk on "Navigating Kink While Feminist," at the 2014 American Culture Association/Popular Culture Association conference, a woman in her 20s raised her hand and asked me if I thought woman-on-woman BDSM was "better" than fem sub/male dom scenarios. I tried to explain how I thought this belief, that certain power/gender configurations in BDSM were somehow superior to others, was ultimately misguided and unhelpful. As I outline further in the chapter on the female dominant, it rests on many incorrect assumptions: that what feminists want is domination, rather than equality; that feminist agency can only be expressed by assuming the dominant position on BDSM; that *anything* about feminism or indeed men and women's real life roles can accurately be expressed through BDSM; and that all submissives are disempowered and all doms complete dictators. However, I understood what made this young woman think this way. Robin Bauer, author of *Queer BDSM Intimacies: Critical Consent and Pushing Boundaries*[33] reported that in his research on BDSM in the lesbian community, one woman said "I'm glad I'm a lesbian so I don't have to have that difficult conversation with myself about whether I'm just doing this because a guy makes me."[34] Although queer BDSM brings with it other issues and objections, further explored in Chapter 7, one refuge it does offer is from the uncomfortable questions regarding female submission and male dominance.

Later on at the conference, I chatted to the young woman who had asked me the question and she admitted that she found any scenes of heterosexual male dom/fem sub BDSM impossible to watch, and only found women-women BDSM marginally easier to stomach. I sympathized with her—I didn't always find it easy, either. Just because I practiced this stuff didn't mean I always wanted to see it. I had been at events which were all male dom/fem sub by invitation, and I actually found it slightly disturbing to be in a room surrounded by women being tied up and flogged by men, however much I told myself all these women were intelligent, consenting individuals enjoying themselves (and who would furthermore go home to normal jobs, lives, pets and taxes that needed paying). I preferred to be at a party where there were a mix of configurations, as then I didn't feel like I'd wandered into a strange cut-off universe where all the women wanted to submit. However, in this thinking I was guilty of the same assumption that Clarisse Thorn rails against when she states, "Even if most women are submissive masochists in bed … there's nothing wrong with that. I don't care."[35] Just because watching other women's submission unsettled me, it didn't mean that anything in those scenarios needed to change, except that I needed to walk away and maybe get myself a drink. The same goes for the young woman I spoke with, and the same goes for those who voted to ban the male dom/fem sub demo from the Christopher Street West fair in 2011.[36] No, we don't always want to see certain images; as Stacey May Fowles says, "When a woman is subjected to (or enjoying, depending on who is viewing and participating) torture, humiliation and pain, many feminists see the six o' clock news, not a pleasurable fantasy."[37] However, this alone is not sufficient grounds for condemning BDSM, female submissives, or art that portrays these things. Why feminism falls at this hurdle when it can be so fantastic at fighting for acceptance for so many other things in women's lives is understandable, but it's also so easily dismantled that it really does seem like it's time to stop the kink-shaming.

So no, I didn't find the perfect female, feminist submissive who doesn't submit for love or money or because she has a history of self-harm or a history of abuse. However, the very fact I felt the need to look for her shows that I was falling into the trap of placing disproportionate weight on women's behavior. Why should it be the responsibility of any woman, real or fictional, to uphold the honor of her entire gender by behaving in ways that made her sexual practices fit on to a feminist tick-list? If I knew that I, as a fiercely intelligent, independent, educated woman who liked to sometimes play the sub, couldn't tick the boxes of being perfectly emancipated in every other aspect of my life, why was I demanding it of anyone else—why was I demanding it of *women who weren't even real?* In the concerns of the young woman who questioned me at the conference, I found my answer. Because we want reassurance. Because. as Clarisse Thorn writes, we have, sadly "learned to associate discussions of female sexual submission with anti-feminism, and attempts to disempower women in other spheres."[38] And this is not an unjustified belief: there are those who do frame female submission in fairly misogynistic terms. As Julie Clawson found, *that book* inadvertently won support from "conservative Christians defending the idea that a man is meant to conquer a woman."[39] In *Justine*, his famous book about the sexual enslavement of a young woman, the Marquis de Sade—often considered the original advocate for sadomasochism—regularly gives voice to the theory that men have the right to sexually dominate women because of their superior physical strength. In an unpleasant echo of those words, a U.S. state representative once said "If a woman has the right (to an abortion), why shouldn't a man be free to use his superior strength to force himself on a woman? At least the rapist's pursuit of sexual freedom doesn't (in most cases) result in anyone's death."[40] But cherry-picking instances of misogyny are all too easy, both in and outside BDSM. The Marquis de Sade may have believed in abandoning all traditional morals, but he was at least an equal opportunity offender: in her PhD on de Sade, Jennifer Lawrence writes, "While the degendering of rape becomes popularized long after the time of the Marquis de Sade, the effect is already present in his work. Both male and female characters are raped in Sade's universe, and both sexes play the role of rapist."[41] De Sade was also, we should remember, an author of fiction, writing about acts far more extreme than anything he ever personally practiced. As for the idea that a woman should feel compelled to change her sexual preferences merely because they might be misappropriated in order to support the misogyny of religious fundamentalists, or the hateful words of a largely forgotten Republican from 19 years ago; well, there would be very few actions left open to women if they heeded any of the thoughtless bile regularly spewed from the mouths of anti-choice right wing politicians.

The point is, those who genuinely want to dominate, humiliate or deprive women of rights will continue to feel that way regardless of how individual women position themselves in their private sexual interactions. Whether you're a top or bottom, it just doesn't matter—a misogynist will find an excuse to disempower you regardless. So yes, it would be great if we could see some pop culture depictions of happy, autonomous female submissives, but even if we were to find them, we might not recognize them, or they might not make us feel much better. Because they don't have the power to magically overhaul the anti-woman or anti-kink preconceptions held by prejudiced people. Plus, we still tend to make such disproportionate demands of female characters (see the way Skylar in *Breaking Bad* is regularly referred to as a bitch and a nag, while her husband Walt is rarely criticized despite regularly endangering his whole family's lives) that even if we found the perfect feminist submissive, we would probably still pick holes in her the way society teaches us to pick holes in women.

So when Prof Breanne Fahs said in her interview with me "The most empowering thing women can do with their sexuality is to consistently maintain a critical consciousness about their own, and others' sexual practices, behaviors, fantasies and thoughts,"[42] I found myself firmly disagreeing. I don't see why women, or submissive women, or any particular group should carry a stronger expectation than anyone else to police their own desires, behaviors or fantasies, apart from obviously ensuring they're safe, legal and do not violate any other human being's boundaries or consent. I feel that placing this asymmetric pressure on women's shoulders merely echoes the demands of conservative and religious fundamentalist societies which make it women's sole responsibility to uphold the murky concept of "honor" (see Meera Syal quote above!). By a similar token, I've also come to agree that it's not pop culture's responsibility to produce the perfect image of the female submissive whose behavior aligns with all our feminist demands. Not everyone is going to be impressed by mainstream depictions of female submission—as I mention in the chapter on the male dominant, for every kinkster who thinks *Secretary* is a great introduction to BDSM, there are others who think it fails to depict consent and negotiation adequately. However, the notion that our culture is so fraught with anti-feminism that we cannot possibly risk showing BDSM between a dominant male and submissive female without every aspect of their relationship adhering to a pre-defined checklist, lest the watching audience (presumed to be entirely ignorant of BDSM, consent or boundaries) interpret it as the condoning of abuse paints a pretty pessimistic picture of pop culture, its producers, its consumers, and society at large.

When I wrote about *Secretary* for a feminist website, the amount of female commenters who said they loved the film and its portrayal of Lee implied that the flawed nature of both the character and the relationship was what made it convincing.[43] If the characters had paused to explicitly negotiate or write out a contract, commenters pointed out, it would have made the film unrealistic and clunky. Women who identified as queer, submissive, totally non-kinky, who admitted to having previously worried how they could reconcile the film with their feminist beliefs, who admitted to finding the film discomfiting but also eye-opening, wrote in vivid and enthusiastic terms about their experience of watching a female character blossom through BDSM. Should their experiences be discounted because someone who already believes consent is a nonsense made up by feminists to stop men getting laid might jump upon the film as evidence that what women *really want* is a good spanking with no questions asked?

As Stacey May Fowles said in her interview with me "Who are we to say what any kind of sexuality should or needs to look like, or to decide what kinds of consensual visual representations are wrong and what are not?" Now that BDSM can be shown on TV, in movies without censorship, and written about in books without them being burned—

and this was certainly not the case till very recently—it's hardly much more progressive to demand that representations of kink fit into a certain template or else run the risk of being condemned as misogynistic. Fowles went on to say, "It is ultimately the responsibility of every viewer to educate themselves … not the responsibility of a handful of sanctioned subs and Doms to censor and police the allowable construction and enjoyment of visual expressions and depictions."

Dykes, Daddies
and Drag Queens

How BDSM and
LGBT People Are Portrayed

When I interviewed various cultural commentators about BDSM and pop culture, one of my standard questions was whether they thought it was easier to be kinky if one was already part of a group considered sexual outlaws—i.e., the LGBT community. Sara Vibes, a sex educator, performer and producer who was named International Ms. Leather 2011, agreed to an extent, saying "If I'm already queer, then what's the different if I'm also poly or kinky?" However, most respondees said no, they didn't think it was any easier to be gay and kinky, but rather that it added a layer of complication. In a world where a heterosexual couple kissing in public is perceived as sweet, but a gay couple kissing publicly is still somehow "ramming it down people's throats," there remains an unspoken expectation that gay people modify their sexual behavior in order to be unthreatening to straight people. Ergo, adding kink into the mix just acts as further confirmation that gay people's sexual behavior is deviant and disturbing. As Cliff Pervocracy said to me, "Being able to say, 'I'm gay but my sex life is totally boring and unshocking, don't worry!' ... gets a vanilla gay person more social acceptance than a kinky gay person."

Perhaps the only real acceptance gay practitioners of BDSM can hope for, from mainstream heterosexual culture anyway, is the assumption that being gay and being kinky go hand-in-hand, because they've both traditionally been viewed as deviations from "natural" sexuality. Writing about the 1990 Spanner trial which saw 15 gay BDSM practitioners accused of actual bodily harm, Paul Ferris says that there was a perception that gay sexuality was just more edgy, and hence BDSM was more likely to be a part of it: "Gay men in general, ran the argument, needed to experiment more than heterosexual couples, whose behavior fell into obvious patterns, conditioned (at least on women's part) by romantic love."[1] The stereotypical assumption here may annoy both gay men and straight women but it is one that's borne out in popular culture. In the latter part of the 20th century, Western media inextricably linked gay male sexuality with leather, uniforms and the suggestion of shady, down and dirty activities involving "unnatural" sexual practices, pain and violence. Several of my interviewees said to me that their first or only experiences with BDSM in pop culture was the association of male homosexuality with kink, to the point where one could be forgiven for thinking that you could only practice it if you were in possession of a big moustache, a leather biker's cap, and a penis.

Frankie Goes to Hollywood decided to co-opt this assumption in the early '80s by accompanying their song *Relax* (already banned on BBC radio for containing the words "suck" and "come") with a video that played into this stereotype by portraying a homosexual S&M orgy. There was leather, there was PVC, there were togas, there were cages, chains and suggestions of golden showers, and a little simulated gay sex thrown in at the end for good measure. Frankie Goes to Hollywood assumed that it would press every homophobic, kinkphobic button of the conservative right wing, and they were right—the video was promptly banned by BBC TV too. The British public, perhaps operating on the prurient assumption that if something gets banned, then it must be interesting, rewarded the moralists by sending the song to number one for five weeks.

Depeche Mode nearly suffered a similar fate with their 1984 song *Master and Servant* with its heavily kinky lyrics (which intriguingly suggest that like real life, sex can never really be about equality), whip and chain sound effects, and leather-strewn video which showed Dave Gahan holding his fellow band members on a chain, but managed to avoid a BBC ban. However, U.S. censors weren't so kind, with a large number of radio stations reportedly refusing to play the song because of its lyrical content.

Leather and the '80s

Yet, despite the censors' belief that gay sexuality topped off with lashings of kink (pun so very intended) was simply too shocking a combination for the viewing public, it appeared that sometimes it actually made it easier for the public to digest. Writing off male homosexuality as deviant meant it could fit nicely in a category alongside the freaky, dirty, warped doings of BDSM practitioners. Indeed, the association of gay men with BDSM turned up in places as mainstream and inoffensive as the *Police Academy* movies. The first four movies contain a running gag whereby various unsuspecting characters are lured into The Blue Oyster, a stereotypical leathermen/bear gay bar. My personal favorite was always the scene in the fourth movie, *Citizens on Patrol* (1987), where unpleasant megalomaniac Captain Harris and bumbling sidekick Proctor are the victims of the joke. They walk in, fully uniformed, only to find themselves surrounded by burly men in leather trousers and waistcoats, police uniforms, motorcyclist gear and cowboy outfits. The punchline is Harris shrieking "Proctor, I don't see a salad bar!" before being forced to dance with one of the aviator-shaded men. Proctor is grabbed by a mustached bar patron and quips, "Nice collar!" before being dragged away to tango with the man. The stereotype of gay male sexuality as predatory, indiscernible from BDSM and threatening to heterosexual men is in full force in this scene, although obviously part of the humor is derived from the homophobia and insecurity of the straight men involved. Although portrayals of gay male sexuality have generally become much more diverse and less caricatured in pop culture since the '80s, the leather-clad daddy still pops his motorcycle hat above the fence now and again in 21st century popular culture. Think Tobias Funke, the closeted therapist of *Arrested Development*, inadvertently dressing as a "leather daddy" in the 2004 episode "Storming the Castle." One of the many running jokes of *Arrested Development* is that despite being married to a woman, Tobias is clearly gay and in denial about it. With BDSM adornments still perceived as the obvious visual signifiers for male homosexuality, what better way to convey this than to place the character in a collar, chains and leather vest?

Much *has* changed, however, in the decades since the *Police Academy* and *Wayne's World* movies played the concept of the leather bar for laughs—the UK introduced, then repealed, homophobic piece of legislation Section 28 (which forbade the "promotion of homosexuality" by local authorities), legalized civil partnerships and then full gay marriage, and lowered the homosexual age of consent in line with the heterosexual one. Thirty U.S. states now issue marriage licenses to same-sex couples, and the recent relief when Proposition 8 in California was finally struck down for good epitomizes the public shift in support for gay equality. Yet much of the socially acceptable face of gayness does seem to align with Cliff Pervocracy's ideal of the unthreatening gay person. Gay people mimicking heterosexual vanilla lifestyles with marriage, children and an SUV does seem less threatening to some (although is still obviously seen as an aberration by those whose vision of "the family" is stuck on a 1950s ideal which probably never actually existed), but gay sexuality itself remains threatening, inextricably connected with darker desires as it is.

There are, of course, those who will say that gay sexuality and BDSM should be unsettling, and that to try and "mainstream" either is to miss the point. As Patti Smith says of Robert Mapplethorpe, a photographer acclaimed in the '70s and '80s for his groundbreaking portraits of male homosexuality, BDSM and black male nudes, Mapplethorpe was never interested in "making it his mission to help the S&M scene become more socially acceptable. He didn't think it should be accepted, and he never felt that his underground world was for everybody"[2] Indeed, while Mapplethorpe's later, luscious portraits of Debbie Harry and Grace Jones may be relatively uncontroversial, his early work—for example, a photograph of one young man urinating in another's mouth—is still unlikely to adorn many people's coffee tables. Mapplethorpe was even the posthumous victim of a 1989 campaign by Senator Jesse Helms, who wanted to prevent the National Endowment for the Arts from funding exhibitions of apparently "indecent and obscene material"—ironically, this actually ended up bringing Mapplethorpe's work to a much wider audience than it had enjoyed before his death.

Threats to Masculinity

Perhaps what unsettled conservatives the most about Mapplethorpe's photography was not its sadomasochistic subjects, but the way the camera casts its most consuming gaze upon the male form. Despite the fact Mapplethorpe also photographed female nudes, his photos of taut, black male buttocks and crouching, prone male bodies unashamedly portray them as delicious spectacles to be feasted upon. The bodies are clearly lithe, strong and muscular, but they are displayed for the gay male (or perhaps straight female!) viewer's pleasure in a way that the male body is rarely depicted. Mapplethorpe was also unafraid to objectify himself in his quest to plunder the world of BDSM, taking self-portraits of himself with his wrists bound, or in another shot, bending over and looking back at the camera with a whip handle inserted into his backside. If homophobia and kinkphobia from straight men have their roots in a fear of men being objectified (like women are) or behaving submissively (like women are expected to), and there's a fair amount of evidence to suggest that they do, then it's hardly surprising Mapplethorpe's work had such power to shock conservative male senators.

As I explored in Chapter 2, threats to heterosexual masculinity are not taken kindly, and are usually neutralized by mocking and emasculating the men in question. Indeed, just as I was writing this chapter a story popped up on my newsfeed saying that Russian singer Yulia Volkova, famous for being part of girl group t.A.T.u who simulated lesbianism and spoke out in favor of gay rights in 2002, had gone on Russian television to say she would want her son "to be a real man, not a fag."[3] She also expressed the double standard towards male and female homosexuality that I will return to later in this chapter "Two girls together—not the same thing as the two men together.... It seems to me that lesbians look aesthetically much nicer than two men holding their hands or kissing." Her words epitomize the basis of homophobia as well as, subconsciously, disdain for submissive men or men who deviate from set gender roles in any way—"The man for me is the support, the strength.... I believe that a man must be a real man." Stunningly, although perhaps not entirely surprisingly considering the recent growth of anti-gay legislation in 21st century Russia, Volkova went on to say that she thought being gay was better than being a murderer or a drug addict, but only a little.

The fear of male homosexuality, and its accompanying fear that men voluntarily being objectified, submissive, penetrated or otherwise "behaving like a woman" will upend masculine identity is what makes gay male BDSM such a potent combination, and goes some way to explaining why it remains possibly the least visible form of BDSM in popular culture.

Keep It Camp and Asexual

For liberal Westerners, it is easy to fool ourselves that attitudes such as Yulia Volkova's are the preserve of backward cultures, but the former USSR is hardly an insignificant dot in the world's economy or culture, nor was it always this retrogressive—its current laws demonstrate an increasing and relatively recent conservatism. This conservatism is also still very apt to quickly rear its head in the Western media if famous homosexual men refuse to keep their behavior acceptably vanilla. In 2009, singer Adam Lambert saw his appearance on *Good Morning, America* cancelled the morning after he gave a BDSM–themed performance of his song "For Your Entertainment" at the American Music Awards. Lambert's performance was a mishmash of BDSM and gay imagery; male and female dancers writhing around in leather harnesses and peephole bras, Lambert leading two male dancers around on leashes, Lambert pressing both male and female dancers' faces to his crotch, and kissing his male keyboardist.

Jos Truitt, writing for *Feministing*, nailed the media hypocrisy perfectly: "Bondage-themed performances seem old hat at awards shows (except, hmm, they are usually headlined by female performers). Seriously, what's the big deal? Oh right. Adam Lambert's male. And gay."[4] The writer suggested that as well as discomfiting an audience ill-at-ease with both overt male gay sexuality and BDSM, Lambert also disrupted assumptions about power roles: "The glam-inspired performance had a male-presenting but femmed-up Lambert dominating strong, muscular men. And we could never accept femme as empowering, especially for a dude person!" Narrow constructions of power dynamics in heterosexuality tend to bleed over into perceptions of both BDSM and gay sexuality—femininity is associated with submission and passivity, masculinity with strength and domination. Butch gay men must therefore always be the penetrating partner in sex, and the dominating partner in BDSM. Language that divides gay men into the "bitch" and the "butch" not only reinforces this bifurcation of roles, but also strongly implies that to be in the feminine position must necessarily be degrading. Heterosexual culture is already made uncomfortable enough by the prospect of two men fucking—the idea of one man volunteering to be collared, put on a leash or roughly made to perform oral sex is just one sacrifice of straight power too many.

Unfortunately, anti–BDSM feminists didn't find Lambert's performance positive in terms of upending gender norms. One commenter on
the Feministing piece said, "Adam Lambert's choreography came off as
abusive and violent," and another went with the even more extreme,
"The fact that it involved a queerman doesn't lessen its contribution to
Rape Culture." Another accused Lambert of sending out the message
"slaves are hot"—even if this were his message, (and we subscribed to
the belief that slaves in BDSM are disempowered or coerced), the
assumption that it's necessarily misogynistic depends on presuming that
the slave in question is always female, which in Lambert's performance
was most definitely not true. I felt that the way Lambert got jumped on
by both left and right wings of the media was more evidence that gay
men can't win when it comes to representing their sexuality in mainstream media. I, personally, applauded Lambert for refusing to be
reduced to a pink, fluffy, camp stereotype—why should gay men's sole
purpose in the media be to stand as bitchy best friends or interior design
and fashion experts? How come (as several of those commenting in support of Lambert pointed out) Janet Jackson can simulate her male dancer
performing oral sex on her and be met little or no comment, while a
gay man is only expected to be out and proud as far as the public nervousness surrounding gay sex and BDSM will allow?

Gays on the Bottom

> "In violent contact sports, men touch each other in furious
> and often wounding intimacy, but the homoerotic implica-
> tions are scrupulously disavowed."—Anne McClintock[5]

When it comes to pop culture depictions of BDSM, there appears
to be a hierarchy of acceptable depictions (echoing Gayle Rubin's hierarchy of acceptable sexual behavior, described further in the chapter
"Who's Vanilla, Who's Edgy"). Girl-on-girl BDSM, from its appearances
in early 20th century erotica, through its 1950s popularity thanks to Bettie Page, and up to Rihanna and Britney Spears merrily wrangling with
other women in their music videos, seems to be one of the most acceptable configurations, possibly because of its lack of challenge to male sexual insecurities (no other penises to compete with, ergo no unflattering

comparisons!). There's also the apparent male erotic attraction to the idea of two women together, although I have to say this is one I've always met with a little skepticism—why would men be turned on by a scenario that so clearly excludes them, unless of course they subscribe to the lesbophobic believe that lesbian sex is not real and that any girl/girl scenario is just waiting for a man to come along and provide the *real* sex? More on this later...

When it comes to this hierarchy of acceptable BDSM, heterosexual kink is generally acceptable to portray, but only within certain parameters—fem dom and male sub scenarios are fine for laughs, male dom and fem sub scenarios seem to make producers more queasy, and seem less likely to be explicitly portrayed, although showing scenes of rough, coercive sex between men and women where consent is questionable (e.g., the much-written about sex scene between Adam and Natalya in the second season of *Girls*) sadly doesn't seem to trouble makers of popular media so much. One thing's for sure though, and that's that gay male BDSM sits at the bottom of the hierarchy, considered the most deviant, disgusting and least media-friendly of all. Even Lady Gaga, mindful of her huge gay following and not afraid to push boundaries in her outfits and videos, limited the scantily clad men in her 2010 music video *Alejandro* to either writhing on their own or with her—despite the deeply kinky and homoerotic image of muscular men stripped to underpants and black PVC stilettos playing with rope, there was no guy-on-guy bondage, no men grappling roughly with each other. Even though director Steven Klein's style of video and photography is described by Susan Kismeric of the Museum of Modern Art as "often sexual in content, or erotic—homosexual or sadomasochistic,"[6] and Klein is renowned for photographing attractive celebrity men such as Justin Timberlake and Brad Pitt with a distinctly sexual and objectifying gaze, he felt, for some reason, unable to take the gay BDSM imagery in *Alejandro* from the merely suggestive to the actual.

This hierarchy of acceptable gender configurations in kink is neatly shown in, of all places, an episode of off-the-wall Canadian "mockumentary" *The Trailer Park Boys*, which originally aired on Showcase in the early 2000s. In the episode "Mr. Lahey's Got My Porno Tape!" less-than-smart protagonist Ricky sees his latest money-making scheme (appearing in adult films) go awry when his nemesis, trailer park supervisor Mr. Lahey, busts the shoot and steals the tape of Ricky's low-budget adventure for blackmail purposes. Ricky's slightly more streetwise buddy Julian goes to Mr. Lahey's trailer to try and get the tape back, and breaks in to find Mr. Lahey dressed as a woman in a black negligee, skirt, heels and wig, with his deputy Randy (who certainly fits the body profile of "bear," as the running joke of him never wearing shirts evidences) wearing a leather hood and bending over a spanking bench with his head in Lahey's crotch. Despite the men protesting first that they're "practicing for a play" and latterly that "this is the first time we've done anything like this," the floggers and slappers hanging on the wall imply differently. Julian keeps his cool and uses the occasion to get Ricky's tape back (and also takes their handcuffs, presumably for evidence!), and even says, "I'm not judging anybody here, all right?" which the viewer suspects is probably true, given the amount of amoral behavior that occurs on a daily basis in the trailer park. In this case, a spot of man-on-man BDSM complete with cross-dressing isn't really of concern to Julian, except for the blackmail purposes it offers. He's not interested in judging, but he knows others will be only too keen. A bit of heterosexual porn featuring Ricky is nowhere near then level of incendiary material that a tape of Lahey and Randy getting kinky will provide, and Julian knows it, marveling "It's gonna be tough keeping that a secret." Gay BDSM—still the ultimate trump card in the blackmail game.

A Man in a Dress Is a Problem

As *The Trailer Park Boys* episode also shows, popular culture has a strained relationship with the concept of men cross-dressing, so it makes sense that it would be doubly pathologized by placing it in a kinky context. As discussed further in the chapter on the male submissive, feminization is still far too readily viewed as being equal to degradation, the conclusion being that only a man who relishes humiliation could possibly enjoy being dressed as a woman.

A glittery riposte to that preconception came in the form of the 2005 movie *Kinky Boots,* which was based on the true story of a Northampton shoe factory turned its failing fortunes around by manufacturing footwear for drag queens and transvestites. The working class, conservative workforce of Price's shoe factory are forced to confront their prejudices as Lola, a tall, burly black drag queen, sashays into their lives and gives them lessons on how to create truly erotic footwear.

Raising questions around consumerism, fetishism (Oh, the shoes! All the shoes!), sexual fluidity and gender roles, *Kinky Boots* situates the fun and sparkle of cross-dressing in the reality of drab, homophobic, transphobic small-town Britain. Lola may strut around the factory brandishing a riding crop, but it's not the swish of her switch which threatens the heterosexual male workers in the family, so much as the presence of a big black man who loves dressing up as a woman. Lola describes how liberating she finds cross-dressing—"Put on a frock and I can sing 'Stand By Your Man' in front of 500 strangers" and how restrictive traditional masculine roles make her feel—"Put on a pair of jeans and I can't even sodding well say hello!" Her predilection for drag has cost her a great deal of heart-ache, with her father disowning her before he died. Lola's own sexuality is ambiguous throughout the film; she implies to factory worker Lauren that she may have a crush on Charlie, the factory owner—"He's had quite an impact on us girls, hasn't he?"—but also implies that her drag queen persona helps her attract women. "Ask any woman what she likes in a man: compassion, tenderness, sensitivity. Traditionally the female virtues. Perhaps what women secretly desire is a man, who is, fundamentally, a woman."

Lola's biggest contribution to the shoe factory is to help its owner identify just what it takes to sell a kinky boot—sex. When Charlie shows her the first prototype boot, a clunky, burgundy boot that she regards in horror, Lola gives him a quick lesson in fetishwear. "RED! Charlie boy. Rule One. RED is the colour of sex, Charlie boy! Burgundy is the colour of hot water bottles! Red is the color of SEX, and fear, and danger...." When Charlie responds, "But they're comfy!" Lola identifies exactly what BDSM practitioners have been telling their baffled vanilla counterparts for centuries—"COMFY?! Sex shouldn't be COMFY!" She also makes some very astute commentary on how fetish objects must act as a representation, a stand-in for the erotic, in order to be marketable: "I don't know what you're used to making around here, Charlie boy, but now you're making SEX! Two and half feet of irresistible, tubular sex." In addition, Lola acts as a spokesperson for shoe fetishists and Freudians alike when she tells Charlie with tantalizing emphasis: "Look to the heel, young man. The sex is in the heel."

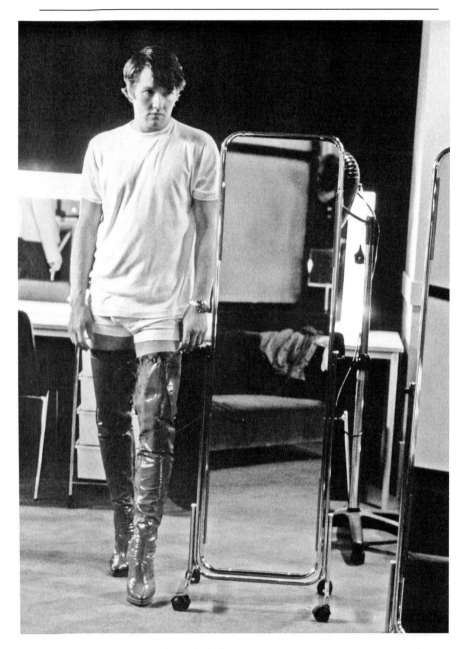

Charlie Price (Joel Edgerton) wrangles with gender, sexuality and PVC in the British comedy *Kinky Boots* (Photofest).

Lola's gender-bending unsettles the more unreconstructed men among the workforce, especially heavy-set Don, who challenges her to an arm-wrestling contest. Don wins, but clearly only because Lola lets him. When he asks her why she didn't keep fighting, Lola says, "I wouldn't want you to walk into the factory and feel that people didn't respect you, Don. I wouldn't want anyone else to know what that feels like." Her parting shot as she walks away is "Change your mind about someone." The storyline of a marginalized person educating a bigot is not a new one—think Goldie Hawn in *Wildcats*, Tom Hanks in *Philadelphia*—but the spectacle of chunky Nick Frost in a sleeveless vest and tattoos, arm-wrestling with a black man wearing a pink blouse, false nails and full make-up is a novel spin on the tale. Nothing has the power to unseat masculinity more than a man who publicly declares his preference for the feminine.

Women are usually portrayed as more sensitive to, and less prejudiced towards, homosexual men, transgender women and cross-dressers; think the fag hag/gal pal, think Kelly in *The Office* telling Oscar that him coming out as gay is "awesome," think Cher in *Clueless* not minding that Christian rejects her because he's gay, as she now has a male friend with whom she can clothes shop. The women of the factory in *Kinky Boots* are more welcoming to Lola, especially Lauren, Charlie's main supporter in his quest to save the factory's fortunes. During a celebration on the shop floor, the women take turns to dance with Lola (to James Brown's *This Is a Man's World*—the makers didn't miss any opportunity for obvious symbolism), who is bending gender more than usual by appearing with short hair, a man's shirt, jockey shorts and then a thigh hair pair of red PVC kinky boots. Lola asks Lauren to dance, but she refuses. Lola draws a red riding crop out of a handy holster (designed as part of the boots ... of course) and slices it through the air at Lauren; Lauren grabs the end and Lola pulls both crop and woman towards her, meeting Lauren in a slow embrace. Swaying slowly, they both look up at where Charlie is watching from his office. It's a scene that oozes sexuality and suggestion, but the question of Lola's sexual preference is never answered in the movie. In one particularly cruel speech, Charlie asks Lola if cross dressing is merely a way of "dodging the question of what sex you get off on...?" Perhaps making the point that cross-dressing isn't necessarily a journey, but an end in itself, the filmmakers portray

Lola as a bisexual, possibly pansexual figure, who refuses to place herself in a neat box just to appease threatened heterosexual men. This is nicely emphasized by one of the closing shots, where Lola walks away arm in arm with both Lauren and Charlie.

As a commentary on BDSM, *Kinky Boots* deals in fairly mild symbolism, but as a comment on the power of gender-bending to unsettle traditional ideas about gender roles, it does go outside stereotypical portrayals as drag queens as either confident sassy mamas or oppressed queer-bashed victims, and sneaks a lot of PVC, thigh-high boots and riding crops in at the same time.

Subtle Suggestions Go Down More Easily

There are, of course, pop culture producers who know how to introduce a reference to gay male sexuality while still managing to fly relatively under the radar. The ambiguity of pop music lyrics make it an ideal medium in which to explore sexual tastes seen as edgy without being censored or condemned. The Smiths, always a group whose lyrics pushed homoeroticism to its very limit despite the fact their lyricist Stephen Morrissey has always refused to confirm his (much suspected homo)sexuality, told a tantalizing tale of wanting to be slapped, shoved and well, "Reel Around the Fountain" with a mysterious partner on their eponymous 1984 debut album. Morrissey writes of wanting to be pinned and mounted like a butterfly and take whatever the object of his desire wants to dish out in a voice that is deliciously and longingly submissive. Presumably to keep the fires of suggestiveness burning, the band have never confirmed what the song is actually about, although they have strenuously denied that its ambiguous references to a child being made old are about child abuse.

Suede, another UK indie band that courted attention via ambiguous sexual imagery (the cover of their debut album in 1994 showed two men kissing), drew interest for the lyrics of their song "Animal Nitrate." The song's name appears to be a pun on amyl nitrate (or poppers, their street name), renowned for use by gay men to make anal sex easier, and also a drug loved by teenagers for its quick and cheap thrills. The lyrics refer to being jumped by an older man, broken bones, chemicals and animals, and the video sees androgynous singer Brett Anderson shaking his hips in a leather shirt unzipped nearly to his navel, alternately kissing then slapping a figure in a pig mask. The kinky imagery is undeniable, even if one doesn't quite catch the references to forceful gay frolics in the lyrics. Anderson later admitted "You know it's about violence and abuse and sex and drugs. It's actually quite a hardcore song."[7] Interestingly, the flooring used in the shot is the same carpet pattern used in the 1980 film *The Shining*, and the Suede video's image of a suited man in a pig mask bending over provocatively seems to echo the *Shining* scene where Wendy sees a man in a dog outfit fellating a man in a tuxedo. One could speculate whether directors Stanley Kubrick or Pedro Romhanyi were deliberately making reference to the fetish "furries" (where people gain sexual satisfaction from dressing up as animals) as well as gay sex...

The UK indie scene, where a certain amount of feyness and effeminacy from men was acceptable (Brett Anderson and Jarvis Cocker were exemplary of the stick-limbed fragility of male indie singers of the mid–'90s), was perhaps an easier place to try and introduce a song about rough gay sex than the mainstream pop charts, although "Animal Nitrate" did make it to number 7 in the UK charts. Yet the other side of the indie scene—the football-shirt-wearing, lager-swilling likes of Oasis, also at their peak in the mid–'90s, was distinctly intolerant of any gender bending. The UK has always had a conflicted relationship with gay male sexuality, with extremely camp celebrities and drag queens (John Inman, Danny La Rue, Dick Emery to name but a few) being beloved in UK popular culture in the '60s and '70s, while overt homosexuality was still publicly condemned, not to mention illegal until 1967. At the time of writing, one of the most popular comedies on TV is *Mrs. Brown's Boys*, where the lead character Mrs. Brown, an elderly lady, is played by a man in drag. Storylines involving gay characters in soap operas are standard in the UK, but just as I wrote about the need to explain female submissives via the need for love, gay sexuality is also often obscured by the mitigating factors of love and romance. Gay sexuality is fine as long as it mirrors the conservative aspects of heterosexuality—marriage, monogamy and the icky bits taking place behind closed doors. When it comes to being able to stomach the idea of BDSM between men, the less sanitized aspects of gay male sexuality still retain great potential to provoke.

Girl-on-Girl BDSM—Just a Bit of Fun

"Lesbian sex is often represented as a form of 'foreplay,' warming women up for men: lesbians are 'liberated' girls who enjoy all kinds of kinky sex, but whose lesbianism rarely withstands the arrival of the male on the scene."—Celia and Jenny Kitzinger[8]

As I've already implied, BDSM between women in pop culture carries many different issues and signifiers when compared to the more unequivocally perceived imagery of gay male BDSM. Yes, it may be seen as less offensive, but the pay-off isn't always so great for feminists or lesbians alike. A cynic might label Britney Spears the ultimate example of a famous woman happy to go "gay for pay," in light of her suggestive writhings with Madonna in the "Me Against the Music" video and her whipping and leading female dancers on leashes in the video for "Work, Bitch." Along with trying to find a pop culture depiction of a female submissive who practiced BDSM for her own pleasure, rather than for love, money or due to abuse, the other holy grail in my research was a mainstream depiction of lesbian BDSM that didn't distinctly cater to the male gaze. Apart from a pleasantly unsensationalized passage in Stieg Larsson's *The Girl Who Played with Fire*, as mentioned in Chapter 1, I really struggled to find popular culture depictions of BDSM between women that weren't between slim, white, young, cisgendered feminine women and which usually looked more like a Calvin Klein photo shoot than anything one might find at the average play party.

My research introduced me to a lot of great non-mainstream examples of lesbian BDSM portrayals, such as The Sex Positive Photo Project, queer feminist sex magazine *Salacious*, Laura Antoniou's *Marketplace* series and Kate Allen's *Alison Kaine* series (four books about leatherdykes in Denver), the existence of which was all heartening to learn. However, in popular culture, diverse depictions of lesbian BDSM were thin on the ground. A commenter on *Bitch* online, "Arsenic Alyss," wrote, "As a butchy dominant leather woman I am used to being vilified in the media." I thought it was probably closer to the mark to say that the butch lesbian kinkster was simply *erased* from mainstream media. As I explore in the chapter on the female dominant, deviation from Western media expectations of female beauty are not generally accepted, even in women who are supposed to be in powerful positions. The female domme must remain attractive to the male gaze at all times by being slim, white, long-haired, identifiably feminine and in figure-hugging, revealing clothes. Fat, short-haired, non-white, transgender or butch dominatrices are

Butch women in BDSM are more likely to be seen in independent movies such as *Mommy Is Coming* (courtesy Shilo McCabe).

145

pretty much impossible to find in mainstream pop culture, even though plenty of them exist in real life.

Rihanna's music video "S&M" does at least make a token effort at diversity, with a large, short-haired black woman wielding a riding crop next to the singer in one of the group scenes. In another scene, Rihanna places black tape over the mouth of another large black woman, who looks frightened, then gently kisses her through the tape and smiles rogueishly. Apart from this, though, the last butch woman I remember seeing in a BDSM scenario in a music video was probably Madonna's *Erotica,* back in the mid–'90s. In the 21st century, gender seems more strictly policed than ever in terms of demands for unthreateningly feminine appearance, especially in the music business, and the hierarchy of acceptable kinks divides even further down when we get to how kink between women is portrayed. Kink between two women who are both considered conventionally attractive is acceptable in mainstream pop culture in a way that kink between butch, androgynous, boyish, or genderqueer women is not.

This refers me back to the suspicion I voiced earlier in this chapter—that the hijacking of female homosexuality as mild titillation for the presumed male viewer is actually evidence of male paranoia about female sexuality. The fear that lesbianism could potentially be more fulfilling to women than heterosexuality is one that poses a great threat to the male ego, at both an individual and societal level. Women not needing or wanting penises, or the men attached to them, is a frightening prospect for those brought up to believe in women's complete dependence on men for personal and sexual fulfillment. This fear is demonstrated in pop culture through films such as *Chasing Amy* (1997), where the sexist and homophobic character Banky claims that lesbianism is just "bullshit posturing" and that "everyone needs dick," or the moment in *Mad Men* where a clearly jealous and threatened Stan says to Peggy's lesbian friend Joyce, "You can never do for a girl what a guy can" (to which Joyce responds to by agreeing and then teasingly licking Peggy's face). So what better way to neutralize the threat that woman-woman sexual couplings pose to men's monopoly on all power and pleasure, than to imply it's *actually all about men?*

I once suggested this theory to a man my age, who didn't disagree with me, but suggested that perhaps the voyeuristic appeal of lesbian sex for men also lay in the lack of any other man in the picture who could be a competitor. There are no other men's bodies to make one feel inadequate, no penises that might be bigger or more satisfying to women than one's own, no worries about having to exhibit similar levels of stamina or sexual competency to a male porn star. A man can also place himself as the imaginary third party in the scenario, although again I've always thought this relegates lesbianism to no more than foreplay, a way of getting two women wet before a man can come and give them a *real* fucking. Which to me, is not a sign of progress or of people becoming more accepting of gay women—rather it just means that lesbianism is only acceptable insofar as it remains appealing to straight men, and its appeal is assumed to lie in its lack of real threat to male sexual supremacy. So far, pretty anti-feminist and homophobic.

The patronizing attitude that lesbian sex isn't "real" compared to heterosexual interactions can bleed over into the kink world. In his research among lesbian BDSM practitioners, Robin Bauer reported one lesbian top saying that her dominance wasn't taken seriously by certain men, precisely because she only played with women. The woman reported to Bauer that more than one man had said to her if she played with men "then you'd submit nicely." This example of sexist role essentialism merely develops upon the belief that sex between women isn't "real" sex until a man comes along: a woman's dominance over another woman is only legitimate until a man comes into the picture, and then apparently the man's naturally superior dominance would cause any female top to immediately become a bottom. The implication that lesbian BDSM is just a pale imitation of true dom/sub power roles (which are only seen as truly authentic when enacted by heterosexual couples, and only then in the case of male dominance and female submission) is both homophobic and sexist, as it rests on a failure to take relationships between women seriously, and a belief that women can never exert as much authority as a man.

When BDSM and feminist blogger Charlie Hale said to me that the BDSM scene can end up replicating patriarchal tropes in terms of its structure and dynamics, they added that a particular example of this is the way female bisexuality is framed. Some of the examples of woman-on-woman kink I saw in the scene definitely depicted lesbianism as nothing other than a sideshow for straight men. For every female couple

I saw playing together explicitly for their own pleasure and no one else's, I saw far too many other instances of submissive women playing with each other while their male doms looked on and even orchestrated the scenes (once even with the men literally, like puppetmasters, guiding the women's arms). Watching two (young, slim, white, cisgender, feminine) naked women wrestling in the center of a ring of men did, frankly, rub me up the wrong way (pun *not* intended). Freely chosen bi-curious exploration was one thing, but this performative faux-lesbianism struck me as anything but. One could argue that the women were exploring a power of their own—the power to transfix men with a bit of flirtatious boob-rubbing—but I thought play was meant to be about the pleasure of the players, not the heavy-breathing voyeurs.

Where this translates into mainstream pop culture is the totally narrow parameters within which women are allowed to participate in lesbian (or more likely faux-lesbian) behavior. They are most certainly not permitted to present as butch, because this brings too much gender disruption into the equation. A masculine-presenting woman can easily be viewed as the substitute for the threatening male, which the viewer of the lesbian spectacle naturally wants removed from the scene. A quick look at the music videos for 30 Seconds to Mars' "Hurricane" or Britney Spears' "Work Bitch" will confirm that only the femme-est of slim, white, long-haired young women are acceptable for any depictions of girl-on-girl kink.

The woman whose appearance is not constructed in a way that implies male approval is her paramount concern is still apparently far too dangerous a figure to be included in pop culture depictions of lesbian sex per se, let alone lesbian BDSM. Although the Netflix series *Orange Is the New Black* has been groundbreaking in its diverse portrayals of lesbians and their relationships, it's still very telling which characters the producers select for sex scenes. Older, butch or fat women are absent from the girl-on-girl writhings, as the focus remains on young, slim, white, feminine women getting busy with each other in showers or in the chapel. To see such a male-gaze-centric vision of lesbian sexuality is disappointing, coming as it does from a show that was otherwise so unapologetic in its focus on women who look, speak and behave differently from how the mainstream media dictates. Whether due to outside pressure to sex the show up, ignorance or indifference to the issues at hand, the makers of OITNB fell at the last hurdle.

Hard-Won Gains

It's easy to forget (and I'm sure many were unaware in the first place) how it was precisely the women who didn't fit in with heteronormative ideals of how women should look and behave who fought both for acceptance of lesbians, and also acceptance of lesbians who practiced BDSM. Navigating layers of sexism, appearance fascism, and opposition from factions one would expect to be supportive (Betty Friedan famously labeled lesbianism "the lavender menace" and initially tried to distance the women's movement from it), lesbians have historically faced a unique set of barriers in gaining visibility and fighting discrimination. As Laura Cottingham points out, being allied with the male gay rights struggle could only take gay women so far—"Like women in the Civil Rights, Chicano Rights and New Left movements, lesbians involved with Gay Rights realized that unless they articulated themselves clearly and distinctly as women, any political issues they faced that diverged from the interests of the men they were working with would be left unaddressed or even sabotaged."[9] Hence lesbians beginning to form their own groups, separate from gay men, in the early '70s.

The fight for gay and lesbian acceptance subdivided further when BDSM lesbians started demanding access to the leather culture that had, till that point, been considered the exclusive territory of gay men. As Gayle Rubin, an outspoken feminist BDSM lesbian, notes in her essay "The Leather Menace: Comments on Politics and S/M,"[10] "When I came out as a lesbian sadomasochist there was no place to go," hence she was forced to start her own group, the lesbian S/M (as BDSM was known in the '70s and '80s) organization Samois. Yet, aside from trying to carve out a space for lesbians in a scene previously reserved for gay men, the bigger fight was for acceptance from other lesbians, especially those who considered BDSM between women "the internalization of heterosexual dominant-submissive role playing [and] an internalization of the homophobic heterosexual view of lesbians."[11] Rubin writes that she ended up having to come out twice—first as a lesbian, and second as a sadomasochist, and furthermore, that "the second coming out was considerably more different than the first." Having fought for acceptance from the heterosexual community, fought to be perceived separately from the gay male community and fought for the acknowledgement that gay

women did not enjoy many of the automatic privileges their male counterparts held, BDSM lesbians now had to fight the belief among many
of their own, that they were sick, brainwashed dupes of the patriarchy.
Rubin writes, "It is especially depressing if a once-progressive movement
in which you have spent your entire adult life is leading the assault. The
experience of being a feminist sadomasochist in 1980 is similar to that
of being a communist homosexual in 1950."[12]

The lesbian and feminist objections to S/M were often intertwined
with a belief that lesbianism was as much political as it was sexual, and
that it therefore had to be practiced in a manner divorced from any
power dynamic that could possibly replicate oppressive heterosexual
interactions. The assumptions that there is such a thing as sex free of a
power dynamic, or that all heterosexuality is necessarily oppressive, or
that BDSM automatically mimics oppression and abuse, are all ones that
have been picked apart by feminists and BDSM practitioners alike over
the decades. Unfortunately, this was not before BDSM lesbians had experienced their fair share of scapegoating and gaslighting.

So when I read a modern online commenter innocently asking,
"How can it be 'conforming to the patriarchy' when a woman submits
to another woman?"[13] I sense that the person can't have done much reading into feminism's recent past, otherwise they'd be well aware that lesbianism has never been seen as a mitigating factor in defenses of kink
by those determined to condemn it. Also, their belief that lesbian BDSM
neatly sidesteps the patriarchy's malign influence in a way that straight
BDSM doesn't also rests on the pretty objectionable belief that lesbianism
is a more enlightened way of having sex, and that heterosexual sex must
necessarily be oppressive, a presumption already dealt with in the previous chapter. Writing in Samois' *Coming to Power*, an essayist by the
name of "Juicy Lucy" demonstrates firsthand that being an S/M lesbian
did not mean automatic admittance to the feminist club, quite the opposite: "I've had friends scream insults at me, tell me I'm to be pitied, like
a man, oppressive to womyn, disgusting, not welcome in their home,
untrustworthy.... I wish lesbians were braver and that we didn't scape-
goat each other so easily."[14] Pat Califia, writing in the same book, recalls
the first time an S/M organization marched in a gay pride parade in the
late '70s. Her group was harassed by monitors who believed that "we
violated a parade regulation excluding images that were sexist or

depicted violence against women,"[15] and a monitor tried to remove a lesbian top and bottom from the parade because the former was leading the latter on the chain.

"Take that chain off that woman!" one of the monitors kept screaming. "Unchain her!"

"I can't," replied the unruffled mistress. "I welded it on myself this morning."[16]

From this, we arrive in the modern world where a woman leading another woman on a chain is just another frame in yet another deeply sexualized music video which may well play in the background at any time of day in a U.S. or European family home. I'm not sure this is the kind of acceptance S/M lesbians fought for or even wanted, but the point is, BDSM between women is not the easy escape from feminist objection that some people seem to believe it is. Far from being uncontroversial, lesbian BDSM was still being labeled as "the measure of our complicity in our own and other people's oppression"[17] by feminists well into the '90s, and continues to be defined thus by a small minority of self-proclaimed radical feminists today (whose writings are now more likely to be found online rather than in feminist anthologies).

History Lessons

One thing I did notice when looking at photographs of vintage kink erotica, and watching films such as *The Notorious Bettie Page* was how, despite there being little understanding or construction of lesbian sexuality in mid–20th century U.S., the default pairing in BDSM photography did tend to be two women. Bettie herself was depicted in both dominant and submissive poses in her photo shoots, alternating between being bound, gagged and chained, and being the bossy figure brandishing the riding crop—but all her play partners were female. At face value, this was, of course, a simple and handy excuse for pornographers to get two women in their underwear into the shot, rather than just photographing a solo model. In this old-style bondage porn, there's plenty of over-the-knee spanking, hair-pulling, wrestling and general "catfight" clichés, but unlike today's BDSM porn, no men. Was male sexuality still seen as simply too shocking to introduce into already outrageous scenes, so the producers had to let something go—and in this case they opted for the safety of woman-on-woman bondage, because female sexuality is perceived as nicer, gentler, and therefore bondage and spanking between women could be perceived as just a bit of fun? In the film about Bettie's life, the male director of a photo shoot certainly enjoys placing himself in the position of the submissive, saying, "I'd like this young lady to look very strict," after one of Bettie's co-stars has warned her, "He's not normal, but he is nice…. You just have to scare him." So why were there no pictures depicting male submissives, nothing to give this man a figure with which to identify?

I've established at length in Chapter 2 just how uncomfortable the idea of a man being the bottom in a BDSM encounter makes many heterosexual men. So does the appeal of girl-on-girl BDSM yet again lie in the lack of a man to compete with in the scene? Girl-girl dom/sub play means that a man doesn't have to worry about seeing one of his own gender humiliated (and god forbid, aroused by it), therefore there will be no uncomfortable questions asked of his own sexuality. It also ticks politically correct boxes insofar as there's no male violence to worry about either—you can get off on seeing a woman dominated without any concern that this is a form of rape or abuse, or an uncomfortable echo thereof, because after all, it's just women playing! Since, as I've mentioned previously in this chapter, many people

Gretchen Mol as Bettie Page in *The Notorious Bettie Page,* in which girl-on-girl kink is a standard image (Movie Stills Database).

still see lesbian BDSM as merely a gentle imitation of *real* dominance and submission, then it follows that women can't be capable of doing that much damage to each other—like nudge-nudge jokes about mud wrestling, no one really wants to see women *hurting* each other, just grappling erotically, right? That's why Britney Spears still has to wear a swimming costume slashed so high no bikini wax will really be up to the job and be tottering on heels while she brandishes a singletail whip at her female dancer's backside in the video for "Work, Bitch." There's only so much damage you can inflict when your own clothing and bodily positioning is restricted by your obligation to appeal to a heterosexual male audience.

Of course, there are lesbians who do choose to dress and act in ways that happen to align with the heterosexual male gaze, both in and outside the BDSM scene, and the fact that the mainstream media only focuses on these women does not automatically render them colluders with the patriarchy. Femme-phobia is not a solution to the erasure of butch women, as it merely moves criticism from one group of lesbians to another. Robin Bauer[18] makes the point that deliberately identifying away from the feminine brings with it a disdain for typically female roles—the fact that so many kinky lesbians use the term "Daddy," whereas one rarely, if ever, hears of lesbians calling themselves "Mommy," implies a possibly unconscious but nevertheless distinct belief that male-identified terms convey dominance much more effectively than female ones. Being lesbian, or being kinky, does not automatically mean that one escapes ingrained beliefs about the superiority of certain gender or sexual roles. This is just one of many reasons why, as I mentioned in Chapter 6, I do not subscribe to the belief that any particular kind of BDSM pairing is "better" than any other. No BDSM practitioner, however divorced from the mainstream they consider themselves to be, can claim that their play takes place in a vacuum. Any potential pairing will bring with it the possibility of simulating sexist, homophobic, or racist situations (as well as classism, ageism, even specie-ism, if we're talking animal play), even if the practitioners themselves consider themselves marginalized. Unfortunately, the meeting of lesbian BDSM and pop culture is precisely where the liberation of female sexuality seems particularly likely to be hijacked in order to support limiting narratives on how women should look and behave.

* * *

Lesbian BDSM in 21st century popular culture occupies a strange space where it oscillates between invisibility and brief, cartoonish depictions with little depth or nuance. It's notably absent from the recent strain of identikit BDSM–flavored erotica including *that book* and its copycats, which are generally determinedly heterosexual in their trajectory. If other women are included in play, it's usually at the behest of the dominant man, and is only a brief foray into sexual adventure for the wide-eyed heroine before she returns to a monogamous relationship with said man. *The Story of O* includes plenty of lesbian BDSM, but it does not stray from this narrative: O agrees to sexual encounters with women precisely to satisfy the voyeuristic urges of her owner, Sir Stephen, and also does so to help lure other women into sexual slavery. This again links into the perception of women as sexually and physically unthreatening to other women; by gaining these women's trust, O can lull them into a false sense of security before they end up being sadistically treated by the men at the deviant chateau of Roissy. There are tender moments in the lesbian BDSM scenes in the book, but they still ultimately seem to serve as a mere stepping stones before the women's "real" submission to men takes place.

In less mainstream kinky erotica, such as Anne Rice's *The Awakening of Sleeping Beauty*, there is plenty of bisexuality (possibly even more between men), but most of the woman-woman configurations consist of sadistic older women punishing the young, attractive beauty for her crime of being, well, just that—feeding into the stereotype of the female domme as old, ugly and jealous of younger women. A recent release by independent, queer and feminist friendly press Cleis, *Safe Word* by Molly Weatherfield, is decidedly more edgy than mainstream BDSM erotica, touching subjects that most BDSM–lite books don't dare (anal sex, pony play, 24/7 captivity), but again the lesbian encounters are asides to the defining relationship with one distinctly domly man, and often tinged with jealousy and resentment.

I remember when I was first looking for BDSM dungeons in Los Angeles, I came across a website showing the mistress of the dungeon— a woman who looked to be in her 40s or 50s, sitting holding reins attached to a bit gag which a naked, twentysomething young woman was wearing (as well as pony hooves), with the older women's spike heel dug into her backside. It occurred to me that the inverse configuration was rarely shown, contributing to the idea that older women dominate younger women out of resentment of their beauty and privilege. Perhaps this is an overly paranoid reading of the stereotype—after all, many male dominants are older than their female partners, and this can be because due to many reasons (wealth, education, seniority at work and social power all tend to increase with age), but we would imagine that youth is considered part of the submissive's attraction, not a reason to want to punish her. Women being pitted against each other in popular culture mean that female sadism can end up being portrayed as a bitter, jealous older woman desperately clawing back some of the power that is automatically conferred upon young, attractive women; and this is not a particularly helpful or accurate portrayal of real BDSM between women.

*   *   *

The obstacles faced, then, of being gay and kinky, are indeed a different set to those faced by the heterosexual community, and must be faced without the protection of straight privilege afforded to men and women who fit heteronormative standards. Gay BDSM has the power to disrupt conservative beliefs about gender roles, power, bodies and the erotic, and in a society still riven with homophobia, its imagery in pop culture remains unsettling. While the hijacking of lesbianism as a tool with which to arouse straight men is bothersome both in and outside of the BDSM community, it does not necessarily make girl-on-girl BDSM less powerful in its potential to threaten heteronormativity. Indeed, the fact straight men are so keen to situate themselves in sexual scenarios that are defined by the very absence of men says much about heterosexual men's fear of being excluded from women's sexual activity. Butch and dominant lesbians particularly retain the ability to unsettle a culture still too ready to associate power with heterosexual masculinity, and this may go some way to explaining their absence from lesbian BDSM in popular culture. This also explains the nervousness with which gay male BDSM is still treated: men bottoming to other men is still an image that unseats the very foundations upon which heterosexual and male supremacy is founded.

8

Consumerism, Switches and Abuse

Different Faces of BDSM

Paying to Play: Kink and Consumerism

In summer 2012, a mooch around the average British shopping mall got a little more interesting. Bookshops were suddenly proffering displays of Anne Rice's reprinted erotic *Sleeping Beauty* series,[1] previously only found on dusty library shelves or accessible via mail order, and *The Story of O, The Sexual Life of Catherine M* and various erotica by Anaïs Nin had magically found their way to the front of bookstores where previously they had either been out of print or hidden in discreet back sections. Booksellers saw that there was an appetite for woman-friendly erotic fiction, often with a suggestion of kink, and so did publishers, who hurried out new versions of old books with tasteful covers (if your idea of tasteful is lots of satin, and heavily symbolic items such as keys, pearls and the odd black stiletto).

Not long after this rapid regeneration of old erotic fiction, there also came a slew of copycat books which mimicked both the storyline and cover art of *that trilogy* so closely that I was slightly surprised copyright lawyers weren't called. I supposed that seeing as *that trilogy* started its life as fan fiction anyway, it would have been a bit rich to start suing people for ripping it off, and given the sales figures, the author and publisher were hardly going to be hurting for money anyway. The blurbs on the back of these books assured readers that they'd be getting more of the same sexy dominant male/submissive female narrative—"Where he leads me, I have no choice but to follow" *(Fire After Dark*, Sadie Matthews); "The bonds of his love transformed me" *(Bared to You*, Sylvia

Day)'; "A devastatingly handsome, utterly confident, pleasure-seeking playboy who knows no boundaries" (*This Man*, Jodi Ellen Malpas)—and the cover art all sticks to the same monochrome suggestiveness that characterized *that trilogy*. Publishers didn't even try to hide the derivative nature of these tomes; the cover of *Fire After Dark* even has a red sticker on it asking "Did Fifty Shades of Grey leave you wanting *more*?" One

In 2012 there was an explosion in *50 Shades* "copycat" books which used similar cover art to appeal to female readers (courtesy Thomas Bliss).

Publishers of erotic fiction know that a comparison to *that book* will immediately attract interest (courtesy Thomas Bliss).

almost feels that there must have been a factory of female writers churning out these books like battery-farmed authors during 2012, as I stopped bothering to count once the number of blatant rip-off titles in bookstores went in to double figures.

It wasn't just the bookstores though. The UK differs from the U.S. with its uneven laws towards adult stores, which vary wildly according to states. Despite the country's reputation for being sexually repressed, Britain has boasted its own chain of female-friendly sex shops, Ann Summers, gracing its high streets since 1970. With 140 stores dotting the British isles, the success of the Ann Summers chain could be said to represent a triumph of marketing over prudery, and is popular with both women and couples. Having always carried a small bondage range, the shop expanded its stock of floggers, blindfolds, ball gags and restraints in 2012, and was rewarded by its sales doubling.[2] Sales of nipple clamps at the stores increased fifteenfold, and I distinctly remember the store selling a "Christian Grey tie," which seemed to me to be an example of what us Brits call "money for old rope." After all, it was just a silvery-grey tie, of the type you could buy in any UK clothing store, yet because the image was now synonymous with *that book* (whose cover is graced by such a tie), it was apparently also a sufficiently erotic garment to be sold in a sex shop. Several years on, you can still buy a "Fifty Days of Play" board game from the store; a friend of mind complained just the other day that she had been spammed with an email offer of "Fifty Shades of Grey condoms," which one has to say does not sound aesthetically pleasing. The 2012 surge in kinky commerce has been credited with saving the fortunes of Ann Summers, whose profits had varied wildly throughout the 2000s and whose bottom line had been hit hard, like many UK retailers, during the post–2008 recession. Kink doesn't just save people's sex lives, it seems—it also saves their businesses.

A Capitalist Dream?

For a culture that considers itself to be pioneering, edgy and clearly distinct from vanilla society, BDSM can be far more closely aligned with the mainstream than its adherents might like to think, and the main indicator of this is its relationship with capitalism. As I've explored in other chapters, many defenses of kink ultimately boil down to the concept of choice, a neoliberal argument which obscures the myriad factors that may limit the range of choices available in the first place—gender, race, disability, class and wealth. The latter two factors were not ones I saw discussed much in my local scene, but there was an awareness, nonetheless, that it cost money to be kinky. People would confess with a guilty grin just how much they'd spent on a pair of hand-crafted floggers, and would commiserate with each other over the compulsion to keep adding to their toybag, an addiction which perpetually left them with barely enough money to make rent. A guy I was seeing kept emphasizing how tight money was for him, yet he kept spending the money to drive to kink events, pay the entry fee, and inevitably come away with yet another addition to his range of domming tools. I myself wasn't generally interested in this conspicuous consumption; I like a bargain, and I've never seen extravagance as something to be proud of. A latex outfit which cost the same as a used car holds no appeal to me, but then not being a latex fetishist, I'm probably never going to see the pleasure gained from such an item as being worth the money. Perhaps I was something of an anti-materialist kinkster, insofar as I felt BDSM should be about the pleasure of play, not the satisfaction of being looked at, the ability to brag to other doms how much you spent on your floggers or the smugness of being able to tell gawkers how much your outfit cost. I saw all these things out on the scene and they generally made me roll my eyes. This rampant consumerism didn't feel countercultural to me, and as someone largely turned off by the materialism of mainstream Western society, I would have preferred a community that considered itself edgy to apply more of a critical lens to its spending habits.

One example of this was a relatively young male dom (or so he called himself) in my local scene who seemed to bring a fancy new piece of expensive equipment to every event, yet never seemed to find a sub with whom to play. This may have had something to do with his way of trailing around the room like a lost puppy brandishing his new flogger or handcuffs; the flashiness of the equipment could not compensate for the distinctly under confident manner of its owner. The phrase "all the gear and no idea" certainly sprung to mind. It didn't seem that different from an unpopular adolescent at school trying to win friends by walking around the playground brandishing the latest iPhone.

A Touch of Class

The expense of decent kink equipment means that the BDSM scene automatically favors those with disposable income. This places the middle classes, the child-free and gay men and women as the group with the most spending power, while the working classes, single parents and ethnic minorities are statistically at a disadvantage. This is another aspect of the kink scene in which the pretense of a level playing field is a decidedly disingenuous tactic. As Carrie, one of Margot Weiss' interviewees says, "[I]t really does take money to play. I don't think that a lot of people who are wondering where they're going to buy their next milk and bread from are going to do that."[3] This is another way in which BDSM culture pays lip service to a community where everyone is equal, yet the reality is decidedly different.

Of course, a marginalized group being sold the ideology of liberation through pleasure is nothing new. Nina Power's tirade against the capitalist hijacking of feminism, *One Dimensional Woman,*[4] bemoans the fact "that the height of supposed female emancipation coincides so perfectly with consumerism" and adds that "if the contemporary portrayal of womankind were to be believed, contemporary female achievement would culminate in the ownership of expensive handbags, a vibrator, a job, a flat and a man."[5] Rejecting the notion that being able to buy sex toys represents anything other than a victory for consumerism (rather than the progress for feminism with which it is often considered synonymous) Power scoffs, "Masturbation is a pre-condition for shopping? Feminism simply *is* one's purchasing power."[6] Like myself, Power has grown up in a country where Ann Summers has made buying a Rampant Rabbit as simple as strolling into your local shopping mall. Of course, this is not necessarily the case in some parts of the U.S.—the sale of sex toys remains illegal in Alabama, and the city of Sandy Springs, Georgia has also passed an ordinance in 2009 forbidding the sale or distribution of "any device designed or marketed as useful primarily for the stimulation of human genital organs."[7] However, Power's broader point remains relevant when applied to the constantly expanding potential of BDSM as a cash generator. The urge to have the newest, shiniest toys, and to keep up with the Joneses at the next play party, means kink can, like feminism, end up reduced from a powerful counter-cultural movement to a mere expression of purchasing power. As "Paul," one of Margot Weiss' interviewees says to her. "We live in a consumer economy; there's never enough. There's no such thing as enough!"[8]

As those who have constructed their own fun kinky worlds with dressing gown cords, clothespins, Saran Wrap, hairbrushes and any amount of everyday household implements can attest, neither clothes nor high-end toys make the man. You don't need gags when stuffing someone's panties in their mouth will do, and for sensation play, why look further than your own freezer or cutlery drawer? And yet pop culture seems unable to deal with kink without treating it as a narrow uniform, a set of tools without which one is not a "proper" practitioner of BDSM. No one really *needs* that expensive leather paddle to be kinky—and if we're talking about psychological forms of BDSM, no one needs any physical artifacts at all. Yet these subtleties are ones that cannot be claimed, packaged and sold back to us, so they go ignored by the market and the media.

Beginnings

There's a tendency to believe that subcultures used to be braver and more anarchic in previous decades, and therefore to romanticize the early entry of BDSM clothing and paraphernalia into the mainstream. BDSM fashion is synonymous with the punk movement of the late '70s, and was epitomized by London's Sex shop, run by Vivienne Westwood and Malcolm McLaren, the latter going on to manage the Sex Pistols. Selling a mix of punk and fetish wear, the shop was renowned for its edginess in a deeply conservative British culture—Adam Ant claims that it was in the back of this shop that he (voluntarily) had the word FUCK carved into his back with a razor blade. Punk fashion, seen as a refreshing alternative to the visually drab flares, blue jeans and plain T-shirts of the mainstream rock bands as the late '70s, was deliberately chaotic, consisting of outfits slashed to pieces and then reconstructed with safety pins, bondage trousers with chains and belts hanging off the legs, plus plenty of studs and leather. John Lydon, aka Johnny Rotten of the Sex Pistols, renowned for his deliberate mishmashing of torn school uniforms, leather, chains, studs and tartan, recalls, "I did a series of photographs in a straitjacket. I really liked being in that straitjacket, so I wanted gear on stage that wouldn't be quite so restrictive but would look like it. That's how the bondage gear came about."[9] Given that BDSM fashion is always presumed to be primarily sexual, the highly-strung Rotten's love of bondage clothing offers an alternative perspective that many wearers of latex, corsets and other restrictive items will echo: it makes them feel safe, caged but in a good way. Singer Chrissie Hynde echoes this, saying of the era, "All the bondage gear wasn't supposed to stimulate you in the sexual sense. It was more of a statement; two fingers up at the Establishment.... These were teenagers who were just trying to say, 'Fuck you!'"[10] Fast forward to an era where bondage gear is merely another accessory in a Beyoncé or Lady Gaga video, and most certainly *is* intended to stimulate the viewer sexually, and one wonders exactly where the subversive potential of BDSM fashion went. Lady Gaga parading around in Vivienne Westwood heels so cripplingly high that they make the toes scream just to look at them seems little more than a statement of purchasing power—how many, if any, of her fans can afford designer labels that high-end?

As already touched upon in Chapter 3, several of Margot Weiss' interviewees complained about younger, newer fetishists competing to be the ultimate kinkster by buying more and more items, missing the organic, DIY element of BDSM that they claim was present in the earlier generations of the '70s and '80s. "As Lady Hilary explained, when she first came out, you had to work to earn your boots, vest, chaps and jacket, and now you just 'go out and buy it. And there's nothing wrong with that, but there's nothing special about it either....'"[11] For this old guard of BDSM, just accumulating latex outfits, custom-made floggers and hand-made spanking benches is missing the point—a spiritual connection to BDSM is needed in order to maintain its intensity, and to retain its powers to unsettle the mainstream.

However, there are those who contest that even in the late '70s, bondage fashion was never as threatening to the mainstream as modern nostalgia likes to make out. Johnny Rotten, who claims that Vivienne Westwood and Malcolm McLaren hijacked many of his original designs and profited by selling them at the Sex shop says, "They were always blabbing on about sex and freedom, but that's exactly what they denied the very people who worked for them, They didn't share their ideas. It was all dictated; this is the way you must wear it ... it's a uniform. It's just a neat little box and so blinkered in its vision."[12] Rotten also notes the irony of people claiming to be punks or anarchists by "paying two thousand pounds for a torn dress with a safety pin on it"[13] (referring to Zandra Rhodes' high-priced punk clothing ranges), and mocks how clueless wannabe punks merely upheld the capitalist system they claimed to be railing against by attempting to buy their identity this way. Rotten himself, from a deeply poor working-class Irish family, claims his habit of wearing ripped clothes either came from having worn the same outfit so long it fell apart, or from destroying his own clothes in fits of rage—certainly plausible given both his deprived background and tightly-wound personality. His observations also tally with how the luxury to purchase an identity is a distinctly middle-class privilege, and echo Margot Weiss' writing on the belief that money can provide a shortcut into the fetish scene: "There is a fine line between becoming a practitioner through the (tainted, inauthentic) buying of an identity versus the (skillful, masterful) use of toys to create a scene,"[14] but those who believe they are on the right side of the line still see it very clearly, and see those on the other side as clueless pretenders to a hard-earned throne.

*   *   *

The Switch and Why BDSM Is Not Black and White

> "Taking the other role at least occasionally gives you an empathy, perspective and understanding that you just can't acquire any other way."—Jay Wiseman[15]

When it comes to mainstream popular culture and its love of simple and easy binaries, the switch in BDSM is often the ugly stepchild—ignored, left out, invisibilized. Yet switch behavior is present in far more BDSM scenarios than simple dom/sub labels allow, and the potential for switching is within us all. In my research for this book I encountered a lot of debate about what constitutes a switch—is Christian Grey one because he was a submissive to an older woman for years, even though in *that book* he identifies as dominant? Is the label "switch" applicable only if one continues to oscillate between the two roles, or can it be applied retroactively? Much like the confusion over whether someone still "counts" as bisexual if they are in a monogamous relationship with a person of the same or different gender, the quibble over what constitutes a switch is a lot less important than the nuance the concept brings to BDSM culture.

I encountered several dominants who agreed with Jay Wiseman that even if one identifies primarily with one role or another, trying the other side made you a better dom because you understood what it was like for the sub. Several people said they never used toys on another person without having tested them on themselves first, which I thought made a lot of sense. This is a level of empathy rarely, if ever, hinted at in mainstream portrayals of BDSM, which usually depict power roles as frozen, unalterable, and often devoid of a real connection between two partners. The concept of the switch implies a fluidity about power roles and sexuality which many find much more accurately aligned with real-life experiences of kink and sex.

The HBO TV series *Girls* was much discussed for its depictions of sex between protagonist Hannah (played by writer and director Lena Dunham) and her decidedly odd partner Adam. In the early episodes, Hannah seems to be on the submissive end of things, albeit without much prior negotiation and sometimes even without consent (in one memorable scene Adam starts urinating on her in the shower, to her shock and disgust). Hannah says of Adam "sometimes I let him hit me on the side of my body" and there are some cringeworthy scenes between them him trying to play the dom by saying "You modern career women, I know what you like," threatening to anally penetrate Hannah, and attempting dirty talk about her being a schoolgirl he is going to send home "covered in come." Hannah's enjoyment of these interactions seems pretty questionable, and it becomes apparent as the series progresses that she would prefer a monogamous relationship rather than these casual hook-ups. However, in episode 5 of series 1, the switching occurs

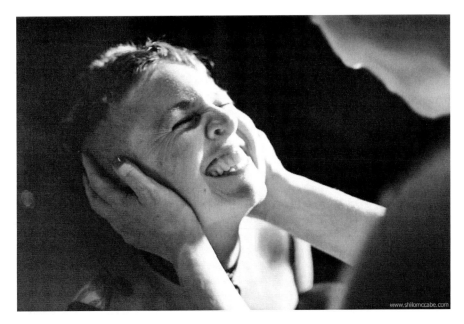

The fun side of BDSM is often absent from pop culture depictions, which prefer stern dominants and cowed submissives (courtesy Shilo McCabe).

and Hannah assumes a dominant role as Adam lies masturbating on the bed. She tells him he's "pathetic and bad and disgusting," criticizes the size of his penis and demands money from him. He agrees to give her $30, she promptly takes $100 from his dresser. Then she demands that he apologize, which he does, sincerely: "I'm really sorry." Far from only getting pleasure from playing the dom, Adam is clearly very aroused in his position as the submissive, moaning with pleasure as Hannah snaps, "You heard me, you filthy boy," and even asking her to step on his balls.

The dynamic between the two continues to oscillate as the show develops, demonstrating that the early assumption by the likes of Katie Roiphe, that *Girls* is simply more evidence that women want to be dominated, is way too simplistic. The switch nature of human sexuality is not a new idea; in his *Three Contributions to the Theory of Sex*,[16] Sigmund Freud wrote, "The most striking peculiarity of [sadomasochism] lies in the fact that its active and passive forms are regularly encountered together in the same person" and "he who experiences pleasure by causing pain to others in sexual relations is also able to experience pain emanating from sexual relations as pleasure." The more we interrogate pop culture depictions of kink and view power roles as organic, evolving and subject to constant change, rather than fixed, inert and unalterable, the more we see switching. Rihanna being tied up in the video for *S&M* was troubling to those who already saw her as a victim after her real-life abuse at the hands of then-boyfriend Chris Brown, but there were much fewer comments on her role as a riding-crop wielding mistress to a puppyish Perez Hilton, or her tying up and gagging a group of reporters. Madonna, a renowned chameleon of pop music, fluidly moved between dominant and submissive roles in her "Human Nature" video (see also the videos to *Express Yourself* and *Erotica* for further switching), and one only has to listen to the lyrics of Alice Cooper's *Poison* to hear the craggy-faced rocker's desire to both hurt and be hurt by his cruel, black lace-wearing lover.

As I discuss in the chapter on the female submissive, the tendency of popular media to jump all over depictions of female submission as evidence of female complicity with sexism usually obscures a much more complex reality. I had to read *that book* myself to discover that Christian Grey had not always been dominant, because not one media commentator mentioned it. Yet that's precisely the twist in the tail of Anastasia Steele's

166

discovery of this complex world of BDSM and its myriad roles—few people ever just stick 100 percent to one role. Her response is predictably one of surprise, since Grey has been at pains to come across as so domly— "He's so overwhelming, so alpha male, and now he's thrown this bombshell into the equation,"[17]—but that's precisely the point. Grey is supposed to be cold, uncaring and devoid of empathy for his sub, and yet: *"He knows what it's like."* The fact no one bothered to mention this in the hundreds of column inches dedicated to *that book* and what it supposedly says about gender, power and sexuality, says a lot more about the journalists creating the conversation around BDSM, and a lot less about *that book's* supposed romanticizing of female powerlessness. It seems E. L. James was actually aiming for some sense of balance in portraying Grey as a former submissive, and in doing so, perhaps more of a realistically fleshed-out character than the 24 hour, perpetually-in-role uber-dom.

Independently produced and queer-themed depictions of BDSM seem to have less trouble with this fluidity, perhaps because moving outside the straitjacket of heterosexual gender binary frees scriptwriters' imaginations more. In Samois' anthology *Coming to Power*, Juicy Lucy writes, "power is in its nature a flowing of energy, an exchange. Sometimes we give and sometimes receive but the energy, the power, always flows. Patriarchy and heterosexuality attempt to freeze power, to make one side always dominant and one side always passive."[18] It might be more accurate, and less offensive to the heterosexual women who the writer assumes must always be in the masochist position, to say that patriarchy and heteronormative standards certainly attempt to freeze power, but it's also true that gay and lesbian BDSM can demonstrate the possibilities for infinite different power configurations when these limiting templates are abandoned. The 2011 film *Mommy Is Coming*, directed by queer black filmmaker Cheryl Dune, certainly has a lot of fun constantly switching the power roles from the expected—butch, cross-dressing lesbian Claudia playing the dom in a pretend hostage scene— to the less conventional—more feminine, delicate partner Dylan harshly dumping Claudia with the words, "When I think of the great loves of my life, you just don't measure up." Dejected Claudia begins to mooch around Berlin as her drag alter-ego Claude, and reaffirms her butch identity as she begins to date Helena, an older femme woman. However, when she goes to a kink club and has a threesome, Claude plays the bottom to a genderqueer couple (one partner presenting as female-bodied, one intersex) and has an incredibly pleasurable time doing so. Dylan later goes to the same club and bottoms to a sadistic butch woman, but doesn't enjoy the experience ("I really felt … not loved at all") compared to the fun, kinky threesome we see her having on the floor of an apartment with some more femme women earlier in the film.

The mix of these different power configurations, gender presentations and outcomes of kink scenes shows how the best way to say anything about kink in a film may be via not trying to say anything *particular*. Instead, Dunye shows the same person switching between dom and sub, between traditionally expected (e.g., that the butch partner will always be the dom) and subversive behavior, and between gender roles, then leaves it up to the viewer to absorb all this. No role is depicted as any better or worse than the other, since what works for one party is a disappointing experience for another. There is no hierarchy of kink in this queer BDSM free-for-all, just the pursuit of pleasure, and of course, that little bit of love. This is the value of the switch—to get the viewer to look past simplistic categories that try to press "pause" on human sexuality when of course it is a constantly playing film. It reminds us that, as Anne McIntosh puts it, "S/M performs social power as both contingent and constitutive, as sanctioned neither by fate nor by God, but by social convention and invention, and thus [constantly] open to historical change."[19]

* * *

Pathology and the Past: BDSM and Abuse

"People in the scene assume that there must be 'some reason' for being submissive, reasons that Anthony elaborates as 'you're fat or you were abused as a child … or there's something missing or there's something that's not quite right … or that you can't say no.'"[20]—Margot Weiss

The misreading of BDSM as indistinguishable from abuse is one that dogs the mainstream public perception of kink. As long as there are those who believe that BDSM is merely a disguise for non-consensual beatings, sexual assault, rape and all manner of coercive, violent acts, there will be a reluctance to accept BDSM's value as a pleasurable opportunity to express the complexities of human sexuality. Neither radical feminists nor conservatives have helped to debunk the former stereotype—rather, they have historically supported the dissemination of it. In her essay "Blood Under the Bridge: Reflections on 'Thinking Sex,'" Gayle Rubin writes how anti-porn feminists presume that there is no such thing as consent to BDSM activities, that "no one could enjoy hot candle-wax dripping on bound breasts; that such experiences could not be part of legitimate lovemaking; and that the act is intrinsically violent."[21] This erasure of consent from BDSM has been a standard tactic employed by its critics: writing about the 1986 Attorney General's Commission on Pornography (usually known as the Meese Commission), Carol S Vance notes how no attempt was made to understand how BDSM functions; "Viewers were unfamiliar with the conventions of s/m sexual behavior and had no access to the codes participants use to read these images." Instead, the Commission imposed its own context: "s/m was non-consensual sex that inflicted force and violence on unwilling victims. Virtually any claim could be made against s/m pornography, and by extension, s/m behavior."

This neatly sums up how BDSM ends up conflated with abuse by those unfamiliar with its practices and its workings. Pop culture representations often do not help to maintain the distinction, instead using BDSM as a stand-in for emotional or physical abuse when it suits them. In an early episode of *Sex and the City*, "La Douleur Exquise," the theme of kink is mixed in with Carrie's faltering relationship with callous alpha male Mr. Big. A fetish-themed party where the buffet is dotted with chained submissives and waiters you can spank, Charlotte's shoe fetish and Carrie's inability to leave a man who won't commit to her—all these are conflated as part of S&M. Carrie asks herself "Why do I keep doing this to myself? I must be a masochist," a reference to the "exquisite pain" of the title. Perhaps this is an honest comment on how all humans have the potential to knowingly put ourselves in situations that are not good for us, but it also runs the risk of equating physical pain/sensation as a means to a pleasurable end, with emotional pain as an end in itself. There are clearly no thrills to be gained from the constant disappointment Carrie experiences with Mr. Big, leading her to throw food against the wall and finally scream "Why does it hurt so fucking much?!" in exasperation. The language of bondage is also inappropriate—"I was the one who tied myself up. Tied myself to a man who was terrified of being

BDSM as therapy: Sabina (Keira Knightley) finds catharsis through spanking from Carl Jung (Michael Fassbender) in *A Dangerous Method* (2011) (Movie Stills Database).

tied down"—and again equates pleasurable restraint with being trapped in a toxic relationship.

Using BDSM as quick and easy shorthand for pain and punishment may appeal to pop culture producers because of the already established misunderstandings surrounding it. Want to show that someone's an emotional masochist? Get out the whips and rope. However, this not only fails to inject any nuance or subtlety to Joe Public's understanding of BDSM, but it also pathologizes BDSM participants as abusers and damaged victims, and puts off those curious or struggling with latent kinky desires from investigating further, lest they get caught up in this clearly abusive and unpleasant world.

Getting Over It

> "On the relatively rare occasions on which I divulged my [research] in professional situations, people winked and giggled, wagered over whether I needed a spanking, or asked

me whether the members of the community had all been abused."—Staci Newmahr[22]

It occurred to me in my research that the mistaken narratives about BDSM and abuse seemed to fall into several categories: the belief I've outlined above, held by some feminists and conservatives, that BDSM simply *is* abuse and therefore something to which no one ever truly consents; the belief that people only practice BDSM because they have been victims of abuse and are therefore working out psychological trauma; and perhaps a third, uneasy suspicion that, while it can be practiced consensually, the BDSM scene gives abusers and predators an easy place in which to hide.

There is very little in pop culture exploring the third concept, although there is an increasing, if deeply fraught, discourse on abusers in the scene, which can be found in the writing of BDSM activists such as Thomas Macauley Miller, Clarisse Thorn, Cliff Pervocracy and Kitty Stryker. Apart from the scene in *Mommy Is Coming* where the sadistic lesbian top with whom Dylan plays admits that she has the potential to kill someone, there is little mainstream media exploration of the fact that the BDSM scene can be a refuge for those who have no respect for limits. Other than the Salon article I mention in Chapter 6, I can't think of any other examples of mainstream journalism about abuse in BDSM. Understandably so: so much energy has been expended on showing how BDSM is *not* about violence, coercion or hatred that pop culture producers would be showing themselves up as reactionary and prudish if they insisted on focusing on those aspects of kink just when it's becoming sexy, cool and media friendly. However, as the existence of campaigns such as the Consent Culture project (tagline: "Because Safe Words Are Sexy") founded by Kitty Stryker and Maggie Mayhem demonstrate, there is certainly an appetite for, if not a need for, a public discourse about abusers lurking in the BDSM scene. Just as this book goes to press, a debate is currently raging about Jian Ghomeshi, a Canadian TV host fired from CBC following allegations of sexual harassment and assault. Ghomeshi has just released a statement on Facebook protesting his innocence and claiming that the only activities he participated in with his alleged victims were part of consensual BDSM. Andrea Zanin, a Canadian BDSM blogger, comments on the case: "A danger inherent in

[BDSM becoming more publicly acceptable] is that the 'don't hate me for being kinky' defense will be used by people who perpetrate non-consensual violence, and that we, as a community, will stand by uncritically.... I don't wish to be complicit in someone's misappropriation of BDSM terminology and codes as a shield for rape and assault."[23]

You Only Like It Because You're Fucked Up

The narrative about all kinky people being damaged victims of past trauma certainly gets a fair bit of airing in pop culture. To get the reference to *that book* out of the way first, it has to be noted that Christian Grey is apparently only a dominant because he was rejected by his parents, seduced by an older woman when he was a teenager, and then dominated by another older woman for six years. His need for control and insistence on not being touched are manifestations of the psychological damage done to him; he's described in *that book* as a victim of sexual abuse, and referred to as "fucked up" more than once. The narrative of victimhood is also often applied, and probably more frequently, to submissives and masochists, especially if they're female. As described elsewhere, the dom/sub relationship between Lee and her boss E. Edward Grey in the movie *Secretary* unfolds against the background of Lee's release from a mental institution and her predilection for self-harm. The fact Lee quits self-harm as she begins a sadomasochistic relationship with Grey can be read as BDSM standing in for the satisfying pain yielded by self-harm; she can still achieve the pain and humiliation she needs, but she now has someone else to inflict it for her. It's a simplistic reading for certain, but there's no denying that the film makes it easy to jump from tormented soul to vulnerable masochist once we've seen that a kinky character has a background of mental instability. The 2011 movie *A Dangerous Method* makes no secret of this connection, depicting BDSM as therapeutic for Carl Jung's hysterical patient Sabina. The ending is positive, insofar as Sabina moves from seeing herself as "vile and filthy and corrupt" for her love of being spanked, to acceptance of herself and her sexuality and a successful career in psychiatry. However, this is only after her relationship with Jung has ended, implying that BDSM merely functions as a cathartic tunnel which the mentally troubled can go through in order to release their demons, but that they will also emerge from the other end and not need any of that weird kinky shit any more.

This is a belief supported by the media's love of articles such as "I'm Gonna Need You to Fight Me on This: How Rough Sex Cured My PTSD,"[24] a 2011 article by Mac McLelland in which she describes how staged scenes of violent, coercive sex helped her work through the trauma she experienced reporting on the aftermath of the Haitian earthquake. McLelland was not raped, nor did she witness rape in Haiti, but she did spend a great deal of time around women who had suffered horrific sexual violence, and spent her time in the country suffering from nightmares, drinking to block out the horror, and beginning to show the signs of post-traumatic stress disorder—dissociation, numbness, constant crying. She writes, "Since I'd left Port-au-Prince, I could not process the thought of sex without violence. And it was easier to picture violence I controlled than the abominable nonconsensual things that had happened to [the Haitian women]." And so McLelland sought out an ex-lover, now a friend, with whom she'd "done this sort of thing before," and asked him to make this idea a reality. Her descriptions of the sex are intense, honest and to those unfamiliar with the fantasies of being overpowered, extremely unsettling:

> … with that he was on me, forcing my arms to my sides, then pinning them over my head, sliding a hand up under my shirt when I couldn't stop him. The control I'd lost made my torso scream with anxiety; I cried out desperately as I kicked myself free…. When I got out from under him and started to scramble away, he simply caught me by a leg or an upper arm or my hair and dragged me back. By the time he pinned me by my neck with one forearm so I was forced to use both hands to free up space between his elbow and my windpipe, I'd largely exhausted myself.

The sense of catharsis experienced afterwards, however, as well as the caring attitude of McLelland's partner, are crucial in balancing what might otherwise sound like a horrifying experience to those who cannot comprehend the concept of consensual non-consent. "After he climbed off me, he gathered me up in his arms. I broke into a thousand pieces on his chest, sobbing so hard that my ribs felt like they were coming loose." McLelland goes on to say that her symptoms eased, that rape scenes in films no longer triggered her flashbacks, and that she was able to report from other war zones where sexual violence was endemic, such as the Democratic Republic of Congo.

On its own, McLelland's story stands as an extremely brave, vivid piece of journalistic storytelling. A woman who has enjoyed this kind of sex runs a great risk in admitting it and writing in detail about it. However, as part of a cultural narrative that tells us no woman could enjoy this kind of sex without there being a psychological reason for it, it's not actually anything new. It stood to reason that McLelland selected a sex partner with whom she had enacted these kinds of scenes before, yet her previous experiences—unlinked to war and rape—are merely treated as a side note. There's a whole other story to be told here, one about women who enjoy sexual scenes of consensual non-consent because they simply find them arousing, and even manage to stay good friends with the men with whom they've practiced such scenes without falling in love afterwards, and yet it's one that the mainstream media seems unable or unwilling to tell.

Furthermore, as several commenters on the article pointed out, placing rough sex in a context with war zones, rape and PTSD only serves to further differentiate it from normal, healthy sexuality. McLelland sounds like she has prior experience with scenes of consensual non-consent, yet this is disregarded in favor of making the experience sound as taboo as possible. Why not simply frame this as just another kinky experience, or at least a natural form of catharsis, rather than something so odd and shameful it needed to be confessed to in the form of such an article? Other commenters agreed, saying that the article was a missed opportunity to normalize kink, and instead fed straight into the persistent belief that BDSM is deviant, uncommon and only has a use in cases of severe mental distress. The article was flagged by Daily Kos a "must-read" and labeled "the best/most disturbing thing you will read" by the blog Feministe, yet the sex was probably the least shocking and troubling part—it read like consensual kink to me. I felt like headlines like this came from the assumption that re-enacting rape fantasies is still taboo and shameful, and this stems from conservative beliefs about female sexuality, as well as about kink.

McLelland's article troubled me precisely because it represented many other articles on consensual violent sex which don't get written or if they do, don't get publicized. It's still not stated often enough in popular media that not everyone in the BDSM scene is an abuse victim, and not everyone in the scene who has trauma in their past is using BDSM to process it. Indeed, in a 2006 study of 132 BDSM practitioners (which included psychometric testing), Dr. Pamela Connolly concluded that compared to normative samples,[25] kinky people suffered lower rates of depression, anxiety and PTSD. Interestingly, they also displayed lower rates of psychological sadism and psychological masochism than non–BDSM practitioners, implying that roles in BDSM play do not necessarily correlate to real-life pathology, or maybe that BDSM provides a release for tendencies that otherwise lead to psychological imbalances when not processed. Similarly, an Australian study of 20,000 men and women[26] found that kink practitioners "report no more sexual difficulties than other people, and men involved in BDSM actually score better on a happiness scale." Perhaps most crucially, the study also concluded that BDSM is "not a pathological symptom of past abuse or difficulty with 'normal' sex" as it still too often presumed to be.

However, as Dr. Meg John Barker points out in their paper "Gender and BDSM Revisited,"[27] "myth busting" can end up being a double-edged sword. Referring to the theories of Shiri Eisner, author of *Bi: Notes for a Bisexual Revolution*, Barker suggests that well-intentioned myth busting can end ultimately up as divisive as the prejudice it seeks to destroy. Trying to speak for the whole bisexual community with statements such as "We are not confused" "We are not just gay and in denial" undeniably is done with good intent, but it leaves anyone who fears they *might* be confused, or gay and in denial, feeling like they have nowhere to turn, and that their feelings are a betrayal of their peers. Similarly, in our keenness to show that BDSM is not synonymous with mental illness or trauma, we can run the risk of erasing those who do use kink to heal. Turning defenses of kink into a binary of "We are all totally mentally healthy!" vs. "We're all traumatized, damaged people" obscures the much more layered reality of human experience and the multiple subconscious or unconscious forces motivating our behavior at any one time. Stacey May Fowles, who has written openly about her past experience of sexual assault, said in her interview with me "I don't believe it is my responsibility, or that I owe it to anyone, feminist or otherwise, to reconcile the fact that I was sexually assaulted with my submissive or masochistic impulses." It's tricky when pop culture does seem to demand a crudely bifurcated answer (*are* you doing it because of abuse or *aren't* you?!), but as I discuss in Chapter 6 regarding the search for the perfect feminist submissive, we should not feel obliged to provide it.

What's Normal?

I expected that BDSM would be pathologized to some degree by conservative forces, namely: a reactionary media desperate for salacious headlines, family values advocates for whom no type of sex other than married, monogamous and obviously, heterosexual, intercourse could be considered "normal," religious fundamentalists. I expected to hear it much less from liberal, left-wing or sex positive camps, and even less from people who were in the BDSM scene. Nonetheless, an intelligent, articulate woman in her 30s who had participated in consensual BDSM relationships told me she still believed that all kinks ultimately must originate from some event that warped people's sex drives. This didn't have to be a major, notable trauma; it might be something barely perceptible, something that didn't even register on one's radar at the time, mixed in as it was with the multiple revelations and humiliations of growing up, but nonetheless, she believed that anyone with a predilection for BDSM had experienced something which resulted in their sexuality deviating from the norm.

In her memoir, *The Surrender*, largely a love-letter to the dominant/submissive dynamic of anal sex, Toni Bentley reinforces this theory by suggesting she enjoys the physical and mental release of the act precisely because of childhood trauma. She writes about her father spanking her as a child, causing her to associate her backside with control, distress and humiliation. Anal sex is a way of reclaiming this body part, and she writes, "Getting ass-fucked is the most extreme form of rebellion against one's parents."[28] She describes one particularly traumatic memory when at the age of four, her father took the banana she was refusing to eat and smeared it all over her face and hair (an experience she believes has led to her complex relationship with humiliation). "The quest for my lost dignity has become a lifelong obsession, a relentless search for the face beneath the banana." Her way of dealing with this upsetting memory is to "embrace her terror of humiliation by choosing and desiring what many is the ultimate act of humiliation: anal penetration. The weapon has become an instrument of pleasure in my adult world." She adds, "To this day, however, I don't finish a single banana without pulverizing it first in the blender."

Still, not everyone who enjoys humiliation or power exchange has such an anecdote in their history, yet there is little room for them in popular culture. One wonders if Bentley's book would have reached publication had it not had contained the requisite explanation for her kinks, the back story, the Freudian root for her love of anal sex. Possibly not; it would certainly be a much slimmer tome, as pages and pages, whole chapters even, are given over to the author's ponderings on her relationship with her backside, and how it relates to her childhood and relationship with her parents. *The Surrender* is subtitled "An Erotic Memoir," but to be flippant for a moment, there's not much that's erotic about paragraphs and paragraphs of psychoanalysis drawing links between adult sexuality and childhood. Unless, of course, age play is your particular kink.

What Hadley and the young woman mentioned above are both implying is something most BDSM practitioners don't want to hear. Kinky people are obliged to spend so much time and energy proving that one is *not* deviant, warped or a damaged victim, that even giving credulity to the suggestion that kink is some kind of sickness feels like admitting defeat. However, I also take issue with the belief that kink must always relate to something broken in our pasts because it seemed to be rest on a false premise: namely, that there is or ever has been any such thing as normal or natural human sexuality. The philosophers St Augustine and Thomas Aquinas believed that only sex acts which carried the possibility of procreation could be considered "natural," immediately ruling out contraception, masturbation, oral sex, anal sex, same-gender sex, sex with anyone infertile and pretty much most of the forms of sex practiced by the average 21st century adult. We all know that it wasn't too long ago that homosexuality was considered a mental illness, a perversion, a deviation from nature that saw even supposedly neutral sexologists labeled its sufferers "inverts," and interracial relationships were also viewed as a threat to the natural order until relatively recently in Western history. Indeed, if we're going to make the statement that kinks must originate from something wrong or broken within people, why not extend the theory to interracial relationships, and suggest that attraction to someone of another race must result from exotification or fetishization?

I can understand why, faced with the feeling that one's own kinks, or those of others, are incomprehensible without some kind of psychological explanation, we resort to talk of normality and "healthy" sexuality. Most of us have interior boundaries drawn, and a glance across FetLife will show that even among BDSM practitioners, deviance is only taken so far—it's pretty common for people to state on their profiles that they are not into any of the Big 5 (urine, feces, blood, animals or children). Yet, sticking just to the concept of consensual fantasy between adults, when we label something kinky, we assume it must have an opposite, or at least a vanilla counterpart: something which has literally been bent out of shape to render it abnormal. And this brings us back to the begged question: what *is* normal? When does regular sex become kinky? When the woman goes on top? When one partner slaps the other's bottom? Or does it still count as normal right up until someone makes it official and purchases a ball gag?

In an episode of HBO drama *Six Feet Under*, when Claire finds out that her new love interest Billy used to have a sexual relationship with his male art teacher, she asks Billy, "Wasn't that a sort of fucked up power dynamic, though?" Billy responds, "There's always a fucked-up power dynamic in sex, isn't there?" That line has stuck with me throughout the decade since I first heard it, because it spoke a truth that most of us seemed afraid to voice. Someone's usually on top in sex, both metaphorically and physically. Someone's usually giving and someone else is taking. It is only when we use that theory to try and say that certain power roles are immutable, that one role is better or worse than the other, or that they should dictate social structures, that we are likely to end up bolstering sexist or homophobic narratives. However, providing we are not attempting to achieve those aims, why then is it so problematic to admit that there are *always* power dynamics at work in sex, and that there isn't always necessarily a clear line between BDSM sex, which just happens to make that dynamic explicit, and sex which takes place without chains, leather or floggers?

Kink is present in the everyday, and the everyday is present in kink, yet we draw artificial distinctions between it and that which we consider normal. As Michael McIntyre points out, just as we don't live lives free from distinctly BDSM power dynamics, nor do we live lives free of masochistic tendencies. McIntyre writes, "Dancers who go *en pointe* are told to 'embrace the pain.' Long-distance runners wear t-shirts reading 'my sport is your sport's punishment.' Rugby players sport bumper stickers reading 'Give blood, play rugby.' A tattoo or a piercing is valued, at least in part, because of, not in spite of, the pain entailed in acquiring it…. In which world do people live lives devoted to the avoidance of pain?"[29]

Unless, then, we are going to assume a freakish psychological root for every activity considered normal, I do not believe that BDSM necessitates the discourse of trauma and abuse that is associated with it any more than the choice to practice martial arts or the decision to eat spicy foods. It may be that everything we do as humans, is, at its roots, some kind of coping mechanism, so why single out kink? Each one of us deals with the traumas inflicted upon us at a wide societal level by corrupt governments, rotten legal systems, inadequate education and healthcare systems and the often malign influences of religion. We must all learn to operate under the distinctly dom/sub, master/slave hierarchy which capitalism imposes upon us. A childhood spanking may well be processed through a BDSM scene; it may equally be exorcised by taking up boxing. However, the scars of a lifetime spent trying to appease the capitalist beast of Western society may be the deepest ones of all, and there may be no activity which can truly provide catharsis from this.

9

Blinding Whiteness?
Race and BDSM

"The vast majority of black women in the United States, more concerned with projecting images of respectability than with the idea of female sexual agency and transgression, do not often feel we have the 'freedom' to act in rebellious ways in regards to sexuality without being punished."—bell hooks[1]

I bought my first dog collar that had the word "SLAVE" embossed on it in silver when I was 19. Back in 2003, in a pre-social media world where I was only tentatively beginning to educate myself with sociology books from the heaving shelves of the university library and had yet to stumble upon blogs where issues of social justice were discussed, the term "white privilege" was totally unfamiliar to me. Buying the collar definitely made me feel nervous for feminist reasons; I already knew I was rampantly opposed to sexism (and would only become more so as my university career progressed) and wasn't quite sure what wanting to wear the item, however recreationally or humorously, said about me. However, the other implications of the word "slave" didn't occur to me until much later.

White privilege, and indeed any other kind of privilege, I would later learn, was the luxury of never having to think about certain issues; my ignorance was demonstration enough that I was indeed the epitome of the blissfully unaware white person. When I wrote about racialized imagery in BDSM for *Bitch*, I was asked to put a disclaimer in the post saying "As a feminist with white privilege, I don't have direct experience with racism in the BDSM community and I can't speak to black women's experiences." I didn't really want to do it, as I felt like it was immediately setting me up to be criticized for having written the piece at all. However, time was ticking, I wanted the piece to go out at a reasonable time of day for it to have a decent-sized reach, and I was aware that I was writing for a U.S. audience where racial issues are very differently weighted to how they are in the UK. So, I agreed. Sure enough, the second comment made on the piece was entitled "Sigh" and the commenter wrote only "Was it like, somehow *impossible* to find a black woman to write about this?"

I tried to understand where this person was coming from, but I felt a bit like I'd been stitched up—I'd been asked to make a disclaimer with which I wasn't really comfortable, and then had been immediately jumped on for doing so. Nowhere else in the blog series had anyone accused me of effectively not having the right to write about an aspect of kink. Incidentally, I can't speak to the experience of dominatrices, male submissives, gay, lesbian or trans kinksters directly either, and I also experience the privileges of presenting as heterosexual, cisgender and traditionally feminine. Yet no one criticized me for writing about butch lesbians or gay BDSM, nor was I ever asked to write a disclaimer about the privilege I held in comparison to those groups. Nevertheless, I tried to understand where this criticism came from—I know that, even though women's voices may still be in a minority in the media, white women's voices are still accorded more weight than their sisters of color. I am in a privileged position, no doubt, of being able to broadcast my views across the internet; however, I found it odd the way *Bitch* only wanted me to apologize for this in one particular instance, and irritating that the commenter hadn't bothered to see my post in the context of a holistic exploration of kink.

Interestingly enough, when I actually looked at the profile of the commenter who had criticized me, I realized that she was also white. This brought to mind a passage in Margot Weiss' *Techniques of Pleasure,* where she mentioned white BDSM practitioners who refused to play the top to a bottom who was a person of color, or who said they would do race play in private but not in public. It seemed that what Weiss identified as "white people's desire to be antiracist, postracial or maybe just PC,"[2] meant that to this commenter, I was transgressing some terrible boundary by writing about race and kink as a white woman. Somewhat illogically, that did not stop the commenter adding her own thoughts to the mix, therefore creating yet more dialogue between white women on an issue she seemed to think only black women should be publicly discussing. However unjustified I felt this criticism was, it showed me that this was a very sensitive topic, and it was very hard to know how to proceed with it.

The problem seemed to stem from the conflating of three concepts—private race play, public race play and racialized BDSM imagery in popular culture. No one quite seemed to be able to sort the three from each other, and therefore the debates about them tended to get a bit circular. Some commenters were unequivocal—blogger Alex Grey writes, "I've never been comfortable with the use of the word *slave* as terminology in the BDSM world, or any world, for that matter. Nobody should be. The history surrounding slavery is too vast and horrific for it to be used for anything other than what it actually is; the oppression and ownership of human beings as chattel."[3] Yet Grey herself is white, and the dictatorial tone of her declaration seems misplaced, even if it is aimed at other white people—surely it's up to those most affected by the history of slavery to dictate how the word is used? Sara Vibes, a black sex educator, performer and producer who practices BDSM is critical of the notion that racialized kink should be policed, especially in a community that, by its very definition, is built upon taboo: "Racism isn't over just like incest isn't over, but people still openly flaunt their Daddy/girl relationship—that could be just as triggering but no one is demanding that couple no longer be allowed to play in [a public] space." Vibes adds that, with regards to racialized language, "If you happen to hear it in the dungeon and that's triggering to you, think about what it's like for me every day, in the street. I'm sorry you have to be reminded of your whiteness and shared American history, but that's how I want to play." Marisol Smalls, another BDSM practitioner of color, adds that she is not concerned with putting a white audience at ease: "Anything racialized or interracial will cause discomfort whether it is BDSM, LGBT, or anything else. Hell, my multiracial children cause discomfort. Racism will always exist and that's the sad honest truth. Those who say it's discomforting are those ones who need to stand in front of a mirror and ask themselves why."

As Aph Ko points out in an article for the website Everyday Feminism,[4] it's well-meaning white people's preoccupation with slavery that does much of the damage in the first place. "The fact that black skin still reminds us of slavery—*while the white, colonialist, appropriative gaze doesn't*—is part of the problem. The only thing that connects enslaved

Grace Jones has often used her body and sexuality in her art: why are her modern counterparts criticized so much more harshly for the way they represent black female sexuality? (Movie Stills Database.)

black women [in history] and sexual black women today is the violent system of white supremacy. Therefore, if we want to make this connection at all, we should center our discussions and critical analyses on the white gaze, rather than black women's bodies and slavery."

183

Jamaican singer and actress Grace Jones has certainly never been shy about using her body, sexuality or the word "slave" in her music and surrounding imagery. One of her biggest hits was the 1985 single *Slave to the Rhythm*, also the title of the accompanying album, and the video is a disconcerting mishmash of shots, including Jones wearing nothing but a beret, standing naked opposite an equally tall, slim, naked black man, a black man spanking a white woman, and a model of Jones' head that morphs into a parking garage and spits out a car. Yet, 21st century commentators seem to have a selective memory when panicking about racialized BDSM imagery in modern music videos, and Jones' use of black bodies, sex, kink and possibly racialized references in 1985 barely get a mention in modern discourse about how women of color should be depicted on screen. Indeed, the lyrics to *Slave to the Rhythm* (written by white men, incidentally) possibly have a more direct link to slavery than any amount of onscreen antics from Rihanna and Ciara, referring to men laboring at chopping wood and chain gang songs.

Such provocative images being sung about by a black woman whose home country was built upon slavery and the back-breaking work of black people who sweated over the sugar plantations would surely result in some kind of outcry were the single released today. Yet, for whatever reasons—a society less keen to analyze racial politics, lack of the internet upon which white people could broadcast their outrage—such older instances of race, sex, kink and the black female body intersecting have gone largely without comment.

Triggers and Taboos

The imposition of troubling imagery upon scenes where the participants are not even trying to conjure up any racialized history is an important point to bear in mind when we look at the panic over racialized BDSM imagery in popular culture: as I've demonstrated, much of the hand-wringing comes from well-meaning white people, and much of the "So what?!" comes from an exasperate black community who are tired of being reduced to nothing but their ancestors' struggle. To me, the most effective way to acknowledge the awesome power of the word "slave" is about listening to those who it truly affects, rather than purporting to speak for them. Mollena Williams, a black BDSM educator and author who speaks openly about her experiences bottoming to white men, points out that her play has historical connotations imposed on it by others, even when there is no such element included in it. In Margot Weiss' *Techniques of Pleasure*, Mo says, "I do race play by default in the eyes of most people." Her first public play with a white top was perceived as race play, even though "it was a straightforward fuckin' rope scene with whips and shit."

Mollena has, however, also written openly about participating in role-playing scenes with an obvious racial tenet, which sound very intense. In her book, *The Toybag Guide to Playing with Taboo* she vividly describes a scene where her own friends helped a white dominant playing the role of "this fucking sadistic redneck asshole"[5] to restrain and threaten her with a knife.

"My eyes were swollen shut from crying, throat swollen and raw from screaming, heart thudding with trip-hammer speed and force … as the knife scraped its way up my belly…. He slapped my face again, but my head wedged into my shoulder didn't even move.

"*Yeah. Another dead nigger. No one will give a shit. No one.*[6]

"And I believed it."

Mollena's scene took place in a dungeon, which while not entirely public, was a space where others could witness this depiction of extreme, murderous racism and hear the hateful language used against her. So how do we reconcile the two? Does the willingness of a black kinkster who enjoys racial epithets being slung at them as part of a scene trump the discomfort of the white viewer? What of the black woman happy to bottom for a white man—is she obliged to change the way she plays, because the power dynamic in their play mimics the white male slave owner and the black female slave too closely?

Interestingly, Mollena does challenge the use of "slave" and the practice of "selling" people at fetish events, saying to Margot Weiss that the casual use of charity slave auctions at kink events made her think that BDSM practitioners should consider what real slave auctions in the Americas might have been like. "What would it be like if you walked into a Society of Janus auction … and then suddenly someone was dragged in for outside kicking and screaming and crying and pleading for mercy, and then stripped naked and inspected … and then sold off, while personally begging for his not to happen?"[7] Weiss adds that forcing people to consider the painful history behind slave auctions "makes sure that racism cannot be denied through neoliberal fantasies of being postracial or colorblind."[8] Other BDSM practitioners of color feel differently: Tijanna, an African American kinkster interviewed by Margot Weiss was simply not interested in accommodating what she saw as a racist tradition, even in order to provoke discourse: "A slave auction! Can't they think of another word? You know, a 'sub auction?' Slave auction! Come on! Shit."[9] This raises the question of how far it's acceptable to impose race play on a watching public, when it is not only white people who may end up distressed by it. It also shows how the distinction between publicly acceptable kinks and private play is often drawn: do what you want behind closed doors, but don't drag it out in public for everyone else to see.

Sara Vibes says she actively enjoys the fact that racialized BDSM is provocative for those around her: "I prefer my race play to go beyond the scene and have the onlookers take a second to think about their role in shared history. And [also be reminded] that it's not over, [that] slavery didn't happen in a vacuum in the South!" For Sara and Mollena, marrying kink and race isn't about blanding either of those things out, quite the opposite. It means harnessing the power of BDSM to confront the white-dominated kinky community (and possibly a mainstream audience beyond this) and not minding who it makes uncomfortable. Racialized BDSM, then—both in the kink scene and in the wider world of pop culture—has the power to dislodge the privileged from their comfortable position, which is why white writers dictating who can and can't use the word "slave" seem to be missing the point on a grand, if well-meaning scale.

However, the other side of the coin, as identified by Tijanna—white kinksters acting as if there is no racialized component to talk of masters and slaves at all—is equally frustrating. When a white "master" tells Margot Weiss, "Most people ... are sophisticated enough to realize that that's a very superficial connection and isn't really terribly relevant,"[10] the white privilege contained within that statement is palpable. Who is a white middle-class man to dictate that there's no real connection between the language of the master and slave, and the suffering of African Americans throughout American history? Isn't that exactly what he *would* say, because to imagine otherwise might unseat him from his comfortable position in an imagined color-blind society? As Chimamanda Ngozi Adichie puts it, black Americans "know an America different from American Whites; they know a harsher, uglier America. But you're not supposed to say that, because in America everything is fine and everyone is the same."[11] The illusion of equality and a postracial society is what allows white people to salve their consciences, but it seems astoundingly presumptuous for a white man to say that black history "isn't terribly relevant" to a scene where racial minorities are underrepresented, and where the language of slavery is perpetually present. It seems especially audacious to make this statement while trying to claim that the BDSM scene *doesn't* have a race problem.

Respectability Politics

> "Because white people have taken black bodies and marked them as deviant and lascivious doesn't mean that our bodies are actually deviant and lascivious. I shouldn't have to live my life by imaginary white rules."—Aph Ko[12]

Just as I found in my research that the asymmetric focus on female behavior and female sexuality mean that women in BDSM are often asked to answer to a higher level of scrutiny than men encounter, being African American seemed to add another layer of demands on one's behavior. In an interview with Andrea Plaid, Mollena Williams quips, "My vagina isn't really interested in uplifting the race,"[13] yet those who demand that black women never dare simulate the power dynamics of slavery either in private or public seem to be asking her (and her vagina!) to do exactly that. As Tamara Winfrey Harris puts it in her 2012 article "No Disrespect" for *Bitch* magazine, "black women carry a double burden, as they are asked to uphold a respectability built on both racist and sexist foundations."[14]

In this sense, then, hysteria over singer Ciara wearing a chain around her neck and allowing Justin Timberlake to yank suggestively on it in the 2009 music video Love Sex Magic, is not so different from those who snarked at Erykah Badu for having children outside of marriage, or actor Angela Bassett sniffily comparing Halle Berry's role in

Monster's Ball to prostitution. Why was Ciara expected to carry 200 years of American history across her shoulders while making a 3 minute video, while her white contemporaries such as Britney Spears and Lady Gaga are left in peace to toy with provocative imagery without anyone telling them "our ancestors are crying inside?"[15] Was not the assumption that Timberlake, or another white man, must have forced Ciara to writhe over Timberlake's lap or briefly be used as human furniture by him, as offensive as any presumed racism in the imagery? As it turns out, the concept in the video was actually Ciara's idea. This, perhaps is the most important lesson when tackling BDSM imagery in pop culture—remembering to separate the artist from the art. Also, the confusion between willing surrender and coerced disempowerment is one that allows BDSM to be mistakenly equated with violence, yet this is the part critics are frustratingly slow to grasp. It's only BDSM when it's consensual, and power can only be consensually surrendered if you have it in the first place. To assume Ciara was merely told what to do by white men in suits when she walked into a studio betrays a perception of black women far

Black women indulging in BDSM play for their own pleasure remains a controversial issue when depicted in popular media (courtesy Shilo McCabe).

more racist or sexist than any scenes of white male top/black female sub race play. As Aph Ko says, "If you can't stop thinking about enslaved black women when you look at me and my body, perhaps that says something about you. If you can't acknowledge that I have my own desires, I can't imagine what else you don't acknowledge about my personhood."[16]

For others, there were bigger issues at stake. When I interviewed racial justice activist Heather M. Carper for this book and asked her about the music video, she responded "Timberlake's disrespect for the Black community goes *way* beyond this video … [his] career is based almost entirely on racial appropriation." Pointing out that any objectification of Ciara that does take place in the video is no more gratuitous than the way women's bodies are generally served up for consumption in pop music videos per se, Carper adds, "I can find far more things to find objectionable in the trajectory of Timberlake's career than this video."

We Don't Want Your Pity

> "None of us have been forced to do this, and all of us can leave at any time. No one brainwashed us into taking part, and the more we do, the more proud we become of our performances."—Avril Nuuyoma, actor, on taking part in controversial *Exhibit B* live installation[17]

As I was writing this book, a controversy in the art and theatrical world began to rage regarding *Exhibit B*, a piece of live art installation/theatre crossover which was exhibited at the London Barbican in 2014. The installation ended up being closed down due to outcry over allegedly racist content. Staged by white South African Brett Bailey, *Exhibit B* was apparently intended to highlight the dehumanizing aspects of the human zoos in which Africans were displayed as objects of scientific curiosity during the 19th and early 20th centuries. The Barbican website states that the black actors standing still as part of the exhibit "confront colonial atrocities committed in Africa, European notions of racial supremacy and the plight of immigrants today.

"As spectators walk past the exhibits one-by-one, to the sound of lamentations sung live by a Namibian choir, a human gaze is unexpectedly returned."[18] Confronting the viewer with real-life visions of oppressed black people in history such as Sarah (Saartjie) Baartman, the "Hottentot Venus" who was treated as an exotic object to be studied by white people both during her life and after her death, the exhibition was described by white critics as "challenging," "essential" and "fearlessly uncompromising."

Writing for *The Guardian*, Kehinde Andrews disagrees, stating, "*Exhibit B* is offensive because it perpetuates the objectification of the black body that is a standard trope of society."[19] Rather than adding the voices of black people to the conversation, it renders them motionless, speechless and objectified, while white people continue to control the means of viewing, perceiving and discussing the black bodies displayed before them. He condemns the artist, a white South African, for being part of a privileged minority, and compares his work to a non-Jewish German making art which fetishizes Holocaust victims. He concludes, "If you pay to see it you are colluding in the worst kind of racial abuse."

The exhibition was shut down after protest marches outside the Barbican and a petition which apparently gained 20,000 signatures demanding the end of *Exhibit B*. However, there are those who disagree that censorship is ever the answer when it comes to confronting the public with uncomfortable truths about racism. Heather M. Carper says, "The argument 'Not in public—other people might be offended' is the same [argument] used to silence people in the LGBT community, or [to stop] interracial dating." Many of the protestors who wanted the exhibition shut down were black, but to assume that there is a "black consensus" on every issue is no more helpful than the presumption that racism is definitely dead and no one need concern themselves any further with it. As "E," a black woman comments, "Black people are not some homogenous mass living one collective life, so sacred cows are bound to differ.... Hell, one part of my family OWNED slaves while the others were enslaved: economics created two very different sets of black people who experienced racism quite differently!"[20]

In an interview with Mollena Williams, Andrea Plaid suggests that the queasiness over confronting racially charged imagery prevents the pain of slavery from being truly processed in the public consciousness: "it's like we hold the painful history as a sacred mythology that is not to be blasphemized." This gives the horror of the past more power over people's words, actions and fantasies by policing them—which is why Mollena says, "You can't heal something in your soul by letting it remain in its original state of pain … it HAS to be touched. Otherwise it will never heal." If the wound in this case is slavery and the objectification and exploitation of black bodies, there seems to be little to gain from censoring it. This is echoed in the words of one of the actors who participated in *Exhibit B,* who describes the exhibition as "a healing process that cannot be communicated with words, for no words can describe the horror and trauma that are transmitted from generation to generation."[21] On a mundane level too, those protesting against the exhibition have also cut short an employment opportunity for black actors—who, because of a white-centric acting industry, will already struggle to find work much more than their white counterparts. Is putting other black people out of work really the most effective way to combat the perceived racism in an art installation?

At the time of writing, an exhibition of female artists' work is scheduled to take place at New York's Ivy Brown gallery. One of the artists being exhibited is Nona Faustine, a black artist whose series "White Shoes" addresses the history of slavery. The exhibition is advertised on the *Wall Street Journal's* arts webpage using one of Faustine's images, where she stands naked except for white stilettos, holding a pair of archaic-looking handcuffs, and staring up at New York City Hall, which is built upon an African American burial ground. The title is "Over My Dead Body." One wonders if there will be similar criticism of Faustine's work, especially for its use of her naked (and some may argue sexualized) body, or if there will be more acceptance of art dealing with slavery if it comes from someone directly affected by the legacy, rather than a white artist.

White Panic

The panic over the objectification of the black form, however willing black people might be to use their bodies as part of art, was epitomized when Tracey Wallace, a white writer for *Policy Mic,* condemned a picture of Russian magazine editor Dasha Zhukova sitting on a chair in the shape of a half-naked black woman. Wallace slammed the picture thus—"This is not art. Not even for a fashion magazine"[22] (intriguingly, her qualification implies that fashion magazines might sometimes get a special pass for using racialized imagery, but apparently not in this case). There seems to be no awareness of the kink theme of human furniture when Wallace writes that the black woman's body is contorted "in a pretzel-like position that for any human being would be insanely uncomfortable." It's also telling what Wallace chooses to highlight about the human chair, when she writes, "The chair, designed to look like a bound black woman, has naturally curly hair and is topless."

As Aph Ko has pointed out above, the discomfort with a black woman being topless or bound is an instinct for which the viewer must take at least some responsibility. Feminist blogger Sarah Woolley, who has written articles in the UK press arguing against censorship of soft porn, points out "it takes more than nudity to cancel out a man's regard for a woman as a human being ... a true woman hater will dehumanize you no matter how you behave or what you wear. That is the nature of prejudice."[23] This can also apply to panic about racist objectification, as Ko states. Why should a topless or bound black female body trouble us any more than the same body but white, or the same body but male? Why should we worry that someone is going to use this sculpture as an excuse for sexism or racism, unless we are already looking to do so ourselves? Some of the most provocative images in Nona Faustine's "White Shoes" series show her completely naked, handcuffed or lying prone in the water with her legs splayed and breasts raised. There are undeniable sexual and kinky overtones to seeing a voluptuous naked black woman in these poses. Yet Faustine is both the holder and the recipient of the gaze: she has created her art using her own body, knowing exactly the power that her naked body has to provoke a reaction. Yes, she is emphasizing the vulnerability of the black body throughout history in order to make the viewer to think about slavery, but she is also using her body to remind us that just because she is standing naked with her wrists cuffed does not mean she is powerless.

Returning to the *Policy Mic* editorial criticizing the black "human chair" sculpture; it's somewhat telling that Tracey Wallace felt the need to highlight the fact the human chair has naturally curly hair. It begged the question: would the chair be more or less acceptable if the black woman/chair had relaxed hair, or was sporting a wig, or colored hair, or hair that is more obviously trying to mimic European hair texture? Is the problem with the black woman being a human chair that she's *too* black, *too* authentic and therefore too discomfiting to a white audience? Would she be less bothersome if she came with straightened hair, because a black woman who tries to alter her "nature" is clearly just an Uncle Tom who isn't so deserving of our sympathy about her objectification? Wallace is condemning this piece of art for objectifying the black female form—yet by focusing on utterly irrelevant areas of the chair/woman's appearance, she is doing exactly the same thing.

Further weight is lent to the theory that a certain branch of feminists, however well-meaning, like to become outraged on behalf of black women without bothering to ask if black women themselves are offended, when one traces the chain back to the original article in which the picture appears. On the website Buro 24/7, the photograph is cropped so that one cannot see the human chair in full—only the upturned legs, which form the "back" of the "chair." Because these legs are clad in black boots, one cannot tell the race of the wearer. One certainly cannot tell that Dasha Zhukova is sitting on what's meant to be a black woman's inverted body. Yet when the photo appears at *Policy Mic*, the crop has been removed to show the whole "chair," so the viewer can get suitably angry about it. While I bridle at the clichéd accusation often thrown at feminists—that we just *want* to be offended by things so badly that we seek to find sexism where there is none—I feel like there may actually be a little validity to this criticism in this case. No one had even seen the black female human chair until Policy Mic drew attention to it. So who really did the objectifying? Who was *really* responsible for highlighting and thus shoving in all our faces a prone, bound black body— the evil Russian fashionistas, or the well-meaning Western journalists?

Art as a Revolt

There was also something of lack of context to Wallace's critique, at least in terms of the art world—the human chair was a direct echo of a sculpture by artist Allen Jones, except in his case the topless woman being used as a chair was white. Jones himself argued that the piece, premiered in 1969, was a piece of cultural commentary, and that the accompanying sculpture series (also including woman as table and woman as hatstand) was partly inspired by the decidedly kinky leather outfits in popular shows such as *The Avengers*, and the accompanying fetishization of the female body. Predicting how fashion and its surrounding imagery would only become more sexualized and extreme as makers strove to be more outrageous than each other, he comments, "Every Saturday on the King's Road you went out and skirts were shorter, the body was being displayed in some new way. And you knew that the following week somebody would up the ante."[24] Jones identifies as a "card-carrying feminist" and says, "I was reflecting on and commenting on exactly the same situation that was the source of the feminist movement. It was unfortunate for me that I produced the perfect image for them to show how women were being objectified."

Jones' defense may seem a little disingenuous to those who believe that his art does not simply identify, but instead replicates and therefore implicitly endorses sexism; there's a tendency to resort to the excuse that "I'm just holding up a mirror to how awful society is" whenever art appears racist, sexist, homophobic or otherwise offensive to a minority. Those unconvinced by this defense will probably also be unmoved by Norwegian artist Bjarne Melgaard's defense of his modern version of the sculpture: in a joint statement with his art dealer Gavin Brown, he claims that such things "exist to destabilize and unhinge our hardened and crusty notions of race and sex and power.... Our tragedy is so evident in our daily experience that Melgaard has nothing left to portray but society in its utter decay."[25]

All that said, the human chair sculpture's positioning in a picture of a rich white woman *can* be read as an extremely apt commentary of the way the first world profits from exploiting the labor of third world populations, where the most deprived people are still disproportionately women of color. The positioning of Zhukova mimics a social hierarchy which still exists even in—one might say *especially* in—the wealthiest, supposedly most progressive countries in the world. She enjoys the privilege of being fully clothed, comfortably positioned, given a voice in a magazine article, whereas the black woman is stripped, voiceless, decorative and exists only to (in this case literally) support the white woman's endeavor. In the U.S. and UK, where the menial labor of women of color as house cleaners, health care aides and restaurant workers allows white women to enjoy high powered executive roles, the picture can be read as a pretty accurate social commentary.

A negative interpretation is not the only option, however, if we take a BDSM reading of the image (and also of Allen Jones' original work). Looking at the sculpture as a kinky artifact disrupts the simplistic assumption that the human sculpture must necessarily represent disempowerment or decay. The fetish of being or using human furniture is a popular if misunderstood proclivity, and the usual narratives surrounding objectification tend to fall down when people try to apply them to this fetish. As I write in more detail in the chapter on the female submissive, the standard feminist condemnation of all female body

Allen Jones' sculpture "Chair" was accused of sexism when it was released in 1969: a 2014 version with a black woman caused an outcry over racism ("Chair," 1969, © Allen Jones, b. 1937. Photograph © Tate, London 2014).

objectification as inherently negative fails to explain the increased pleasure, satisfaction and mental wellbeing that BDSM practitioners gain from consensual objectification. Feminists unused to BDSM imagery may well be horrified by "human furniture" websites such as Decorative Girls, but those in the kink scene will simply see a certain kink represented, and one which can be arousing to both men and women. (Professor Antony Whitehead, who has studied the issue of male submission, said that men who liked to serve as human chairs to their female dominants reported feeling safe and grounded when being sat on.[26]) Also, it's easy to cherry-pick instances of objectification. To make the Grace Jones comparison again, where is the outrage over a picture of Jones' face being sliced with a scalpel by a white hand, and then altered so her mouth opens grotesquely wide in the Slave to the Rhythm video? Why are we not equally bothered about Jones' head being used as a parking garage, which spits out and then later swallows a speeding car, her dark, glossy lips closing suggestively around it?

Perhaps the answer is that few white commentators would dare to criticize the assertive, androgynous, 5'10" Jones (who once physically attacked a white male interviewer live on TV for turning his back on her!) for objectifying herself in her videos, whereas a silent, blank-eyed sculpture is an easy target. However, this selective outrage shows how objectification is not necessarily a one-street populated only with voyeurs at one end and victims at the other; indeed, those who consensually objectify their own bodies as part of BDSM—or like Nona Faustine, as part of their art—would argue strenuously there are no victims at all. The media's tendency to reduce all interactions to simple binaries of oppressor/oppressed, especially in the case of race, is often too blunt a tool to address the fluidity of how power moves back and forth between parties in a BDSM exchange.

This is a subtlety hinted at when the actors who participated in Exhibit B made a statement in their defense:

At first glance … it is easy to assume that we are nothing but objects, repeating the worst of the racist and dehumanising aspects of the human zoos referred to in the petition(s) to cancel the exhibition.

Standing, exhibited in this manner, we can state explicitly that we are not objects during the exhibition. We are human, even more so when performing.[27]

Somewhere out there may be a black woman who agreed to model for Bjaarn Melgard so he could create his human chair sculpture. To value that woman's choice as less important than the outrage of a white writer says much more about racism and patronizing white attitudes towards black people than any amount of bound or silenced black bodies.

Men of Color and BDSM

Much of the controversy surrounding race and BDSM is situated with depictions of women of color in submissive positions and white men in dominant roles. Much less is ever said about the reverse configuration, or scenarios involving dominant black men and submissive white women, and even less still about BDSM between men of different races.

The most immediate explanation appears to be that, as Heather Carper puts it, "most depictions of 'subversive' cultures still fit within the dominant narrative of Whiteness." Furthermore, the imagery of black men preying sexually on white women has a different, but equally troubled, history in the American imagination—one only has to think of Emmett Till, or *To Kill a Mockingbird,* to see how black men have been persecuted for their uncontrollable sexuality, which is framed as a malignant force aiming to corrupt white female purity. Aside from an episode of *Married with Children* ("England Show aka Wastin' the Company's Money") which briefly shows a black man in a studded leather vest popping up at an S&M club to offer "a drink ... or a spanking?," and a fantasy scene in *Scrubs* where Elliot asks Turk to spank her because "I've been BAD!," I struggled to think of any instances in mainstream Western culture where black men are portrayed as kinky at all.

We could theorize that this is because black male sexuality is *already* seen as dominant and aggressive by its very nature, therefore to clothe black masculinity in the trappings of BDSM would be a fairly redundant act. Given the racist white assumption that black men are automatically threatening and violent, an assumption used to vindicate those who shoot unarmed black men (Trayvon Martin and Michael Brown are just two of the most recent victims of this belief, but it has a long history in

America and to an extent, in the UK too) it doesn't seem too incredible to suggest that the still mainly white controllers of pop culture view black men as perpetual sexual aggressors. The narrow slice of hip-hop culture that is viewed by the white community is what ends up defining black male behavior, and as a result black masculinity is still too often associated with sexism, violence and mindless materialism. In a 2005 interview, Noel Gallagher of British rock group Oasis justified his hatred of hip-hop thus: "When you see the videos of some guy throwing 100 dollar bills over a naked woman lying on a bed with a dog leash around her fucking neck ... what the fuck is all that about? That to me doesn't seem to be right.... Back in the '70s and '80s, if that was done by a rock 'n' roll band, it'd be called sexist and there'd be shock, horror and outrage. For some reason, hip-hop artists tend to get away with that."[28]

Funnily enough, Gallagher's quote implies that hip hop videos are already BDSM–flavored, although he is using this instance to illustrate the sexist objectification with which he believes hip hop is synonymous. So far, so stereotypical—although many feminists and cultural commentators might say Gallagher is not entirely off-base. Snoop Dogg did appear at the 2003 MTV awards accompanied by two black women on leashes and predictably caused plenty of outrage, including accusations that he was glorifying human trafficking. However, attention-seeking tactics on the red carpet are one thing; the total lack of consideration given to non-white sexuality in popular culture is quite another. What of the black male dominant who doesn't live into a baggy pants-wearing, blunt-smoking stereotype of a misogynist "pimp"? What of the black male submissive who wants to reject the toxic demands of alpha masculinity and submit, possibly to a white or black woman, without being accused of upholding white supremacy? What about the black man who wants to practice BDSM with other men? These figures are all conspicuous by their absence from popular culture.

Perhaps, like the well-meaning whites described earlier, pop culture producers are—whether rightly or wrongly—queasy at the idea of depicting these figures because they believe the risks of getting it wrong are simply too big. While some in the art world may have feted Robert Mapplethorpe's homoerotic photography of black male nudes for moving the (often invisibilized) black male body into the public consciousness, other black activists were unimpressed. Kobena Mercer accused Mapplethorpe of "racial fetishism"[29] and dehumanizing objectification of the black male body. When an artist is white and the objects of his gaze are black, his motivation is assumed to be privilege and voyeurism, not the breaking of taboos. Is it the case that the stakes are just too high, and no one wants to put their head above the parapet to try and depict black men and kink lest a firestorm of criticism rain down on their heads from people of all races?

It's possible, but it seems unlikely that this is the entire reason, or even most of the reason, that the sexuality of people of color, especially men and LGBT people, remains either invisibilized or grotesquely stereotyped in popular culture. As Marisol Smalls in her interview with me "The media [still] sees BDSM as a 'white' alternative lifestyle." All the women of color I spoke to pointed out that black representation in pop culture is so limited to begin with that it's a pretty tall order to expect effective depictions of people of color practicing BDSM. If the person of color never gets to be the princess or the hero in vanilla fiction, then it's unlikely they're going to be placed as a central character in a kink story either. The lack of representation then, mostly appears to result from white heterosexuals continuing to dominate media produc-tion, and therefore endlessly centering social narratives around their own experiences, secure in the knowledge that no one will demand that they stop to consider who they may be leaving out of the frame.

That trilogy is indeed about as white and middle-class as one can imagine, and white-dominated kink scenes appear to be the norm both in the UK and the U.S.[30] During six months of regularly going to events including play parties, munches and fetish markets in the UK, despite these all taking place in areas with significant Asian and Afro-Caribbean populations, I counted one black woman and one Asian man among all the white faces. The events I went to in the States were considerably more diverse, but it was still fair to say that the default skin color in the BDSM scene was one that matched my own. This contradicted the self-perception of the BDSM scene as more enlightened, liberal and wel-coming than mainstream society, and made me wonder whether people of color felt that the scene was truly open to them. There were also ques-tions of economics to consider—as I've mentioned in Chapter 8, the fact that BDSM requires the disposable income most likely to be available to the middle classes means that groups more likely to be living in poverty are going to be underrepresented in the BDSM scene. Seeing as ethnic minorities in the UK are 40 percent more likely to be living in poverty than their white counterparts,[31] this tallies with the theory that the expenses of kink means that it excludes those without spare cash to spend on toys, clothes and attending events.

* * *

There are many worlds to consider when trying to parse the issue of racialized imagery in kink; a real-life world of racial inequality, a history some feel is too painful to be simulated, a media given to simplistic and reactionary takes on pop culture, a BDSM culture that's not always as enlightened as its members like to think, and a vocal group of black women and men who refuse to be told how to express their sexuality. It is an explosive mix, so much so that some people didn't even think I, as a white woman, should be writing about it. It would be churlish then, to end the chapter on a quote from another white woman, even though I think Laurie Penny's words have more than a little relevance when considering how to approach racialized kink imagery in pop culture: "It is terrifically difficult to achieve radical ends by conservative means, and censorship is invariably conservative."[32] However, I'll leave the last words to a woman whose writing, talks and words to me have been absolutely invaluable in analyzing BDSM, race and sexuality.

> "I have spoken with the ancestors. They are delighted that I can FUCKING CHOOSE to do this for a few bloody hours. I can go into the Big Ass Ice Cream Parlor of Racism and have a sample spoon, and leave. I'm not trapped there being force fed the Rocky Road Ice Cream of Oppression until I am sick. It is ALL about CHOICE.... Understand this one thing and then you'll be well on the pathway."—Mollena Williams[33]

Afterword

I always thought I'd write a book about feminism one day; it didn't occur to me until very recently that it might be about BDSM too. When I started a feminist blog as a repository for all my rants against the disdain for women that I saw displayed in newspapers, magazines, TV shows, movies and music videos, I certainly hoped that one day I'd be able to bring my writing together in some kind of coherent form—I just didn't realize that it would involve such a melding of the personal and political. But so it goes; perhaps you can't truly get up in arms about something until pop culture knocks on your door and you realize it's trying to take down your feminism and shame your sexuality.

As a white, largely heterosexual, cisgendered, able-bodied white woman, I really can't complain that I'm so terribly underrepresented in popular culture. However, when idle media speculation starts trying to use a healthy expression of sexuality to disempower, to shame, to reduce, to marginalize not just me, but anyone whose preferences don't fit what they're supposed to (or fit too easily into a model that can be hijacked to support sexism, racism or homophobia), then I'm going to sit up and take notice. Some of my interviewees told me they were so exhausted from having to justify what they do and how they fuck that they just refused to engage with their critics, or even with pop culture, any more; I'm glad to say I haven't quite reached that place yet.

I understand why it might be easier to hide, though. It's still a risk to come out as one of those people. As I'm writing this conclusion, the front page story on this week's edition of my local newspaper is about a male nurse stealing patient details to send a "sex text" to a woman he found attractive. The offending text is given in full, and it's about spanking. Once again, a news story about the acts of idiocy to which sexual frustration will lead is given an extra dash of spice by throwing in a little kink. Not only is the guy by implication a predator, a disgrace to the medical profession and unable to control his randiness, but he's obviously a bit twisted too. Because he wants to spank someone. Ladies and gentleman of the jury, the case rests—he's a perv, and therefore he must deserve whatever he gets. Whether it's actually in the public interest or not to disclose all the dirty details of this somewhat sad case seems to have come a decided second to the assumption that a bit of BDSM will get you a front page story, regardless of the human casualties scattered along the way.

Hopefully—depending, perhaps on how this book is received—I won't ever lose a job, a friend or my sanity over BDSM. I'm blessed with open-minded, loving friends, a family that doesn't care (and thankfully doesn't want to know) what I get up to as long as I'm happy, and an occupation where I have more freedom than most to wear, do and say exactly what I please. Yet still, while writing this book, when people asked me what it was about, I often kept my answers vague. Out of feminism, pop culture and BDSM, the first two were often the only ones I mentioned. Partly because, well, no one really wants or needs a side of kink with their coffee when your mother is asking you to tell her friend what your new book about. But also partly because I've been a feminist long enough to know that the personal will be made political whether you like it or not, and that female freedom is not yet so secure that our bedroom habits can't be seized upon and used to try and disempower us.

I could have filled this whole book with one long and furious polemic about those who use kink to try and do exactly that, and left every other aspect of BDSM alone. I still want to grab and shake (perhaps tie up, perhaps flog? OK, no...) every person who seizes upon women practicing kink as an excuse for retrogressive gender politics, be they the well-meaning feminist condemning sexual options she's never explored for herself, the pearl-clutching conservative or the het male dom sleazing on the new female sub at a play party. When a female sub told me she thought submission was just "women's true nature," I marveled at the irony—not just of a confident, outspoken mother and grandmother in her early 40s who worked as a pro-domme telling me her true nature was submissive, but at her failure to recognize that however sexy it felt to play at being the sub, she was still in control of every aspect of her life. Because if she hadn't been, she wouldn't have been standing in a pub, wearing clothes of her own choosing, spending her own money, with a drink in one hand and a piece of cake in the other, free to have a conversation with me. Power willingly surrendered can be an erotic fantasy for both sexes: however, having no vote, no money, no voice, no reproductive control and no custody of one's children is not actually anyone's real fantasy, however masochistic they may be. If submission was really women's true nature, it's something of an inconvenient fact, then, that we fought for and achieved the erasure of all such sexist traditions. Some women (and indeed this isn't reserved to the BDSM community by any means—just have a look at the hashtag #IDontNeedFeminism or the Tumblr Women Against Feminism) may well be using that freedom to stand around and say that what we all secretly want is a return to the 1950s, or the 1900s, but a mischievously smiling part of my brain suggests that, were there any genuine attempts to actually wrest personal control away from those women, they would turn decidedly un-submissive and would savagely bloody the face of those trying to disempower them.

Having restrained myself from writing one epic rant on such frustrations, I am glad I trained my sights elsewhere, because it made me realize that people were making a fuss about *that book* for the wrong reasons. What that book supposedly signified about men, women, gender relations and kink was less important than what it failed to say and who it failed to depict. It was white, heterosexual, middle-class kink taking place within ridiculously narrow parameters. It was held up as representative of BDSM, when in fact it actually represented no one. Especially not queer people, people of color, working-class people, those whose bodies don't conform to Western beauty ideals, those who play longer and harder than any book or movie could ever hope to show, those who practice BDSM and sex without love or romance and are happy that way, those who dom because they like it, not because they were hostage to an evil older lover for six years, those who sub because it's fun and sexy and not because a billionaire came along and asked them to. I am glad to have been able to find and actually speak with some of those people: I know there are many more of them out there. I am glad to have found some pop culture examples, however few, which attempt to depict the full and thriving kaleidoscope of kink and ways of practicing it that are out there.

The larger woman is just one of many characters I wish I'd seen more of in pop culture kink imagery (courtesy Shilo McCabe).

Sometimes the search was disappointing. The hairless, flawless bodies of young white women in rope, showing off their breasts or performing oral sex peppering FetLife's Kinky and Popular often made me think: and *this* is supposed to be the place for alternative sexuality? What am I seeing here that I wouldn't just see in regular porn? Perhaps the lack of images depicting tied-up men, gas masks, fisting or other more edgy practices was because those who got off on them were out in the real world acting them out, rather than sitting at a computer clicking "Love" on yet another picture of a young, slim white woman. I expected kink to be portrayed unimaginatively in pop culture; I didn't expect images of it to be so tedious within the communities in which it's actually being practiced, but the default settings from the real world still tended to creep in. I do believe that if I spent the rest of my life searching for images of BDSM that included people who aren't models, who aren't aged 18–24, who aren't white, aren't cisgender, who have body hair, women who don't present as traditionally femme, men being submissive, queer people and trans people, and looked at only those images for the rest of my days, on balance I still would have seen more images of the slim white young submissive woman. Because they really are everywhere. And Lord, do they get boring after a while.

Still, it's perhaps understandable that with any subculture, the attempts to bring it over to the mainstream will inevitably default to using that subculture's most acceptable face. The mainstream media, especially in still-repressed and much-hypocritical Britain, just aren't ready to deal with men who get off on wearing nappies, or fat queer women with shaved heads, or black women who truly own their sexuality. That's no reason not to still demand that the bigots get over themselves and accept sexual difference, but it does mean that there are many configurations of kink that we're not likely to see on our TV or movie screens any time soon, apart from possibly in strictly caricatured, mocking fashion. As Stacey May Fowles said in her interview with me, "The soundbite or word-count-dictated world becomes unduly obsessed with … the more cartoonish side of [kink], in the interest of selling copies or gaining pageviews." Rihanna or Britney Spears in PVC is a sure way to achieve clicks through a side-serving of kink: kinky people whose appearances don't conform to the neat categories in which the media likes to place people, especially women, are much less likely to get airtime.

I rarely refer to anything I learned during my philosophy degree, (mostly because I preferred to spend my time in the sociology department reading about feminism and sexuality, and I guess it shows), but it seems that Wittgenstein's theory of language games applies here to an extent. Just as the Austrian philosopher proposed that language is only meaningful to those who are playing the same game as you (hence there can never be any real consensus between, for example, adherents of science and religious believers), I am not sure I can say anything particularly meaningful to those who firmly believe that pop culture is so unsalvageably sexist, racist and homophobic that it is pointless to try and wring any positive examples from it. Similarly, I am not sure I'll ever be speaking the same language as those who consider exploring the erotics of power anti-feminist, evidence of patriarchal brainwashing, or inconvenient evidence of hard-wired sex roles that feminism would rather forget. Perhaps in that sense I am, then, refusing to engage to some degree, but that's because you can only spend so long trying to play rugby with a tennis ball. I recognize that I may never be playing the same game as people who genuinely believe any of those things, but I also suspect there are those who aren't that invested in the game, who just wandered on to the pitch and got caught up in the excitement, and perhaps through my writing I can entice them over here to a different rule set, some other players.

It's a shame that one of my favorite pop culture artifacts, TV series *The Wire*, didn't include any explicitly kinky references, as it would have been great fun to write about it in this book. It definitely, however, included some hot sex scenes, an eye-watering amount of violence, and a lot of memorable one-liners. One from Omar Little, everyone's favorite scar-faced gay gangster, would go well here: "It's all in the game."

Thank you for playing with me.

Chapter Notes

Preface

1. Katie Roiphe, "Working Women's Fantasies," *Newsweek*, April 16, 2012. Accessed October 18, 2014. http://www.newsweek.com/working-womens-fantasies-63915.

2. Maya Dusenbery, "What Katie Roiphe Gets Wrong About 'Fifty Shades of Grey' and Fantasies of Sexual Submission," Feministing, April 16, 2012. Accessed October 18, 2014. http://feministing.com/2012/04/16/what-katie-roiphe-gets-wrong-about-fifty-shades-of-grey-and-fantasies-of-sexual-submission/.

3. "Thoughts on Feminism and the Politics of Kink," Catherine Scott, All That Chas blog, May 14, 2012. http://www.allthatchas.blogspot.co.uk/2012/05/thoughts-on-feminism-and-politics-of.html

4. "The Fantasy of Acceptable Non-Consent: Why the Female Sexual Submissive Scares Us, and Why She Shouldn't." In *Yes Means Yes! Visions of Female Sexual Power and a World Without Rape*, edited by Jaclyn Friedman and Jessica Valenti, 117–125. California: Seal Press, 2008.

Chapter 1

1. *The Confessions of Jean-Jacques Rousseau* (1782) 2006, http://www.gutenberg.org/files/3913/3913-h/3913-h.htm.

2. Helena Kennedy, *Eve Was Framed: Women and British Justice* (London : Chatto and Windus, 1992), 262.

3. Kennedy, *Eve Was Framed*, 261.

4. Anne McClintock, "Maid to Order: Commercial S/M and Gender Power." In *Dirty Looks: Women, Pornography and Power*, edited by P. Gibson and R. Gibson, 227. Italics McClintock's.

5. Laurie Penny, *Meat Market: Female Flesh Under Capitalism* (Hampshire: Zero Books 2011), 22.

6. Germaine Greer, *The Whole Woman* (London: Random House, [1999] 2014) 385.

7. M_K, commenter on Catherine Scott, "Thinking Kink: The Politics of BDSM Fashion" *Bitch* magazine, August 1, 2012. Accessed October 17, 2014. http://bitchmagazine.org/post/thinking-kink-the-politics-of-bdsm-fashion-beyonce-sex-feminist-magazine-kinky-clothes.

8. "Karen B," commenter on Catherine Scott, "Thinking Kink: The Politics of BDSM Fashion" *Bitch* magazine, August 1, 2012. Accessed October 17, 2014. http://bitchmagazine.org/post/thinking-kink-the-politics-of-bdsm-fashion-beyonce-sex-feminist-magazine-kinky-clothes.

9. Penny, *Meat Market*, 23.

10. http://www.romantasy.com/index.html?BodyURL=ZXQ/cyboutique/corset/men.html

11. Margot Weiss, *Techniques of Pleasure: BDSM and the Circuits of Sexuality* (Durham, NC: Duke University Press, 2011) 191.

Chapter 2

1. Weiss, *Techniques of Pleasure*, 176.

2. Comment on Catherine Scott, "Thinking Kink: The Appeal of the Submissive Male" *Bitch* magazine, July 2, 2012. Accessed October 1, 2014. http://bitchmagazine.org/post/thinking-kink-the-attraction-of-

the-submissive-male-feminist-magazine-bdsm-sex.

3. BBC News, "Mosley Wins Court Case Over Orgy," July 24, 2008. Accessed October 1, 2014. http://news.bbc.co.uk/1/hi/7523034.stm.

4. Bob Gruen, quoted in *Rotten: No Irish, No Blacks, No Dogs*, John Lydon with Keith & Kent Zimmerman (London: Plexus, 1994), 136.

5. Paul Ferris, *Sex and the British: A Twentieth Century History* (London: Michael Joseph, 1993) 270.

6. Anne McClintock, "Maid to Order: Commercial S/M and Gender Power," *Dirty Looks: Women, Pornography and Power*, Eds. P. Gibson, R. Gibson (London: BFI, 1993), 207.

7. Staci Newmahr, *Playing on the Edge: Sadomasochism, Risk and Intimacy* (Bloomington: Indiana University Press, 2011) 183.

8. *Ibid.*

9. "Race Play Interview Part II," April 2009. Accessed October 12, 2014. http://www.mollena.com/2009/04/race-play-interview-part-ii/.

10. Weiss, *Techniques of Pleasure,* 177.

11. McClintock, "Maid to Order," 214. Emphasis mine.

12. McClintock, "Maid to Order," 213.

13. McClintock, "Maid to Order," 213–214, italics McClintock's.

14. Newmahr, *Playing on the Edge,* 115.

15. Clarisse Thorn, "50 Shades of Grey," "Fight Club," and the Complications of Male Dominance. April 20, 2012, accessed October 1, 2014. http://clarissethorn.com/2012/04/20/50-shades-of-grey-fight-club-and-the-complications-of-male-dominance/. This essay also appears in *The S&M Feminist*, 2012, self-publication via Amazon.

16. Weiss, *Techniques of Pleasure,* 177.

17. Nancy Friday, *Men in Love. Men's Sexual Fantasies: The Triumph of Love Over Rage* (London: Arrow Books, 1980), 473.

18. Weiss, *Techniques of Pleasure,* 248.

Chapter 3

1. "Where Do We Stand on Pornography?" Roundtable, *Ms.* magazine, January/February 1994.

2. From comments thread on *Thinking Kink* post "Is Vanilla Sex Boring? Who Gets to Decide?" http://bitchmagazine.org/post/thinking-kink-vanilla-sex-bdsm-feminist-magazine-sexuality, accessed May 20, 2014.

3. Anonymous, commenter, *ibid.*

4. Interviewee "J," quoted Weiss, *Techniques of Pleasure* 171.

5. "Thinking Kink: No, Female Submission Doesn't Mean Oppression," July 11, 2012. Accessed October 12, 2014. http://bitchmagazine.org/post/thinking-kink-female-submissive-pop-culture-sub-dom-feminist-magazine-sexuality.

6. Dossie Easton and Janet W. Hardy, *The New Bottoming Book* (Emeryville, CA: Greenery, 2001), 11.

7. Shere Hite, *The New Hite Report* (London: Octopus Publishing, 2000), 557–558.

8. *Peep Show*, season 3, episode 1. Dir. Tristram Shapeero. First aired November 2005, Channel 4, UK.

9. *Friends*, season 7, episode 20, "The One with Rachel's Big Kiss." Dir. Garry Halvorson. First aired April 26, 2001.

10. "Fifty Shades Stimulates Ann Summers Sales," *Financial Times*, August 4 2012. Accessed October 10, 2014. http://www.ft.com/cms/s/0/ffc2738a-dd74-11e1-aa7b-00144feab49a.html#axzz3lhtjrkaI.

11. Newmahr, *Playing on the Edge,* 44.

12. Weiss, *Techniques of Pleasure,* 73.

13. Speech given by Gayle Rubin at the graduation ceremony for the Journeyman II Academy on October 4, 1997, http://black-rose.com/cuiru/archive/4-2/oldguard.html. Accessed May 14, 2014.

14. Weiss, *Techniques of Pleasure,* 125.

15. Rihanna, "S&M," music video 2011, dir. Melina Matsoukas.

16. Matt Elias, "Rihanna's 'S&M' Video Director Responds to Controversy," MTV news, February 3, 2011. Accessed October 20, 2014. http://www.mtv.com/news/16572

50/rihannas-sm-video-director-responds-to-controversy/.

17. Madonna, "Human Nature," music video, 1995, dir. Jean-Baptiste Mondino.

18. 30 Seconds to Mars, "Hurricane," music video 2011, dir. Bartholomew Cubbins.

19. Britney Spears, Work Bitch, music video 2013, dir. Ben Mor.

20. Pat Califia, "When the Playroom Become a Nursery. S/M Fetish People Who Choose to Parent," *Speaking Sex to Power* (California: Cleis Press, 2001).

21. From comments thread on *Thinking Kink* post "Is Vanilla Sex Boring? Who Gets to Decide?" http://bitchmagazine.org/post/thinking-kink-vanilla-sex-bdsm-feminist-magazine-sexuality,accessed May 27, 2014.

22. https://www.gov.uk/government/publications/the-notifiable-occupations-scheme-revised-guidance-for-police-forces.

23. Details of the case (and permission to write about it) provided by Backlash UK, "an umbrella organisation providing academic, legal and campaigning resources defending freedom of sexual expression."

24. http://www.backlash-uk.org.uk/?p=925.

25. http://www.legislation.gov.uk/ukpga/2008/4/part/5.

26. Caroline Davis, "Former Boris Johnson aide cleared of possession of 'extreme pornography,'" *The Guardian*, August 8, 2012. Accessed October 10, 2014. http://www.theguardian.com/uk/2012/aug/08/boris-johnson-aide-extreme-pornography-cleared.

27. Gayle Rubin, "Thinking Sex: Notes for a Radical Theory of the Politics of Sexuality" in Carol S. Vance (ed.), *Pleasure and Danger: Exploring Female Sexuality* (London: Pandora Press, 1992), 281.

28. Myles Jackman, "Extreme Porn Trial: Consensual Sex and the State," *The Guardian,* August 8, 2012. http://www.theguardian.com/law/2012/aug/08/extreme-porn-trial-simon-walsh.

29. Breanne Fahs, *Performing Sex: The Making and Unmaking of Women's Sexual Lives,* SUNY, 2011.

Chapter 4

1. Laurie Penny, 2014. *Unspeakable Things: Sex, Lies and Revolution,* London: Bloomsbury, 64.

2. Sigmund Freud, 1920. *Three Contributions to the Theory of Sex,* Project Gutenberg eBook 2005. Accessed October 10, 2014. http://www.gutenberg.org/files/14969/14969-h/14969-h.htm.

3. http://50shadesisdomesticabuse.webs.com/.

4. Weiss, *Techniques of Pleasure*, 176.

5. Sophie Morgan, *The Diary of a Submissive* (London: Penguin, 2012), 246.

6. Yasmin Alibhai-Brown, "Do Women Really Want to Be So Submissive?" *The Independent,* July 1, 2012.

7. Karen Gordon, "Mommy Porn," August 11, 2014. Accessed October 20, 2014. http://joiedemidvivre.blogspot.co.uk/2014/08/mommy-porn.html?spref=tw.

8. Toni Bentley, 2005. *The Surrender: An Erotic Memoir* (New York: Ecco), eBook.

9. "Of the Flesh Fancy: Spanking and the Single Girl," Chris Daley, 2002. *Jane Sexes It Up: True Confessions of Feminist Desire,* ed. Merri Lisa Johnson (Berkeley, CA: Seal Press).

10. E. L. James, *Fifty Shades of Grey* (London: Random House, 2011) 172.

11. Belle de Jour, 2006. *Secret Diary of a Call Girl* (New York: Grand Central), 55.

12. Pauline Reage, *The Story of O* (London: Corgi Press, 1970), 22.

13. *Ibid.*, 120.

14. *Ibid.*, 121.

15. "Why Stockholm Syndrome Could Be a Total Myth," Erin Fuchs. October 2013. *Business Insider.* Accessed September 9, 2014. http://www.businessinsider.com/stockholm-syndrome-could-be-a-myth-2013-10.

16. McClintock, "Maid to Order," 207.

17. Heather Corinna, "An Immodest Proposal," in *Yes Means Yes!,* 184.

18. Jesse Bering, *Perv: The Sexual Deviant in All of Us* (London: Doubleday 2014), 138.

19. Gayle Rubin, 1981. "The Leather Menace: Comments on Politics & S/M" from *Coming to Power,* ed. Samois.

20. P. Dancer, P. Kleinplatz & C. Moser, "24/7 SM Slavery" in *Journal of Homosexuality*, 2006, 50, quoted in "Norming BDSM," Kathryn Klement and Ellen M. Lee (paper presented at PCA/ACA national conference, Chicago, April 17, 2014).

21. Mrs. White/Robert Evans, "5 Myths About Prostitutes I Believed (Until I Was One)," Cracked.com, December 12, 2013. Accessed October 3, 2014. http://www.cracked.com/article_20734_5-myths-about-prostitutes-i-believed-until-i-was-one_p2.html.

22. Lesley Hall, *Hidden Anxieties: Male Sexuality, 1900–50* (London: Polity, 1991) 173.

23. Lynne Segal, "Sweet Sorrows, Painful Pleasures: Pornography and the Perils of Heterosexual Desire" in *Sex Exposed: Sexuality and the Pornography Debate*, eds. Lynne Segal and Mary McIntosh (London: Virago, 1992), 77.

Chapter 5

1. Aurora Snow, "My Kink Nightmare: James Franco's BDSM Porn Documentary 'Kink' Only Tells Part of the Story," *The Daily Beast*, August 30, 2014. Accessed September 6, 2014. www.thedailybeast.com/articles/2014/08/30/my-kink-nightmare-james-franco-s-bdsm-porn-documentary-kink-only-tells-part-of-the-story.html.

2. *Secret Diary of Call Girl*, Series 1, Episode 4, dir. Yann Demange. First aired ITV 2, October 18, 2007.

3. *The Story of O*, 48. Emphasis mine.

4. Mollena Williams, *The Toybag Guide to Playing with Taboo* (Emeryville, CA: Greenery Press 2010), 76. Emphasis Williams'.

5. Weiss, *Techniques of Pleasure*, 82.

6. *Ibid.*

7. Weiss, *Techniques of Pleasure*, 83.

8. Rachel Kramer Bussel, "Beyond Yes or No: Consent as Sexual Process," *Yes Means Yes: Visions of Female Sexual Power and a World Without Rape*, eds. Jaclyn Friedman & Jessica Valenti (California: Seal Press 2008), 49.

9. Newhmar, *Playing on the Edge*, 163.

10. *SM 101*, Jay Wiseman (Emeryville, CA: Greenery Press, 1996).

11. Cliff Pervocracy, "Why I Didn't Just Call the Cops," February 22, 2012. Accessed September 26, 2014. http://pervocracy.blogspot.co.uk/2012/02/why-i-didnt-just-call-cops.html.

12. Tracey Clark-Flory "When Safe Words Are Ignored," Salon.com. January 29, 2012. Accessed September 26, 2014. http://www.salon.com/2012/01/29/real_abuse_in_bdsm/.

Chapter 6

1. *The S&M Feminist*, Clarisse Thorn, Self-published, 2002. Essays can also be found at www.clarissethorn.com.

2. *Ibid.*, 140.

3. "Women Who Read Fifty Shades of Grey Are More Likely to Have Abusive Partners and Eating Disorders, Study Finds," *The Independent*, August 23, 2014. Accessed October 14, 2014. http://www.independent.co.uk/arts-entertainment/books/news/women-who-read-fifty-shades-of-grey-are-more-likely-to-have-abusive-partners-and-eating-disorders-study-finds-9687440.html.

4. Julie Clawson, 2014. "Fifty Shades of Hope: Finding Healing Power in a Cultural Phenomenon" (paper presented at the ACA/PCA National Conference, Chicago, March 16–19 2014).

5. Clawson, "Fifty Shades of Hope," 9.

6. Laurie Penny, *Unspeakable Things: Sex, Lies and Revolution* (London: Bloomsbury, 2014), 116.

7. Clawson, *Fifty Shades of Hope*, 9, emphasis mine.

8. Meera Syal, *Life Isn't All Ha Ha Hee Hee* (London: Anchor 2000), 202.

9. Cassandra Damm (Gender Studies alum, Loyola University), speaking on BDSM/Fetish studies panel, ACA/PCA March 2014.

10. Professor Breanne Fahs, author of *Performing Sex: The Making and Unmaking of Women's Erotic Lives*.

11. *Ibid.*

12. Cory Silverberg, "Weird Sexual Science: Erotica, Evolutionary Theory and Women Who Like Porn," About.com. Accessed October 14, 2014. http://sexuality.about.com/od/sexualscience/a/sexual_science2.htm.

13. "Sex Doesn't Sell: Neither Does Violence," Accessed October 14, 2014. http://www.spring.org.uk/2007/06/sex-doesnt-sell-neither-does-violence.php.

14. "Sexy Celebrity Ads Are the Worst Thing Companies Can Do for Their Sales," Ira Kalb, *Business Insider*, Feb. 21, 2013. Accessed October 14, 2014. http://www.businessinsider.com/despite-what-you-believe-celebrities—sex-doesnt-sell-2013-2.

15. "A Cock of One's Own: Getting a Firm Grip on Feminist Sexual Power." Sarah Smith, *Jane Sexes It Up: True Confessions of Feminist Sexual Desire*, ed. Merri Lisa Johnson (Avalon, New York, 2002), 300.

16. "Somebody's Fetish: Self-Objectification and Body Satisfaction among Consensual Sadomasochists," Katherine Martinez (paper given at PCA/ACA national conference, Chicago, April 17 2014). Also a forthcoming article in *Journal of Sex Research*.

17. Kozee & Tylka, 2006; Mitchell & Mazzeo, 2009; Moradi, Dirks, & Matteson, 2005; Tiggemann & Slater, 2001, quoted in Martinez, "Somebody's Fetish."

18. Yasmin Alibhai-Brown, "Do Women Really Want to Be So Submissive?"

19. *The S&M Feminist*, Clarisse Thorn, self-published, 2002. Essays can also be found at www.clarissethorn.com.

20. "Race Play Interview: Part I," April 6, 2009. Accessed October 14, 2014. http://www.mollena.com/2009/04/race-play-interview-part-1/.

21. McClintock, *Maid to Order*, 225, emphasis mine.

22. Prof. Breanne Fahs.

23. Newmahr, *Playing on the Edge*, 183. Emphasis Newmahr's.

24. *Skins*, Season 6, "Franky," Channel 4, 2012.

25. Newmahr, *Playing on the Edge*, 184. Emphasis Newmahr's.

26. Newmahr, *Playing on the Edge*, 79.

27. Margot Weiss. *Techniques of Pleasure: BDSM and the Circuits of Sexuality* (Durham, NC: Duke University Press, 2011), 175.

28. Comment on "No, Female Submission Doesn't Mean Oppression," Bitch online, July 11 2012. http://bitchmagazine.org/post/thinking-kink-female-submissive-pop-culture-sub-dom-feminist-magazine-sexuality.

29. Newmahr, *Playing on the Edge*, 79.

30. Weiss, *Techniques of Pleasure*, 161.

31. Stacey May Fowles, "The Fantasy of Acceptable Non-Consent: Why the Female Sexual Submissive Scares Us, and Why She Shouldn't," *Yes Means Yes! Visions of Female Sexual Power and a World Without Rape*." Eds. Jaclyn Friedman & Jessica Valenti (California: Seal Press 2008).

32. "Where Do We Stand on Pornography?" Roundtable, *Ms.* magazine, January/February 1994.

33. Robin Bauer, *Queer BDSM Intimacies: Critical Consent and Pushing Boundaries* (Basingstoke: Palgrave Macmillan, 2014).

34. Robin Bauer, "The Future of Research on BDSM and Gender from a Queer Perspective" (paper presented at BDSM & Gender Research Network Launch, London October 24, 2014).

35. *The S&M Feminist*, Clarisse Thorn (self-published, 2002), 138. Emphasis Thorn's. Essays can also be found at www.clarissethorn.com.

36. All discussions and sources on this incident are on FetLife, which prevents me from reproducing or naming any of them here. My understanding from my research is that after complaints from women about BDSM demos depicting male dom/female subs in the 2010 Christopher Street West fair in Lost Angeles (an LGBT/alternative sexuality pride event), the organizers, Erotic City, voted to exclude this configuration from kink demonstrations in the 2011 fair, while still permitting fem dom/male sub, male-male and female-female kink demonstrations.

37. Stacey May Fowles, "The Fantasy of Acceptable Non-Consent," 123.

38. *The S&M Feminist*, Clarisse Thorn,

Self-published, 2002. 140. Essays can also be found at www.clarissethorn.com.

39. Clawson, "Fifty Shades of Hope," 9

40. Stephen D. Foster, Jr., "Meet the Republican Who Made the Worst Rape Quote of Them All." Addicting Info, Feb. 28, 2014. Accessed October 27, 2014.

41. Jennifer Lee Lawrence, "Sade-omizing Sexuality: Deconstructing the Gender Binary Through the Sadian Sexual Predator" (PhD diss., University of Pittsburgh 2013)http://d-scholarship.pitt.edu/18280/1/Lawrence_Jennifer_dissertation.pdf.

42. Prof Breanne Fahs, author of *Performing Sex: The Making and Unmaking of Women's Erotic Lives.*

43. Catherine Scott, "Secretary and the Female Submissive," *Bitch* magazine, July 13, 2012. http://bitchmagazine.org/post/thinking-kink-secretary-feminist-magazine-film-sex-bdsm-kink-movies

Chapter 7

1. Paul Ferris, *Sex and the British,* 282.

2. *Just Kids*, Patti Smith (London: Bloomsbury 2010), 235.

3. Tatu "Lesbian" Makes Homophobic Slur: All the Things She Said Singer Says She Wouldn't Accept Her Son If He Was Gay," *The Independent*, September 19, 2014. Accessed October 6, 2014. http://www.independent.co.uk/news/people/tatu-lesbian-makes-homophobic-slur-all-the-things-she-said-singer-says-she-would-not-accept-her-son-if-he-was-gay-9743697.html.

4. Jos Truitt, "It's OK Patriarchy, I Understand Adam Lambert Made You Feel Funny," *Feministing*, November 25, 2009. Accessed October 6, 2014. http://feministing.com/2009/11/25/its-ok-patriarchy-i-understand-adam-lambert-made-you-feel-funny/.

5. McClintock, *Maid to Order*, 222.

6. Simon Dumenco, "Fashion Photographer Seeks Models/Celebrities for a Little Rough Play," *New York* magazine, undated. Accessed October 6, 2014, http://nymag.com/nymetro/shopping/fashion/features/n_10371/index1.html.

7. Barnett, David, 2003, *Love and Poison* (London: Carlton Publishing), 109.

8. "'Doing It': Representations of Lesbian Sex," Celia and Jenny Kitzinger, *Outwrite: Lesbianism and Popular Culture,* ed. Gabriele Griffin (London: Pluto Press, 1993), 11.

9. Laura Cottingham, *Lesbians Are So Chic* (London: Cassell, 1996), 7.

10. Gayle Rubin, "The Leather Menace: Comments on Politics and S/M" from *Deviations: A Gayle Rubin Reader* (Durham, NC: Duke University Press, [1981], 2012).

11. Diana Russell, "Sadomasochism as a Contra-Feminist Activity," quoted in Rubin, *The Leather Menace*, 123.

12. Rubin, *The Leather Menace*, 124.

13. "Supertwee," commenter on post "No, Female Submission Doesn't Mean Oppression," Catherine Scott, July 11, 2012. Accessed October 6, 2014. http://bitch magazine.org/post/thinking-kink-female-submissive-pop-culture-sub-dom-feminist-magazine-sexuality.

14. Juicy Lucy, 1981. "If I Ask You to Tie Me Up, Will You Still Love Me?" *Samois: Coming to Power.* ed. Members of Samois, Boston: Alyson, 39.

15. Pat Califia, 1981. "A Personal View of the History of the Lesbian S/M Community and Movement in San Francisco" in *Samois: Coming to Power*, 252.

16. *Ibid.*, 253.

17. Kitzinger & Kitzinger, "Doing It," 24.

18. Robin Bauer, "The Future of Research…."

Chapter 8

1. Cristina Merrill, "Anne Rice's Erotic Sleeping Beauty Trilogy Republished, and the Timing Couldn't Be Better," *International Business Times*, July 11, 2012. Accessed October 10, 2014. http://www.ibtimes.com/anne-rices-erotic-sleeping-beauty-trilogy-republished-and-timing-couldnt-be-better-722167.

2. Sarah Butler, "Ann Summers Credits Fifty Shades Trilogy for Run on Nipple Clamps," *The Guardian*, March 14, 2013.

Accessed October 15, 2014. http://www.theguardian.com/business/2013/mar/14/ann-summers-fifty-shades-trilogy.

3. Weiss, *Techniques of Pleasure*, 107.

4. Nina Power, *One Dimensional Woman* (Hampshire: Zero Books, 2009) back cover blurb.

5. Power, *One Dimensional Woman*, 1.

6. *Ibid.*, 35, emphasis Power's.

7. Emily Shire and Lizzie Crocker, "The Town Where Your Sex Toy Could Land You in Jail," *The Daily Beast*, May 30, 2014. Accessed October 6, 2014. http://www.thedailybeast.com/articles/2014/05/30/the-town-where-your-sex-toy-could-land-you-in-jail.html.

8. Weiss, *Techniques of Pleasure*, 125.

9. *Rotten,* Lydon, 153.

10. *Rotten*, Lydon, 71.

11. Weiss, *Techniques of Pleasure*, 126.

12. *Ibid.*, 155.

13. *Rotten*, Lydon, 197.

14. Weiss, *Techniques of Pleasure*, 126.

15. Jay Wiseman, *SM 101* (Emeryville, CA: Greenery Press, 1996).

16. Freud, *Three Contributions to the Theory of Sex*, eBook.

17. James, *Fifty Shades of Grey*, 155, italics James'.

18. Juicy Lucy, "If I Ask You to Tie Me Up..." 32.

19. McClintock, *Maid to Order*, 210.

20. Weiss, *Techniques of Pleasure*, 176.

21. Gayle Rubin, "Blood Under the Bridge: Reflections on 'Thinking Sex,'" *Deviations: A Gayle Rubin Reader* (Durham, NC: Duke University Press, 2011), 208.

22. Newmahr, *Playing on the Edge*, 201.

23. Andrea Zanin, "Poor Persecuted Pervert?" Sex Geek. Accessed October 27, 2014. http://sexgeek.wordpress.com.

24. "I'm Gonna Need You to Fight Me on This: How Rough Sex Cured My PTSD" Mac McLelland, *Good* magazine, June 28, 2011. Accessed October 6, 2014. http://magazine.good.is/articles/how-violent-sex-helped-ease-my-ptsd.

25. Connolly, P.H.; Haley, H.; Gendelman, J.; Miller, J. (2006). Psychological Functioning of Bondage/Domination/Sado-Masochism Practitioners. *Journal of Psychology and Human Sexuality*, 18(1), 79–120. http://www.tandfonline.com/doi/abs/10.1300/J056v18n01_05#.VDL1go10zIU.

26. "Kinky? You Can't Beat It" *Sydney Morning Herald*, April 16, 2007. Accessed October 6, 2014. http://www.smh.com.au/news/national/kinky-you-cant-beat-it/2007/04/16/1176696736407.html?page=2.

27. Dr. Meg John Barker, "Gender and BDSM Revisited" (paper presented at BDSM & Gender Research Network Launch, London October 24, 2014).

28. Bentley, *The Surrender*, Ebook.

29. Michael McIntyre, "Rethinking *The Body in Pain*" (Paper presented at ACA/PCA national conference, Chicago, April 16, 2014).

Chapter 9

1. bell hooks, "Madonna: Plantation Mistress or Soul Sister?" from *Black Looks: Race and Representation.* 1992. Accessed October 29, 2014. http://xroads.virginia.edu/~drbr/hooks.txt.

2. Weiss, *Techniques of Pleasure*, 209.

3. Alex Grey, "The Appropriation of Slavery in the BDSM World." Accessed October 15, 2014. http://retroqueer.wordpress.com/2014/08/06/the-appropriation-of-slavery/.

4. Aph Ko, "3 Reasons to Stop Bringing Up Slavery Every Time Black Women Assert Sexual Their Autonomy," *Everyday Feminism*, September 26, 2014. Accessed October 2, 2014. http://everydayfeminism.com/2014/09/slavery-black-women-sexual-autonomy/?utm_content=buffer575d1&utm_medium=social&utm_source=facebook.com&utm_campaign=buffer, [italics Ko's own].

5. Mollena Williams, *The Toybag Guide to Playing with Taboo* (Emeryville, CA: Greenery Press, 2010), 76.

6. Williams, *The Toybag Guide*, 80. Italics are Williams' own.

7. Mollena Williams in Weiss, *Techniques of Pleasure*, 210.

8. Weiss, *Techniques of Pleasure*, 211.

9. Weiss, *Techniques of Pleasure*, 197.

10. Weiss, *Techniques of Pleasure*, 197.

11. *Americanah*, Chimamanda Ngozie Adichie, 2014. Ebook.

12. Ko, "3 Reasons…." http://everyday feminism.com/2014/09/slavery-black-women-sexual-autonomy/?utm_content=buffer575d1&utm_medium=social&utm_source=facebook.com&utm_campaign=buffe.

13. "Race Play Interview: Part I," April 6, 2009. Accessed October 14, 2014. http://www.mollena.com/2009/04/race-play-interview-part-1/.

14. Tamara Winfrey Harris, "No Disrespect," *Bitch* online, undated. Accessed October 15, 2014. http://bitchmagazine.org/article/no-disrespect.

15. Andrea Plaid, "Your Sex Acts-and Partners—Aren't Uplifting the Race," *Racialicious*, April 3, 2009. Accessed October 2, 2014 http://www.racialicious.com/2009/04/03/your-sex-acts-and-partners-arent-uplifting-the-race/.

16. http://everydayfeminism.com/2014/09/slavery-black-women-sexual-autonomy/?utm_content=buffer575d1&utm_medium=social&utm_source=facebook.com&utm_campaign=buffer.

17. "Exhibit B: Is the 'Human Zoo' Racist? The Performers Respond," *The Guardian*, September 5, 2014. Accessed October 20, 2014. http://www.theguardian.com/culture/2014/sep/05/exhibit-b-is-the-human-zoo-racist-the-performers-respond.

18. http://www.barbican.org.uk/theatre/event-detail.asp?ID=16226.

19. Kehinde Andrews, "Exhibit B, the Human Zoo, Is a Grotesque Parody: Boycott It." *The Guardian*, September 12, 2014. Accessed October 20, 2014. http://www.theguardian.com/commentisfree/2014/sep/12/exhibit-b-human-zoo-boycott-exhibition-racial-abuse.

20. Comment on LeatherTBird, "Race Play: It's NO Laughing Matter," Mollena.com, June 2009, accessed October 6, 2014. http://www.mollena.com/2009/06/race-play-a-dissenting-viewpoint/.

21. "Is the Human Zoo Racist?" *The Guardian*, Sept. 2014.

22. "Shocking Editorial Features White Editor Sitting in 'Black Woman Chair,'" Tracey Wallace, *Policy Mic*, January 21, 2014. Accessed October 2, 2014. http://mic.com/articles/79603/shocking-editorial-features-white-editor-sitting-in-black-woman-chair.

23. Sarah Woolley, "Leave Jelly Wrestling Alone, Cambridge Feminists," May 9, 2013, accessed October 9, 2014. http://sarahwoolley.tumblr.com/post/49992237383/leave-jelly-wrestling-alone-cambridge-feminists.

24. "Allen Jones: The Day I Turned Down Stanley Kubrick," *The Telegraph*, October 8 2007. Accessed October 20, 2014. http://www.telegraph.co.uk/culture/art/3668398/Allen-Jones-The-day-I-turned-down-Stanley-Kubrick.html.

25. "Bjarne Melgaard and Gavin Brown Say "Racist Chair" Is Nothing Compared to Global Warming," *Blouin Artinfo*, January 22, 2014. Accessed October 2, 2014. http://blogs.artinfo.com/artintheair/2014/01/22/bjarne-melgaard-and-gavin-brown-say-racist-chair-is-nothing-compared-to-global-warming/.

26. Professor Antony Whitehead, "Manhood and Men's Masochism in Relation to Women: Early Northern Study Group Findings" (Paper presented at BDSM & Gender Research Network Launch, London October 24, 2014).

27. "Exhibit B … The Performers Respond." *The Guardian*, September 5, 2014.

28. "Noel Gallagher: Hip Hop Is a Fake Form of Music," *Gigwise*, November 14, 205. Accessed October 9, 2014. http://www.gigwise.com/news/10487/noel-gallagher-hip-hop-is-a-%22fake-form-of-music%22.

29. Kobena Mercer, "Just Looking for Trouble: Robert Mapplethorpe and Fantasies of Race," in *Sex Exposed: Sexuality and the Pornography Debate*, eds. Lynne Segal and Mary McIntosh (London: Virago, 1992), 99.

30. Weiss, *Techniques of Pleasure*, 92. Newmahr, *Playing on the Edge*, 17.

31. "Poverty, Ethnicity and Place." Stave Garner and Gargi Bhattacharyya, May 2011. Accessed October 6, 2014. http://www.jrf.org.uk/sites/files/jrf/poverty-ethnicity-place-full.pdf, 9.

32. Penny, *Unspeakable Things*, 171.

33. "Race Play Interview, Part I."

Bibliography

Barker, Dr. Meg John. "Gender and BDSM Revisited." Paper presented at BDSM & Gender Research Network Launch, London October 24, 2014.

Belle de Jour. *Secret Diary of a Call Girl.* New York: Grand Central Publishing, 2006.

Bentley, Toni. *The Surrender: An Erotic Memoir.* New York: Ecco, 2005.

Bering, Jesse. *Perv: The Sexual Deviant in All of Us.* London: Doubleday, 2014.

Califia, Patrick. *Speaking Sex to Power: The Politics of Queer Sex.* California: Cleis, 2001.

Clawson, Julie. "Fifty Shades of Hope: Finding Healing Power in a Cultural Phenomenon." Paper presented at the ACA/PCA National Conference, Chicago, March 16–19, 2014.

Corinna, Heather. "An Immodest Proposal." In *Yes Means Yes! Visions of Female Sexual Power and a World Without Rape,* edited by Jaclyn Friedman and Jessica Valenti, 179–192. California: Seal Press, 2008.

Cottingham, Laura. *Lesbians Are So Chic.* London: Cassell, 1996.

Daley. Chris. "Of the Flesh Fancy: Spanking and the Single Girl," Chris Daley, 2002. In *Jane Sexes It Up: True Confessions of Feminist Desire.* Edited by Merri Lisa Johnson. New York, Avalon, 2002.

Easton, Dossie, and Janet W. Hardy. *The New Bottoming Book.* California: Greenery, 2001.

Ferris, Paul. *Sex and the British: A Twentieth Century History.* London: Michael Joseph, 1993.

Fowles, Stacey May. "The Fantasy of Acceptable Non-Consent: Why the Female Sexual Submissive Scares Us, and Why She Shouldn't." In *Yes Means Yes! Visions of Female Sexual Power and a World Without Rape,* edited by Jaclyn Friedman & Jessica Valenti, 117–125. California: Seal Press, 2008.

Freud. *Three Contributions to the Theory of Sex.* Project Gutenberg (1920), 2005.

Friday, Nancy. *Men in Love. Men's Sexual Fantasies: The Triumph of Love Over Rage.* London: Arrow Books, 1980.

Greer, Germaine. *The Whole Woman.* London: Random House, [1999] 2014.

Hite, Shere. *The New Hite Report.* London: Octopus Publishing Group, 2000.

James, E.L. *Fifty Shades of Grey.* London: Random House, 2011.

Kennedy, Helena. *Eve Was Framed: Women and British Justice.* London: Chatto and Windus, 1992.

Kitzinger, Celia and Jenny. "'Doing It': Representations of Lesbian Sex." In *Outwrite: Lesbianism and Popular Culture,* edited by Gabriele Griffin. London: Pluto, 1993.

Klement, Kathryn, and Ellen M. Lee "Norming BDSM." Paper given at PCA/ACA national conference, Chicago, April 17 2014.

Lee Lawrence, Jennifer. "Sade-omizing Sexuality: Deconstructing the Gender Binary Through the Sadian Sexual Predator" Ph.D. diss., University of Pittsburgh, 2013.

Lydon, John, with Keith & Kent Zimmerman. *Rotten: No Irish, No Blacks, No Dogs.* London: Plexus, 1994.

Martinez, Katherine. "Somebody's Fetish: Self-Objectification and Body Satisfaction Among Consensual Sadomasochists." *Journal of Sex Research.* Jan. 2015.

McClintock, Anne. "Maid to Order: Commercial S/M and Gender Power." In *Dirty Looks: Women, Pornography and Power*, edited by P. Gibson and R. Gibson, 207–229. London: BFI, 1993.

Mercer, Kobena. "Just Looking for Trouble: Robert Mapplethorpe and Fantasies of Race." In *Sex Exposed: Sexuality and the Pornography Debate*, edited by Lynne Segal and Mary McIntosh. London: Virago, 1992.

Newmahr, Staci. *Playing on the Edge: Sadomasochism, Risk and Intimacy.* Bloomington: Indiana University Press, 2011.

Ngozi Adichie, Chimamanda. *Americanah.* London: Fourth Estate, 2014.

Penny, Laurie. *Meat Market: Female Flesh Under Capitalism.* Hampshire: Zero Books, 2011.

_____. *Unspeakable Things: Sex, Lies and Revolution.* London: Bloomsbury, 2014.

Power, Nina. *One Dimensional Woman.* Hampshire: Zero Books, 2009

Reage, Pauline. *The Story of O.* London: Corgi, 1972.

Roiphe, Katie. "Working Women's Fantasies," *Newsweek*, April 16, 2012.

Roquelaure, A. N. (Anne Rice). *The Claiming of Sleeping Beauty.* London: Little, Brown (1987), 2012.

Rousseau, Jean-Jacques. *The Confessions of Jean-Jacques Rousseau* (1782), 2006.

http://www.gutenberg.org/files/3913/3913-h/3913-h.htm.

Rubin, Gayle. *Deviations: A Gayle Rubin Reader.* Durham, NC: Duke University Press, 2011.

_____. "Thinking Sex: Notes for a Radical Theory of the Politics of Sexuality" in *Pleasure and Danger: Exploring Female Sexuality,* edited by Carol S. Vance. London: Pandora, 1992.

Samois: Coming to Power. ed. Members of Samois, Boston: Alyson, 1981.

Thorn, Clarisse. *The S&M Feminist.* Self-published, 2012.

Weatherfield, Molly. *Safe Word: An Erotic S/M Novel.* California: Cleis Press, 2003.

Weiss, Margot. *Techniques of Pleasure: BDSM and the Circuits of Sexuality.* Durham, NC: Duke University Press, 2011.

Whitehead, Antony. "Manhood and Men's Masochism in Relation to Women: Early Northern Study Group Findings." Paper presented at BDSM & Gender Research Network Launch, London, October 24, 2014.

Williams, Mollena. *The Toybag Guide to Playing with Taboo.* California: Greenery, 2010.

Wiseman, Jay. *SM 101,* California: Greenery, 1996.

Index